Picking Up the Broomstick

The "Charge" comes to each of us in a different manner. It is that moment in our lives when we feel the Magick of the Universe for the very first time . . . coursing through us . . . and we know beyond all real and imagined shadows that this calling to the mysteries is indeed there. That it is truly there, and not a whimsical flight from reality.

—Silver RavenWolf

This book has been written for the New Generation of Witches. It answers the questions most asked by those individuals who have taken up Craft study in the past ten years and who will become interested into the year 2000. Valuable information is provided for the solitary beginner, whose ranks are growing, as well as the coven initiate.

Representing the author's personal study, this book follows the Craft in its solitary form. It does not follow a specific tradition, nor are the teachings and insights gathered from any particular book or specific individual. Therefore, this text is ideal for anyone (male or female) who is interested in practicing either the religious or scientific paths of the Craft, or both.

The choice of following the path of spiritual enlightenment through Witchcraft is one that should be entirely your own. You, and no other person, are in control of your destiny. To enter the Craft, even if you think that it is just to dabble, is a decision not to be made lightly or immediately. Some of you will go on to join small covens, others will join one of the Wiccan Churches that are springing up across the nation. There are those who will continue to practice the Craft alone, and of course, there will be a few individuals who will migrate to other magickal religions.

Whatever your reason is for "picking up the broomstick," this book presents several areas of eclectic study, gives you the leading edge on terminology and allows you plenty of room to grow at your own pace.

About the Author

Silver RavenWolf is the Director of the Wiccan/Pagan Press Alliance, a network of Pagan newsletters, publishers, and writers. "It keeps me pretty busy," she explains, "but I adore it. Writing and publishing are important to the Pagan community. The editors supply the life line for growth, change, and acceptance of magickal people. Positive religions like Wicca are the heartbeat, but the editors are the arteries of the community."

Currently Silver works for a local newspaper and is active in her home town. She has been involved in various aspects of the Craft since she was seventeen years old. In November of 1991 she received her First Degree from Bried Foxsong of Sacred Hart and is on the rolls of the International Red Garters. She also carries Second and Third Degree status from the Temple of Hecate Triskele of the Caledonii Tradition, and now heads the Black Forest Clan in four states. Silver was eldered by Lord Serphant of the Family of Serphant Stone on 29 June 1996 at the Puff Gathering in North Carolina. Her hearthstone coven is known as Coven of the Wolf.

Born on 11 September 1956, Silver is a true Virgo; she adores making lists and arranging things in order. She emphatically tells us that Virgos do not like house-cleaning or laundry. Definitely a lady of the nineties, she's hard to pin down. "I spend a great deal of my time with my four children," she says. "They come first in my life. Everyone else has to take a number and get in line after that."

To Write to the Author

If you wish to contact the author or would like more information about this book, please write to the author in care of Llewellyn Worldwide and we will forward your request. Both the author and publisher enjoy hearing from you and learning of your enjoyment of this book and how it has helped you. Llewellyn Worldwide cannot guarantee that every letter written to the author will be answered, but all will be forwarded. Please write to:

Silver RavenWolf
%Llewellyn Worldwide
P.O. Box 64383, Dept. L791–X
St. Paul, MN 55164-0383, U.S.A.

Please enclose a self-addressed, stamped envelope for reply, or $1.00 to cover costs.
If outside U.S.A., enclose international postal reply coupon.

To Ride a Silver Broomstick

New Generation Witchcraft

Silver RavenWolf

2003
Llewellyn Publications
St Paul, Minnesota 55164-0383, U.S.A.

FIRST EDITION
Twentieth Printing, 2003

Cover painting: Lisa Iris
Illustrations: Silver RavenWolf
Book design and layout: Jessica Thoreson

Library of Congress Cataloging-in-Publication Data

RavenWolf, Silver, 1956-
        To ride a silver broomstick: new generation witchcraft / Silver
RavenWolf.
            p.   cm.
        ISBN 0-87542-791-X
        1. Witchcraft. 2. Paganism. 3. Magic. I. Title.
BF1572.R385   1993
133.4'3 — dc20   92-38151
                                                        CIP

Llewellyn Publications
A Division of Llewellyn Worldwide, Ltd.
P.O. Box 64383, St. Paul, MN 55164-0383
www.llewellyn.com

Printed in the United States of America

To those who dance to a different drummer,
And dare to make their dreams come true . . .
I will always love you, Dad!

To my husband, Ervin Trayer,
I couldn't have done it without you!

Other Books by Silver RavenWolf

Beneath a Mountain Moon (fiction)
To Stir a Magick Cauldron
Witches Runes (formerly The Rune Oracle) (with Nigel Jackson)
Angels: Companions in Magick
Teen Witch
American Folk Magick: Charms, Spells & Herbals
To Light a Sacred Flame: Practical Witchcraft for the New Generation
Silver's Spells for Prosperity
Halloween: Customs, Recipes, & Spells
Silver's Spells for Protection
Witches' Night Out (fiction)
Teen Witch Kit
Siver's Spells for Love
Murder at Witches' Bluff
Witches' Night of Fear (fiction)
Witches' Key to Terror (fiction)

In Spanish

Hechizos para el amor
Hechizos para la prosperidad
Hechizos para la protección

Forthcoming

Solitary Witch (Llewellyn, 2003)

Table of Contents

Preface

*The Charge of
the Goddess*

It is Midsummer Night's Eve — the longest day of the year. This a unique time, full of unlimited power and mystery.

You are standing in a large, secluded clearing, banked on three sides by the dark, evergreen skirts of Earth Mother. Behind you expands a rolling corn field in the cycle of infancy.

Above you hangs the moon. She is full and heavy, dripping her milk-white light on the planet below, like a mother's breast that anticipates the nurturing of a child. The remainder of the heavens expands about the glowing orb, velvety and black, pricked by a multitude of winking stars.

You take a deep breath — heavy-sweet with the odors of a cooling summer day. The field, the dark, the sounds of the night, the forest and the moon all collide in time that does not exist.

As you look around the clearing there comes the realization that you are one among many — old and young, robust and slender. They, as you, have come from many distant places to be here this night. A sea of faces, each barely masking the taunt anticipation behind them, utters whispers that merge with those of the nocturnal insects. An atmosphere of peace and unity with both worlds prevails.

A hush, like the roll of a soft wave, moves across the crowd. Silently, the people form a circle. A lone cloud scuttles to greet the face of the moon and veils its brilliance for a second.

In the darkness, man, woman, and child join hands. As the light once again filters down among the people, you hear the awed murmur of the crowd.

The center of the circle, empty only moments before, is brilliantly lit by the aura of a single woman.

She is like no other. You search your memory, but you can remember no equal, neither in this life time or in any slips of memory that your stingy brain has allowed you to recall.

Her stance is straight and proud. Her strong yet delicate arms rise to the heavens, drawing down the light of the moon into her breast. Into her soul.

She is swathed in shimmering material that any human has yet to make; you marvel at how it ripples about her, like fine flesh that kisses the night.

Some in the crowd see her as a raven-haired beauty; others see her as a white-blonde princess. Yet there are those who observe a fiery, red-headed warrioress. To you her skin appears a musk-honey color, but to the man next to you it shines with polished ebony.

It is then you realize that you are connected to the thoughts of all in the Universe. To look upon her radiant face is to have the air stolen from your lungs, and you gasp, eyes fluttering in mild fear of drowning in the logic of nothing. The sensation flashes by; you are left with steady breath and a pumping heart.

To look within her is to experience the Divine . . . The Goddess!

The logical mind does not well accept the creative premise of divinity. Therefore, you internally debate whether you are looking upon human flesh or a figment of the heavens. You have been told by others that the human is Aradia, Queen of the Witches. Some have said she is the incarnation of the Goddess herself, others say she is the daughter of the Goddess, as She could not enter her full self in human flesh.

Regardless of the debate, you know that you have waited a very long time to see her. Although the humans here are total strangers to you, you finally feel that you are home. This is the place where you belong.

She speaks. Her silver voice rings loud and true. In amazement you watch as the tallest trees around the clearing bow down in reverence as she begins The Call:

> *Hear my words and know me! I shall be called a million names by all who speak! I am Eternal Maiden! I am Great Mother! I am the Old One who holds the immortal key! I am shrouded in Mystery, but am known to every soul!*

She lowers her arms and holds them open toward the people circled around her. A small girl-child in the crowd cries out in fear, erupting the peace of the circle. Her horrified mother attempts to remove the child as the little one breaks into a lusty squall.

But Aradia only smiles and beckons the small one to her. She holds her arms in a cradling position, and where they once were empty, the child now materializes, encircling the child to her breast. The mother is left guiding only empty space from the circle.

If there was one among the crowd who does not believe in her reality, it surely blossoms in that moment, as the child nestles into Aradia's shoulder in peaceful contentment.

Still holding the child, Aradia gestures one elegant arm to the sky and speaks:

Hear my words and know me! Whenever the moon rises in the Heavens shall my children come to me. Better it be once a month when the moon is full, shall ye assemble in some secret place, such as this, and adore the spirit of I. I, who am the Queen of Witches!

And under my watchful eye, my children shall be taught the mysteries of Earth and Nature, of the ways of all Magick! That which is unknown shall be known, and that which is hidden shall be revealed, even the secluded soul shall be pierced with my Light. From my cauldron shall be drunk all knowledge and immortality!

She pauses to caress the head of the girl-child, then lowers her gently to the ground. The tot scrambles quickly back to its mother, the cherub face serene, radiant, and blessed.

Aradia begins to glide slowly around the circle of people, looking intently into many shadowed faces. She speaks:

Ye shall be free from slavery and ye shall dance, sing, and feast. Music shall surround you, for mine is the ecstasy of the spirit, and mine is also the joy of the earth!

Her eyes grow large and luminous and her voice flares with raw power as she proclaims:

I do not demand sacrifice! For behold, I am the Mother of all living things!

She places the palm of her right hand on one man's forehead. She shouts:

Create and heal!

Then softens her voice and winks at another:

Be strong, yet gentle.

She turns quickly to an old woman:

Be noble, yet reverent.

She then tips the chin of an attractive young lady:

Bring forth and replenish.

And pivots with a seductive laugh. She moves about the circle, touching each individual, murmuring encouragement of hopes and dreams, laying aside fear and hatred.

And, as does the cycle of the Moon ever begin to wax and wane and to grow forth again, as do the seasons from one to the next flow in smooth rhythm, from sowing to reaping, to seeming death and rebirth . . . so will my children know their own pattern in both worlds!

Your heart begins to beat its own primal rhythm as she moves — no, glides — toward you. Your stomach does those familiar flippity-flops when you realize it is you she has singled out. She stands but a breath in front of you. You feel her warmth envelop you with the perfume of musk, or is it lavender? She is so beautiful you think your eyes will never see normally again.

Her hand delicately touches your shoulder, sending a rapturous vortex of power jolting down your body, then building in your belly. She speaks in a whisper that, amazingly, all can hear:

And ye shall say these words . . .
I Will love and harm none.
I Will live, love, die, and live again.
I Will meet, remember, know,
and embrace once more.
For the free will of ALL, And with harm to None
> *As I will*
> *It now is done*
> *So mote it be!*

You speak the words. The people speak the words. She backs to the center of the circle, never appearing to move; but there just the same. Her power churns through every molecule of your system.

The circle begins to fill with drifting notes of pan pipes, whirling into a foggy spiral toward her. Where she once stood alone, now solidifies a towering being — half beast, half man. His body is covered in fine, golden iridescence. His bronze, muscular arms encircle her gently, as if she were made of the lightest faery wing.

Two large, twisting horns protrude from His head, glowing with a light that appears to be all its own. His visage does not frighten you, for you realize that this is the God, the consort of the Lady, and that he is the golden half of her silvery being.

They smile deeply at one another. Their separate bodies slowly melt together into a single, blazing entity of light. And the human circle is plunged into darkness.

Your fearful heart turns your eyes to the heavens, but it is only another cloud that has passed before the face of the moon.

The light returns almost as quickly as it was stolen. Perhaps . . . not quite as mystical as before. All eyes turn to the center of the circle.

And it is bare.

·☽ ☾·

Note: The original "Charge of the Goddess" was written by Doreen Valiente for use in Gardnarian rituals. It has been so loved by the entire Pagan community that it has become a common part of many holiday ceremonies. This variation contains the major precepts of her idea, but puts it in story form. It is a beautiful tale to share with both adults and children, as it depicts the Goddess and God in the manner in which we believe in them, not in the negative light in which our general society has often put them.

Silver
Ravenwolf
1990 ©

Introduction

It is an accurate statement that the followers of Witchcraft do not usually pros-
elytize, which means you aren't going to find us standing on your local street
corner, thumping our Books of Shadows. Nor do you have to worry about
jumping out of the shower to answer our serene and smiling faces at the door
with your clothes stuck to various uncomfortable places on your wet body.

But just because we (hopefully) aren't the forcible type doesn't mean that
we don't exist. Trying to find us, though, can sometimes be rather tricky. And
honestly, that's part of the fun.

Witchcraft is definitely an enjoyable practice. There is no fear, no hatred,
no cowering at Divinity. Each of us has the right to enjoy all that the Universe
has to provide. Therefore, this book has been designed to take you to the
avenue of experiencing Witchcraft in its natural form.

I could entice you by saying, yes, after reading and practicing various
aspects of this book you can get the money you need, the love you desire, etc.,
but I would come close to sounding like the 900 numbers that I usually roll my
eyes at; I'm sure you do, too. Who ever heard of something coming from nothing without a catch?

Well — believe it or not — me. Except you must understand that there is
no such thing as nothing. Even nothing is something, really.

This book has been written for each person as an individual, whether you
belong to a coven, practice solitary already, or are just beginning and haven't
decided exactly what you want to do. It's focus is on the single person, often
called solitary, and how they can practice both the science and religion of the
Craft, whether they belong to a group or not.

It speaks plainly and simply about living as a Witch, not just practicing rituals or invoking spells on Tuesday, or Thursday, or whatever.

It is also a very important testimony of one woman . . . me. If Witchcraft
and magick didn't work for me, you wouldn't be reading this book. Now before
you hurriedly flip through the pages because you think I zapped it up without

any stress or strain and you want to do the same, let me assure you that it took an immense amount of work to attain my goal.

Yes, there was definitely magick afoot in my life as I worked on this manuscript. The odds of a mother of four submitting her first manuscript to the publishing company at the top of her list and having it accepted without the usual hassle of numerous rejection letters are slim indeed. It wasn't just my magick, or hopes and dreams that brought this book to you, it was the magick of those many people who are in need of such a text.

What I am trying to stress is that I'm just like you. I'm a normal, everyday-type person. Well, sort of. Everyone likes to think they are special, right?

I live in the real world that has such neat items as rent, phone bills, electric bills, family upsets, car problems, and bank snafus. Not to mention the biggies, like war, crime, and sometimes uncooperative neighbors.

My point is that I can take this real world and superimpose upon it the world of illusion (which isn't really), in order to either fix or prevent many of life's difficulties — or even better, create happiness and well-being for both myself and others.

I can do this, and so can you . . . if you really want to. And that is the fundamental key. To want and to need simultaneously leads to success without researching the subject for the next twenty years; an idea that doesn't sound promising to anybody. Who wants to wait that long to achieve their goals? I'd rather sit in my rocking chair ticking off the things that I have achieved rather than mourn over an expanse of wasted years and unfinished business.

Witchcraft is a natural and practical aspect of being. If followed properly, it doesn't hurt anybody, and helps many. It meshes easily with the cycles of the Universe. You can obtain health, wealth, and well-being. Just ask me!

Blessed Be,

Jenine E. Trayer
aka Silver RavenWolf
31 October 1991

Section One

Background
Shadows

Picking Up the Broomstick

The "Charge" comes to each of us in a different manner. It is that moment in our lives when we feel the Magick of the Universe coursing through us for the very first time, and we know beyond all real and imagined shadows that this calling to the mysteries is indeed there. It is not a whimsical flight from reality.

The choice to follow the path of spiritual enlightenment through Witchcraft should be entirely your own. You, and no other person, are in control of your destiny. To enter the Craft, even if you think that it is just to dabble, is a decision not to be made lightly or immediately.

This book represents my personal study of the Craft in its solitary form. "Solitary" meaning it has just been me, myself, and I — one who for various reasons, practices the art and science of Witchcraft alone. It does not follow a specific tradition, nor are the teachings and insights gathered from any particular book or individual. Therefore, this text is ideal for anyone (male or female) who is interested in practicing either the religious or scientific paths of the Craft, or both.

I have kept from using specific deities whenever possible to enhance your own studies. Therefore, this text may also be used for training initiates in the different traditions, as well as a useful learning tool for Pagan children who are nearing their dedication ceremony, which usually occurs sometime around puberty.

You will find very little history of Witchcraft in this volume because it has been designed as an active, hands-on book. I am one of those people who likes to cut to the chase and learn how to do something without extraneous information that I may or may not use. The information that I feel is important for me may be dry and boring for you.

However, I am not suggesting you bypass our history. It is necessary to become familiar with the Craft of the past in order to prepare your way into the Craft of the future.

In the back of each chapter you will find a suggested reading list. It is not essential to read every book on the list, or read them in the order given. Choose the titles that appeal to you. Try to read at least some of the books as you work through the various chapters, as they will enhance and accelerate your studies.

In Appendix 1 I have provided some of the recent milestones in Craft-related events. Why any history at all? Although you may not be interested in the political side of the Craft, it does exist, and since we know ignorance is not bliss you should be aware of who has been working for both solitaries and coveners alike.

Remember, though, that all history is in the hands of the writers who provide it. No single event is seen in exactly the same way by everyone, even the participants. Most histories of centuries ago which are available today were written by the victors, not the other way around.

Each chapter also contains written exercises. None of them are difficult, but all of them are important and should be completed. Please make an effort to do them in the order they are given. I suggest that, before you continue, you purchase a notebook that is sturdy enough to weather hard use. A ring binder is nice so you can move pages around when the need arises. We'll cover various types of record keeping later on, but you will begin using this notebook shortly.

While studying Craft information, please realize that you are a unique individual. Lessons come not only from texts, but from every-day life as well. In applying your new knowledge, you will gain wisdom and insight into the many worlds around you. Be patient. Don't push yourself. Let it come naturally. And . . . by all means . . . enjoy yourself!

Typecasting

Unlike many other systems of belief, Witchcraft allows you to play. This may sound silly to you, but mental recreation is necessary for the growth of a healthy mind.

Your first exercise is an imaginary one. Often, when people ask me the definition of the words "Witch" or "Witchcraft," I first ask them a question in return: "What do you think a Witch really is?"

Their answer defines their limitations for me. It also allows me to clear away any glaring misconceptions from the onset, and then move into a reasonable definition that they will understand. The key phrase here is "that they will understand." In the future, when you are called upon to explain the nature of the Craft (and you will be), always remember to speak with clarity. Don't fill their heads with buzz-words and incomprehensible data. Short and sweet will serve you better.

Before continuing in this book, write an imaginary let[...] though you may be an old hand in the practice of Witchcraft[...] hold some surprises for you. Thinking about what we are [...] defining this through a limited vehicle, such as pen an[...] entirely different things.

On the first page of your new notebook, begin the letter by telling me what your definition of the word "Witch" is. In the second paragraph, describe the word "Witchcraft."

In the third paragraph, write your general knowledge on how you feel society in general accepts the practice of Witchcraft, and why this is so.

Close your letter by listing one major goal you would like to complete before you finish this book. This goal can be spiritual, mental or physical; it is your choice. Sign and date the letter.

What Witches Are Made Of

An unenlightened individual will tell you that the bulk of Witches in our society today are people who seek solace in a specialized group which relates better to fantasy than to reality . . . their reality, that is.

There are three words in our language that come to mind that mean something different to everyone. They are "love," "happiness," and (of course) "divinity." There are many more, which is just the point I am trying to make here. Everyone's experiences, thought patterns and feelings are different. That is what makes us all unique. What is right for you may not be proper for someone else.

One of the major precepts of the Craft is that all entities deserve to operate as they please and indulge in what makes them happy and comfortable, as long as it doesn't harm anyone else.

Therefore, it is not necessary that your "truth" conform to anyone else's. Conversely, you cannot expect the world to conform to your truths, either.

A person is made up of what he or she believes in. I think that what those beliefs entail was summed up perfectly by the Council of American Witches in their Spring Witchmeet of 1974, held in Minneapolis, Minnesota. Their statement, entitled "Principles of Wiccan Belief," was adopted in an effort to inform and educate both the general public and fledgling Witches like us.

I have reprinted it for you because I feel that it is the most concise document I have seen to date that sets forth our beliefs in an understandable manner.

Unfortunately, the Council of American Witches disbanded in that same year, but this does not mean the efforts they made are inconsequential; quite the contrary! Other groups and organizations continue to function or have formed since then and carry on the ideas they put forth. Appendix 2 of this book gives a current list of these organizations as well as their addresses, should you wish to contact them in the future.

The following pages reprint the Principles of Belief. Don't skip it, even if you have been in the Craft for years. Take the time to read it, word for word.

on't scan it. Each year you should reaffirm these beliefs in some way, whether it be through personal ritual or group gathering. You could choose one of our major holidays, or simply pick the day of your dedication or another special day.

Principles of Belief

The Council of American Witches finds it necessary to define modern Witchcraft in terms of the American experience and needs.

We are not bound by traditions from other times and other cultures, and owe no allegiance to any person or power greater than the Divinity manifest through our own being.

As American Witches, we welcome and respect all life-affirming teachings and traditions, and seek to learn from all and to share our learning within our Council.

It is in this spirit of welcome and cooperation that we adopt these few principles of Wiccan belief. In seeking to be inclusive, we do not wish to open ourselves to the destruction of our group by those on self-serving power trips, or to philosophies and practices contradictory to these principles. In seeking to exclude those whose ways are contradictory to ours, we do not want to deny participation with us to any who are sincerely interested in our knowledge and beliefs, regardless of race, color, sex, age, national or cultural origins, or sexual preference.

We therefore ask only that those who seek to identify with us accept these few basic principles:

1. We practice rites to attune ourselves with the natural rhythm of life forces marked by the phases of the Moon and the seasonal quarters and cross-quarters.
2. We recognize that our intelligence gives us a unique responsibility toward our environment. We seek to live in harmony with Nature, in ecological balance offering fulfillment to life and consciousness within an evolutionary concept.
3. We acknowledge a depth of power far greater than is apparent to the average person. Because it is far greater than ordinary, it is sometimes called "supernatural," but we see it as lying within that which is naturally potential to all.
4. We conceive of the Creative Power in the Universe as manifesting through polarity — as masculine and feminine — and that this same creative Power lives in all people, and functions through the interaction of the masculine and feminine. We value neither above the other,

knowing each to be supportive of the other. We value sexuality as pleasure, as the symbol and embodiment of Life, and as one of the sources of energies used in magickal practice and religious worship.

5. We recognize both outer worlds and inner, or psychological worlds — sometimes known as the Spiritual World, the Collective Unconscious, the Inner Planes, etc. — and we see in the interaction of these two dimensions the basis for paranormal phenomena and magickal exercises. We neglect neither dimension for the other, seeing both as necessary for our fulfillment.

6. We do not recognize any authoritarian hierarchy, but do honor those who teach, respect those who share their greater knowledge and wisdom, and acknowledge those who have courageously given of themselves in leadership.

7. We see religion, magick, and wisdom-in-living as being united in the way one views the world and lives within it — a world view and philosophy of life, which we identify as Witchcraft or the Wiccan Way.

8. Calling oneself "Witch" does not make a Witch — but neither does heredity itself, or the collecting of titles, degrees, and initiations. A Witch seeks to control the forces within him/herself that make life possible in order to live wisely and well, without harm to others, and in harmony with Nature.

9. We acknowledge that it is the affirmation and fulfillment of life, in a continuation of evolution and development of consciousness, that gives meaning to the Universe we know, and to our personal role within it.

10. Our only animosity toward Christianity, or toward any other religion or philosophy-of-life, is to the extent that its institutions have claimed to be "the one true right and only way" and have sought to deny freedom to others and to suppress other ways of religious practices and belief.

11. As American Witches, we are not threatened by debates on the history of the Craft, the origins of various terms, the legitimacy of various aspects of different traditions. We are concerned with our present, and our future.

12. We do not accept the concept of "absolute evil," nor do we worship any entity known as "Satan" or "the Devil" as defined by Christian Tradition. We do not seek power through the suffering of others, nor do we accept the concept that personal benefits can only be derived by denial to another.

13. We work within Nature for that which is contributory to our health and well-being.

·☾ ☽·

Get out your notebook and write down those concepts that either you do not understand or do not agree with, and why. Keep this page handy as you study further, and tick off those things that become clear to you and those that remain questionable.

Be sure that you re-read the Principles of Belief whenever you are in doubt of your position, either magickal or political. Most of us do live by and adhere to these thirteen principles; much like the Ten Commandments of the Christian religion, they serve their purpose well. Remember to sign and date this entry.

How Did I Get Here?

Although people have asked me numerous times just exactly how I got to be a Witch, I often wonder myself how I wandered on this path, and when. For me, trying to pinpoint it is difficult.

When I was little, I saw angels (which were naturally discounted by my parents as an upset stomach). I also had a constant feeling that I somehow didn't belong. I went through that "maybe I'm adopted" syndrome, but that didn't wash. I'm the spitting image of my mother. In fact, after she died, a friend of hers saw me in a bank and thought she was seeing my mother's ghost instead! That was an interesting experience.

When I was thirteen, an older family member gave me a deck of Tarot cards because she scared herself when she read them. No, they didn't tell her she was going to die, they told her about some important life events that were to come that she hadn't planned on! Hence, I got the cards.

When Sybil Leek's book *Diary of a Witch* came out, I ate it up. I had always been told that Witchcraft was evil, bad, part of the devil's work, etc. This book told me an entirely different story. I thought this was me, but because this was only one book and I had several years of standard religion drilled into my head, I was doubtful.

Around the same time, I visited my grandfather. As I sat by his chair eating cookies and drinking iced tea, he told me that at least one of my ancestors had been a Pennsylvania Dutch Pow-Wow artist. These people were known for their healing techniques. Years later, when I questioned him on the subject again, he denied it.

And so my own saga goes. My point is that everyone comes to the Craft in a different manner, and there is no one correct way to reach this juncture in your life. Often, your decision is made up of thousands of things that have happened over the years, that finally culminate into the knowledge of, "Gee, this really is me! This is what I am."

·☾ ☽·

Turn now to the third page in your notebook and write down how you came to this point in your life. What needs are you feeling right now? What do you feel you will gain by studying the Craft? What do you fear you may lose if you continue on this path? Be perfectly honest with yourself. If you are not, don't waste the ink in your pen or the lead in your pencil. You are not ready to enter the study of Witchcraft. Looking at both the bright side and the dark or shadow areas is extremely important in your progress.

To succeed in any endeavor, we must understand what qualities make us weak, and those that show our strength. Take your time and meet yourself eyeball to eyeball. You won't regret it!

Coven initiates are given a year and a day to determine entrance into the Craft. First, you may not like what an individual is teaching, how it is being taught, or have a distaste for someone else who is a member of the group. Human interaction can be both wonderful and painful. To subject yourself to pain for the sake of elusive forbidden knowledge that may or may not exist is not the way of the Craft.

Likewise, others may have the same feelings about you. An individual who opts for the Solitary path does not have this restriction. It is perfectly acceptable to begin your self-training as a Witch and discover along the way that you prefer some other type of esoteric study. The Craft, as any religion/science, is not for everybody. Your right to choose is the glorious benefit of being an individual.

I personally like the year and a day concept, and suggest exactly one year and one day from today (write today's date on the fourth page of your book) you re-read the notes you have taken during your study of this book. I assure you that you will be amused, astounded, and very proud of yourself. Even if you desire not to become involved with the Craft after finishing the text, I still encourage you to re-read your notes one year hence. You may be shocked at the accomplishments you have made on the path you have chosen.

Under today's date, write your own statement of purpose and a promise to yourself that you will re-read your notes in one full turn of the wheel.

Summary

In this chapter we have briefly covered the definition of Witch and Witchcraft. You have learned that by following the Principles of Belief, modern-day Witches can fit in quite nicely with the rest of society.

The Principles of Belief also show that we are not a bunch of crazies hovering over that proverbial cauldron, plopping in bats' wings and toad legs, living in a mystical cave somewhere atop Mount Whatever. We think logically, we plan wisely, and we show compassion for our brothers and sisters.

We care about the planet, the welfare of our children and those of others, the aged, animals, and the state of world political affairs. We are often the first in the fray to speak up for these rights, or the few who volunteer to help the community when it is needed.

When you pick up the broomstick, you take hold of both personal and community responsibility. Since you are one of the few, it is necessary for you to become a role model for others in our society. To tell your friends, family and acquaintances that you are a Witch without truly studying the Craft is a travesty of all you are supposed to believe.

Although the practice of the Craft is fun and enjoyable, the choice to enter such an environment is serious business. Your final choice must be made carefully and wisely.

Suggested Reading List

Margot Adler, *Drawing Down The Moon.* Beacon Press.
> One of the most comprehensive modern texts on Witchcraft offered today.

Scott Cunningham, *The Truth About Witchcraft Today.* Llewellyn Publications.
> An excellent book to give to friends and family; designed to ease fears and provide accurate definitions of our practices.

Doreen Valiente, *The Rebirth of Witchcraft.* Phoenix Publishing.
> Information on the resurgence of the Craft in England as seen through Doreen's personal experiences.

Witchcraft, Satanism and Ritual Crime, Who's Who and What's What. Church of All Worlds.
> An inexpensive booklet offered by this organization in an effort to educate the general public and remove the negative connotations around the Craft.

Joseph Campbell, *The Power of Myth.* Doubleday.
> An extensive dissertation on myth and belief in ancient and modern cultures.

Getting Acquainted

Which Witch Is Which?

Just as no single Witch is a stereotype, neither does his or her personal observance of the religion fall into a precise, pre-structured category. Even if one belongs to a Tradition (sometimes referred to as a "Trad") the very nature of the Craft allows much freedom in the celebration of your chosen pantheon of Gods and Goddesses.

"Tradition" means exactly what you think it does; a practice handed down from human to human. In this case, it means a way of celebrating the God and Goddess by the use of semi-structured guidelines passed down through the years, with various modifications to suit the needs of the group along the way.

Listed below are some of the different Traditions and sects Witches use today, along with a brief description of each.

Alexandrian Tradition: Founded in England during the 1960s, Alex Sanders referred to himself as the "King" of his Witches. The rituals are said to be modified Gardenarian.

British Traditional Witch: A mix of Celtic and Gardenarian beliefs. Most famous organization at this time is the International Red Garters. British Traditionals move mostly from within the Farrar studies (the famous Witch husband and wife from England.) They too are fairly structured in their beliefs, and train through the degree process. Their covens are also co-ed.

Celtic Wicca: The use of a Celtic/Druidic pantheon mixed with a little ritual Gardnerian, and heavily stressing the elements, nature and the Ancient Ones. They had a vast knowledge of and respect for the healing and magickal qualities of plants and stones, flowers, trees, elemental spirits, the little people, gnomes and fairies.

Caledonii Tradition: Formally known as the Hecatine Tradition, this denomination of the Craft is Scottish in origin, and still preserves the unique festivals of the Scots.

Ceremonial Witchcraft: Followers of this Tradition uses a great deal of ceremonial magick in their practices. Detailed rituals with a flavor of Egyptian magick are sometimes a favorite, or they may use the Qabbalistic magick.

Dianic Tradition: First pinpointed by Margaret Murray in 1921 in "The Witch-Cult in Western Europe," this term appears to include a mixture of various traditions. However, their prime focus in recent years is on the Goddess, and has been pegged as the "feminist" movement of the Craft.

Eclectic Witch: Look in any personals column in a Craft-oriented newsletter or journal and you will see this catch-all phrase. Basically, it indicates that the individual does not follow any particular Tradition, denomination, sect, or magickal practice. They learn and study from many magickal systems and apply to themselves what appears to work best.

Gardnerian Tradition: Organized by Gerald Gardner in England in the 1950s. Just why is this fellow so darned important? Gerald was one of the few people so determined that the Old Religion should not die that he took the risk of publicizing it through the media. Under all the hype, I truly believe he understood that the young needed the Craft as much as the Craft needed a new generation to survive.

Note: Both the Alexandrian and Gardnerian Traditions follow a more structured route in ceremony and practices. Usually, they are not as vocal as other Witches and are careful both in screening and the practice of their Craft. Therefore, if you are ever invited to visit or join either circle, do not expect the High Priest or Priestess to spill his or her guts during your first encounter. They adhere to a fairly foundational set of customs.

Hereditary Witch: One who can trace the Craft through their family tree *and* who has been taught the Old Religion by a relative who was living at the same time. Channeling doesn't count. How far one has to go back on the family tree to meet the conditions of the first part of this definition is debatable. Family Trades (another name for Hereditary Witches) occasionally adopt individuals into their dynasty. This decision is never a light one, and usually stems from the lack of offspring to carry on the line, or the high regard they hold for the person in question. The ceremony is intricate and important. After all, it is not every day you can pick your relatives! It is much like the marriage of an individual into a family.

Kitchen Witch: You will hear this term every once in a while. Basically, this type is one who practices by hearth and home, dealing with the practical side of religion, magick, the earth and the elements. There are some who groan loudly at this type of terminology, viewing it as degrading or simply inappropriate. Just remember that the Old Religion started somewhere, and most likely the kitchen (or cookfire) was the hub of many charms, spells, healings, and celebrations. After all, where does everyone congregate during the holidays? Grandma's kitchen has always produced magickal memories for humanity; visions of Mother making that something special for a sick child still holds true today for many of us.

Pictish Witchcraft: Scottish Witchcraft that attunes itself to all aspects of nature: animal, vegetable, and mineral. It is a solitary form of the Craft and mainly magickal in nature with little religion.

Pow-Wow: Indigenous to South Central Pennsylvania. This is a system, not a religion, based on 400-year-old Elite German magick. Pow-Wow has deteriorated to a great degree into simple faith healing. Although Pow-Wow finds its roots in German Witchcraft, few practicing Pow-Wows today in Pennsylvania follow the Craft or even know the nature of its true birth.

Satanic Witch: One cannot be a satanic Witch because Witches do not believe in satan.

Seax-Wica: Founded by Raymond Buckland in 1973. Although of Saxon basis, it was authored by Raymond himself without breaking his original Gardnerian oath. Raymond Buckland's contribution to the Craft is a significant one. Not only did he develop a Tradition that is more than acceptable to many individuals, he also has written a large volume of textbooks on different magickal aspects and practices of the Craft, thereby enhancing many lives in a positive direction.

Solitary Witch: One who practices alone, regardless of Tradition, denomination, or sect. Solitaries come in various forms. Some were at one time initiated into a coven and eventually chose to extricate themselves from that environment and continue practicing a particular Tradition or sect by themselves. A solitary can also be an individual who has no desire to practice with or learn from a coven structure, but still may adhere to a specific Tradition or sect through the teachings of another. For example, a member of a Hereditary Family may choose to teach a close friend the art and science of the Craft, but choose not to adopt them as a Family member for any number of reasons. And finally, a solitary Witch can be a person who has decided to tough it out on their own, learning from books, networking, and fellow Witches of different Traditions. These people have the ability to pick themselves up and brush themselves off, and live to try again. More and more individuals are selecting the solitary path rather than that of group interaction. Another name for a solitary Witch is "Natural Witch." You may hear this word from time to time as well.

Strega Witches: Follows a tradition seated in Italy that began around 1353 with a woman called Aradia. Of all the traditional Witches, this group appears to be the smallest in number in the United States; however, their teachings are beautiful and should not be missed.

Teutonic Witch: From ancient time the Teutons have been recognized as a group of people who speak the Germanic group of languages. Culturally, this included the English, Dutch, Icelandic, Danish, Norwegian and Swedish peoples. This is also known as the Nordic Tradition.

The Wiccan Witch: So far in this rundown of Witches you may have noticed that I very rarely use the terminology "Wiccan," and that many of the definitions — other than individuals' names and dates — are derived from my own understanding of each term. I have listened to and read many arguments for and against the use of the words "Wiccan" and "Witchcraft." I will tell you quite honestly that I have used both words when discussing my faith, depending on the recipients of my conversation. There are those that feel the term "Witch" is an egotistical one. Maybe so. Different words mean different things to a variety of people. Each individual must draw their own conclusion as to the terms they use to describe themselves. I personally like the word "Witch" very much. To me, it means mystery, healing, power, special, different, balance, and history. It means knowledge, secrets, the earth, and a bond with both the male and female sides of myself. The word "Wiccan" does not give me those feelings. It projects a different set of associations —

weaving, church, New Earth, wicker furniture (don't ask me why) and
the movie *The Wicker Man* (which although I despised, I fully understand). It also means "front," a way to bring the public into accepting
our belief system for what it actually is, not what their preconceived
ideas of a word dictates to them. Both words have their strong and weak
points. It is simply how you view them that makes the difference. Neither definition is better than the other; you must choose for yourself.

·☾ ☽·

These, by all means, are not all the types of Witches you will meet, but it does
give you a general idea of what people like to call themselves.

Take out your notebook now and copy down the names of various types of
Witches along with a brief version of the definitions given. Leave some space
after each definition so that when you learn more about a different type, you
can add it to your notes.

Mixing Witches

There is one more term I would like to to think about — New Generation of
Witches. It does not mean the children of the Craft (although it can in some circles). Generally, it encompasses those individuals who have joined the Craft
within the past year or two of their lives. Rather than using the term initiate,
which leads one into the realm of covens and groups, New Generation of
Witches refers to those individuals who are progressive and learning the field
of Witchcraft.

An exciting aspect of the American Craft is its flexibility — as long as you
allow it. It is conceivable that one Witch could in fact practice many magickal
aspects of the Craft.

You will find Witches who use more than one type of magickal system in
any given week! For instance, they may use an Egyptian Hathor's Mirror incantation to turn evil away from themselves one day, use a Havamel rune inscription to bring a friend health or success; and then on the Full Moon follow a
specific Tradition ritual (let's say Strega), as well as use that Tradition in all of
their holiday celebrations.

You will also find people who double definitions when they describe
themselves. I've heard of "Druidic Witches," or statements like, "I'm a solitary
Witch who leans heavily on the Dianic Tradition." Keep in mind, however, that
because they lean heavily on one Tradition or another does not indicate that
they have been initiated by a group into that Tradition.

There is no end to the combinations that will make you happy, successful,
and at peace with humankind. Just because you begin by studying Gardnerian
does not mean you cannot read or learn about Dianic, or use the practices
together, if you so choose.

To operate within any society or belief structure, one must be familiar with its given parameters. The New Generation of Witches should learn the wisdom of "daring to be silent" when a situation dictates. Likewise, they will need the fortitude to "speak up" when the need arises.

Summary

It is necessary to study and research any topic in which you would like to study in detail. The definitions provided here are a good primer for you, but are by no means inclusive.

If you are unfamiliar with a Tradition or sect in which you become involved, do some homework. If someone tells you they are a Strega Witch and you don't know or remember what that terminology means, ask them for a definition. Don't keep quiet because you don't want the other person to fear you are inferior. No one person is an expert on every subject in the world. By interacting with others, we expand our knowledge base. Learn to keep an open mind when discussing the various aspects of the Craft with others.

My father once told me that my approach to religion was through the back door. Well, that may be true. But at least I am happy with my choices and comfortable with my practices, and he agrees with me that I don't seem any worse for wear!

Remember that no matter what "type" of Witch you grow to be, you are a representative of all Witches in the eyes of the general public. Be careful what you say when referring to the Craft and keep generalities to a minimum. Remember that the Craft is full of differences in opinion and belief, just like anything else.

Suggested Reading List

Rhiannon Ryall, *West Country Wicca*. Phoenix Publishing.

Raymond Buckland, *The Tree: Complete Book of Saxon Witchcraft*. Llewellyn Publications.

D. J. Conway, *Celtic Magic*. Llewellyn Publications.

Marion Weinstein, *Positive Magick*. Phoenix Publishing.

Stewart Farrar, *What Witches Do*. Phoenix Publishing.

Zsuzanna Budapest, *The Holy Book of Women's Mysteries*. Windo Press.

Magickal Jargon

Learning to Speak the Lingo

Whether you are in the world of sports or the sphere of artists, all fields have their own special buzz-words. The Craft world has tailored language, as well. Listed below are those words that you will come into contact with frequently during your studies. Give them the once over to begin, then turn to the exercise at the back of this chapter.

adept: An individual who through serious study and accomplishments is considered highly proficient in a particular magickal system. A person can be an adept at Egyptian magickal practices, but a total failure at practical kitchen magick.

Akashic records: In the early part of this century the famed psychic Edgar Cayce brought to general society the thought form of Akashic records. Supposedly, there is a giant data base somewhere that can be accessed for information on subjects such as past lives, healing, and other magickal/spiritual practices. This record system cannot be accessed by material equipment, such as a PC networking with a larger computer. In this case, the mind of the psychic or Witch accesses the data through Universal connections.

altar: A special, flat surface set aside exclusively for magickal workings or religious acknowledgement.

amulet: Usually considered an object of protection that has been charged to deflect specific negative energies or thought forms. Amulets can be made of feathers, plants, beads, etc. The horseshoe and the four-leaf clover are two examples of amulets.

ankh: An Egyptian hieroglyphic that is widely used as a symbol for life, love, and reincarnation. It is depicted as a cross with a looped top.

Aradia: A champion Italian Goddess sworn to protect her people against the aggression of masculine faith and its persecutors during the reign of medieval terror. The original Aradia was a female Christ figure in Italy who taught around 1353. She was imprisoned more than once, escaped several times and eventually disappeared. The second Aradia you will hear about is Leland's *Aradia,* a book detailing information from an Italian Gypsy Witch. The third Aradia is the daughter of Diana and Lucifer (God of the Sun). She is considered the Queen of the Witches.

Arcana: The two halves of a Tarot deck. The Major Arcana consists of 22 trumps depicting dominant occurrences in our lives. The Minor Arcana consists of 56 suit cards (sometimes called the lesser Arcana) that assist in fleshing out the trump situations, or indicate smaller occurrences in our lives. See also **Tarot cards.**

astral: This word conjures lots of definitions. To keep it simple, let's describe it as another dimension of reality. I have heard it referred to as "dream-time," which I think is an excellent label. This reference is from the Australian Aboriginal people and their teachings, which are well worth your further study.

astral travel/projection: The process of separating your astral body from your physical one to accomplish travel in the astral plane or dreamtime.

athame: A cleansed and consecrated ceremonial knife used in ritual work by Witches. The knife is never used for blood-letting, and rarely used for cutting anything on the material plane.

Balefire: You don't get to see too many of these today. In country settings its function was both magickal and practical. Holidays at which you would most likely see this type of celebration are Beltane, Midsummer, Lughnasadh and Mabon.

bane: Another word for bad, evil, destructive.

banish: To magickally end something or exorcise unwanted entities. To rid the presence of.

bi-location: This is an interesting practice. You use a type of astral projection to travel in everyday reality by retaining the capability to be aware of your present surroundings. Synonymous terms are **over-looking** and **mind-travel.**

bind: To magickally restrain something or someone.

Blood of the Moon: A woman's menstrual cycle. If this cycle occurs over a Full or New Moon (and you can arrange that) she is far more powerful than during any other time of the month, as long as she acknowledges this strength within herself. For too many years women have been told that they must regard their cycle with an unkind eye, calling it a curse when actually it is a boon. Society has so dictated this to them that many feel weak, tired and disoriented because they are supposed to. Wrong. If you can rearrange your thinking on this matter, the Blood of the Moon can pack a powerful wallop for you. If you feel spacy, try grounding.

Book of Shadows: A relatively new term for the collection of information in book form for a Witch's reference. Much akin to a magickal cookbook. Another name for this text would be **grimoire.**

bolline: A curved, white-handled knife used for practical magickal purposes such as cutting. For instance, the knife can be used to harvest herbs, cut a branch for a wand, inscribe candles, etc.

Burning Times: You will hear this often. It is in reference to a historical time from around 1000 CE through the 17th century when it is said that over nine million people were tortured and burned by church and public officials on the assumption that they were the Christian version of Witches. This turned into an extremely profitable venture, as all land and property was seized from the accused individual and portions given to the accuser (in reward fashion) and the remainder seized by the church officials. Historians indicated that the majority of people tortured and murdered were women and children.

Cabala: Also seen as **Kabbala(h)** and **Qabala.** The ancient Hebrew magickal system.

Call: Invoking Divine forces.

chakras: Seven major energy vortexes found in the human body. Each is usually associated with a color. These vortexes are: crown — white; forehead (third eye position) — purple; throat — blue; chest — pink or green; navel — yellow; abdomen — orange; groin — red. Smaller vortexes are located in the hands and feet, as well.

Charge, The: Originally written in modern form by Doreen Valiente, it is a story of the message from the Goddess to Her children.

channeling: This is a New Age practice wherein you allow a disincarnate entity to "borrow" your body to speak to others either through automatic writing or verbally. Channeling does not have a very good track record simply because it is difficult to prove and the information imparted is usually not about things that can be "tested." Subjects normally involve distant prophecy, what the after-life is like, the structure of other dimensions, words of wisdom that everybody really needs to know before it is too late, etc. Channeling is the new buzz-word for mediumship. The best known and most accurate medium within our present century was the late Edgar Cayce. Most book stores still carry some of his material and it is well worth your time to read. Channeling is not the same as contacting the dead for information or help.

charms: Can either be an amulet or talisman that has been charmed by saying an incantation over it and instilling it with energy for a specific task.

Cone of Power: Psychic energy raised and focused by either an individual or group mind (coven) to achieve a definite purpose. The most interesting Cone of Power raised in recent history was that of the Witches of England who stood together, despite their differences, to turn Hitler back from the shores of their beloved country.

cleansing: The act of removing any negative energy, vibrations or images from an object or place by utilizing positive, psychic energy.

consecration: The act of blessing an object or place by instilling it with positive energy.

coven: A group of thirteen or fewer Witches that work together in an organized fashion for positive magickal endeavors or to perform religious ceremonies. The **covenstead** is the meeting place of the Witches, and is often a fixed building or place where the Witch can feel safe and at home.

Days of Power: Although usually referred to as **Sabbats,** there are other days throughout the year that can be considered days of power. These days can be triggered by astrological occurrences, your birthday, a woman's menstrual cycle (also known as the **Blood of the Moon**), or your dedication/initiation anniversary.

dedication: Unlike the initiation ceremony that brings one into an order, the dedication of a Witch is that process where the individual accepts the Craft as their path, and vows to study and learn all that is necessary to reach adeptship in a given tradition. In a dedication, you consciously prepare yourself to accept something new into your life and stick with it, regardless of the highs and lows this action may produce.

deosil: Clockwise movement. Most rituals and ceremonies, even spells, call for deosil movement at some point in their construction.

divination: The art of using magickal tools and symbols to gather information from the Collective Unconscious on the nature of people, places, things, and events in the past, present and future.

dowsing: The art/science of using a pendulum or stick to find the actual location of a person, place, thing or element. Dowsing can also be used to answer yes or not questions, and quite a science has developed by holding a pendulum over a specially designed chart to answer specific questions on life patterns.

Drawing Down the Moon: A ritual used during the Full Moon by Witches to empower themselves and unite their essence with a particular deity, usually the Goddess.

Earth magick: A practical form of magick wherein the powers and forces of Earth Mother are used to conduct magickal workings or celebrations. Usually items associated with the Earth and nature hold a particular significance in the ritual or spell.

Elder: Many Wiccan organizations have a group or board of Elders who oversee the operations of the church and its variety of functions. These people have usually gained their positions through a combination of their abilities which may include education, experience, magickal adeptship and counseling.

elements: Usually counted as four: Earth, Air, Water and Fire. However, many Witches add Spirit or Akasha to this category, as well. Each element has a direction within a magick circle or working: East = Air; South = Fire; West = Water; North = Earth; Center = Spirit or Akasha.

Enchantment: A magickal object that must be kept absolutely secret and hidden from all human eyes and affects a hidden aura. Enchantments must be charmed first. Gems and magickal writing are good items to use for Enchantments.

evocation: To call something out from within.

familiar: An animal who has a spiritual bond with a Witch; often is the family pet. Familiars can also be entities who are created to protect your home from the astral.

fascination: A mental effort to control another animal or person's mind. It has been referred to as "mind-bending." Although the technique of fascination runs a borderline when considering humans, it should not be totally trashed. Using it for a love spell would be unethical, and much like committing psychological rape. But if you found yourself in an unsafe situation where your person (or friend or family member) is in real physical danger, I wouldn't have the guts to tell you not to use all the tools and skills available to you.

Gaea/Gaia: Greek Goddess, now meaning Earth Mother or Mother Earth. Environmental action groups use this term almost as much as we do, if not more these days.

Green Man: Another name for the God, as in his kingdom of the forest.

Guardians: Ceremonial magicians use the **Guardians of the Watchtowers** or **Guardians of the Four Quarters**. Some Witches use them, too. There are those that see these Guardians as ugly little biddies, such as lizards, dragons, etc. But I have always envisioned them as the angels Michael, Ariel, Raphael and Gabriel.

handfasting: A Wiccan or Pagan marriage ceremony.

initiation: An experience that so transforms the individual that their concept of personal and worldly reality has been altered. A dedication ceremony should not be confused with an initiation.

invocation: To bring something in from without.

Karma: The belief that one's thoughts and deeds can be either counted against them or added to their spiritual path during several life times. In Sanskrit it means "action." Follows the law of cause and effect.

left-hand path: I never heard this one until I started networking across the country with other magickal individuals. It is a term that points to those people who feel that they are justified in using magick for purposes that are not constructive to other human beings. It is a reference that they are possibly a self-serving individual. Conversely, the **right-hand path** is considered positive in nature.

macrocosm: The world around us.

microcosm: The world within us.

magic(k): The art and science of focusing your will and emotions to effect change both in the world around you and the world within you. Magick is neither good nor evil, positive nor negative. It is the use of the power that determines the path it will take.

magick circle: A circular boundary drawn in visionary blue flames or white light that protects the Witch from outside forces while conducting ritual magick. One must never step outside the circle while performing a ritual unless the appropriate precautions have been take to cut a door. Nor should anyone step in during a ritual, unless they are following a pathway made for them. The door is usually cut with the athame or wand. This circle should never be left hanging after your ritual is over. This means that it must be closed just as ceremoniously as it was opened. The magick circle is considered the doorway between the worlds and allow us to move between the two. Some Witches draw the circle in the physical, either permanently on the floor or for temporary use with herbs, sand, salt, chalk or a nine-foot cord. The circle is still cast with blue or white light by the High Priestess/Priest or individual designated to do so. In some covens, the person is in charge of a particular quarter is responsible for preparing the area before the coven members arrive. This includes cleaning the area, cleansing, consecrating, and making sure all the necessary supplies have been transported to the location.

magickal systems: Can refer to Traditions, denominations, sects, or pantheons. It is a basic set of guidelines relating to specific Gods and Goddesses or cultural traditions.

New Age: Usually refers to mixing metaphysical practices with a structured religion.

Pagan/Neopagan: Follower of a nature-based religion. The term **Neopagan** means "new Pagan" and is not a popular term. It seems to be a direct result of the New Age lingo.

pantheon: No, we are not talking about a building, but a collection or group of Gods and Goddesses in a particular religious or mythical structure. Examples are: Greek pantheon, Roman pantheon, Egyptian pantheon, Teutonic pantheon, etc.

pentacle: A circle surrounding a five-pointed, upright star (known as a pentagram). Worn as a symbol of a Witch's belief and used in magickal workings and ceremonies. Each point on the star has a specific meaning: Earth, Air, Fire, Water and Spirit. Pentacles are never worn inverted in the Craft. Many Witches consider this blasphemy of their faith. However, an inverted pentagram is used in some second degree initiations, not to indicate evil, but to fulfill a function of growth.

Priestess: A female dedicated to both the service of her chosen deity(ies) and humankind. A **High Priestess** is the feminine leader of a coven or Wiccan organization and plays the role of Goddess in certain ceremonies. A solitary Witch can be a Priestess by dedicating herself to a particular God or Goddess.

Priest: A male dedicated to both the service of his chosen deity(ies) and humankind. A **High Priest** is the male leader of a coven or Wiccan organization and plays the role of the God in certain ceremonies.

Note: Neither male nor female has dominion over the other in the Craft. The High Priest and High Priestess in a coven environment should work as a balanced team. On occasion they draw in the energy of the God and Goddess respective to their sex in order to further a positive magickal working or celebrate a holiday. These people must be skilled in magick and ceremony, but they also need maturity, wisdom and a great degree of humility. They are required to be diplomatic and merciful when the situation demands. Their job is not an easy one. You will hear reference to the Great Rite, wherein the High Priest and High Priestess magickally draw in the energy of the God and Goddess through sexual interaction, either simulated or real. However, if intercourse actually takes place, it is almost always done in privacy, out of sight of the other coven members. In the 1970s sexual intercourse among coven members was prominent in some traditions. In the 1990s with the threat of the AIDS virus and society's shift to more conservative views on sexuality, actual intercourse is not as widely practiced. I would also like to add that sex magick is not a requirement for any individual to practice Witchcraft.

reincarnation: The belief that one has lived before in another lifetime.

ritual: A focused mental/physical ceremony to either honor or thank one's chosen pantheon, or to perform a specific magickal working or act.

runes: A set of symbols that are used both in divination and magickal workings. There are several types of runes with different origins. A few are the Norse, Scandinavian and Germanic runes. Unlike the Tarot, they are an integral part of a magickal system with its own pantheon, should you care to use it. They can function as an alphabet and are useful in vision questing, dream recall and controlling your environment.

scrying: A divination method using specific tools such as a bowl of inked water, a mirror, crystal ball, etc., where the diviner "sees" either normal visual pictures, mental visual pictures, or information without any pictures at all!

sigil: A magically oriented seal, sign, glyph, or other device used in a magickal working. The most powerful sigils are those that you create yourself. Sigils can be used on letters, packages, clothing, on paper tucked in your pocket, etc.

Skyfather: Assigning deification to the sky as a male entity. Although shamanistic in its origin, I personally think it compliments Earth Mother perfectly and refer to it often. Skyfather is also used by several Native American belief systems.

skyclad: In some traditions, for example the Alexandrian, it is the act of celebrating or doing a magickal working in the nude. This should not be misconstrued with sexual contact. There are many solitaries that prefer to work skyclad, feeling that the absence of clothing leaves their energy unhindered during the ceremony.

spell: Extended mental and emotional energy spoken aloud, written, spoken to oneself, drawn or even danced. To work, it should be clear, concise, focused and emotional. The need must be present to bring any spell to a successful culmination.

spiral: The sacred spiral plays an important part in magickal workings. It is the symbol of "coming into being." A spiral dance celebrates the spiral symbolism.

talisman: An object that has been magickally charged in order to bring something to the bearer. Such an item could be a gemstone to win a court case, or a drawing to put in your pocket that will bring good luck.

Tarot cards: A set of 78 cards which carry pictures and symbols used to connect the diviner with the collective unconscious. No one knows the specific origin of the cards, and there are many beautiful decks now on the market. Although the Rider/Waite deck is well known, I prefer the Witches' Tarot or the Robin Wood Deck. The cards can be used to determine the past, present and future of an event or person and can become powerful tools in magickal workings and rituals.

Tarologist: One who is adept at the art and science of handling the Tarot.

vision questing: Using astral projection, bi-location, or dreamtime to accomplish a specific goal. Also called **pathworking**.

webweaving: Networking with other magickal people through conversation, in writing, or by computer to gather information to mutually assist each party in their studies and life goals.

Wheel of the Year: One full cycle of the seasonal year, beginning with the Samhain celebration.

widdershins: Counterclockwise motion used in some magickal workings or ceremonies.

working: As in **magickal working.** The process of using magick to reach a desired positive goal.

·☾ ☽·

These words by no means encompass all the terminology of the Craft. Various Traditions and covens have their own terminology that they do not share with those outside their circle.

Get out your notebook now and transfer these words along with their definitions as you understand them. Leave space after each word for adding information in the future.

You may have noticed that I have not included words like Esbat, Sabbat, specific holidays, Full and New Moons, etc. These will be covered in later chapters.

Summary

The jargon presented here is to familiarize you with the Craft in general terms. Many of these words will appear again in this book. These are the words that I had to either look up or ask about when I began my study in the Craft.

Never be afraid to ask questions. If someone thinks you are foolish because of it, they themselves are truly the fool.

Religion vs. Science

It is my personal opinion that most people are attracted to the Craft not by its religious content, but by its scientific and technological allure. There are a few individuals that would gasp at that statement, but one must consider that the intricacies of the religious aspect are not well known to the general public. If they were, we would not experience the heavy weight of prejudice like we do.

Science is another matter. Examples of the science of the Craft are telepathy, spell-casting, divination, astral travel, dowsing, etc. The outside world is more likely to hear and become interested in the technology of the Craft because it appears to be less threatening in nature than a new religious structure that is different from their own. I use the terminology "new" because the preconceived ideas most people hold of the Craft are incorrect, and the truth of our religion would be a new reality to them.

When these people study our "science" with seriousness, sometimes along the way spiritual enlightenment enters the picture, usually with the force of an exploding bomb. This shock does not always lead them directly into the Craft, but it usually guides them to some type of magickal religion, whether it be Shamanism, Eastern Religions, etc.

Dealing with the New Generation of Witches puts an individual in an extremely unique position; much like those people who were forced into early Christian acceptance, they bring their previous beliefs with them, whether they like it or not. The difference here is that the Craft does not demand you give up everything you believe in just to accept it as a religion. There is no need to hide where you came from and what religion you grew up with.

Today, the majority of individuals interested in the Craft have come from mainstream religious backgrounds. To expect them to immediately drop or re-shape the God-form they have always known, and give him some buddies to work with from mythological structures, does not often rest well in the pre-programmed mind. Hence, we see the allure and the interplay of the scientific or technological aspects of the Craft, and the need for many new Witches to use a great deal of ceremonial magick in their rituals.

The science of the Craft acts as a buffer against total, immediate reconstruction of the spirit of the individual. The different technologies can be tested, analyzed and neatly labeled, allowing the individual to understand that they are in control because they can define their own parameters.

Science tells us that the human mind, if programmed properly, can accomplish astounding feats. Witchcraft teaches the same concept, and it is this ideology that draws people to it. It is the exciting consideration that humans might really be in charge of their own destiny!

Witchcraft is both a set of scientific principles and a religious structure. I have found that people who enter the Craft on the basis of science discover religion, and those that are looking for a comfortable religious doctrine discover the science (even though some won't readily admit it to you). The Craft is the ultimate combination of both principles.

You will find that some Witches rely heavily on one principle or the other. This does not present a problem unless they refuse to accept the other half, denoting an entirely internal problem of analysis on their part, not yours.

In the Craft, there is room for everyone. There are those Witches who practice the Craft strictly within scientific boundaries. They use a great deal of high magick and consider the holidays ceremonies. There are those that practice it in a very spiritual manner with little use of tools, depending upon their minds and their close associations with various deities. These people use the Craft for self-healing and empowerment, and are more open to ideas like channeling, the existence of Angels, talking with the dead, other dimensions, even UFO's and Star People.

There are Witches who practice the Craft in a strictly religious form and are not at all happy about the technical side of the Craft, although they use it through religious observance whether they want to admit it or not.

People drift to different facets of the Craft either by pre-programmed ideas that are difficult to let go, or to fill a specific need at the time. There is nothing wrong with this, unless others try to make their truths yours.

There is room for everyone in the Craft, which is what makes it so unique in the first place. If you are like me, you came to the Craft by studying the psychology and motivation of the mind, gradually moved into spiritual education, and finally accepted it as a religion. Not everyone follows the same path.

You must accept what is acceptable to you, not what is acceptable to the High Priestess in the coven in the next town, or the solitary that practices two cities away and visits you once every six months.

This concept is sometimes difficult for the New Generation of Witches to understand. They so desperately want to do things the right way so they can be considered a real Witch that they fail to give their own opinions the benefit of the doubt.

Conversely, there are new Witches who have brought too much of their previous prejudices along with them and find themselves in extremely hot water from time to time, simply because they fail to understand that an integral part of the Craft is the ability for everyone to have an open mind, not just a few.

I have sat in the presence of coven matriarchs who are livid that anyone would practice Witchcraft without strict religious overtones. I have shared meals with individuals that would never dream of patterning their own study of the Craft with even a hint of religious theology or conviction. Each of these people are following their own paths and learning their own lessons along the way.

When you are dealing with any religion or form of esoteric study, you will find it colored with human ideas and attitudes that are as varied as the personalities of the people involved. Be patient and understanding with the differences in opinion you will encounter. This, in itself, is a valuable lesson as you journey forward.

Get out your notebook now and set aside three pages. On the first page write "Science," on the second write "Religion," and on the third write "Religion vs. Science."

On each page, write a short paragraph on your feelings on the subject. Be sure to sign and date each entry. Put them back in your book and re-read them next month, then two months hence. Check to see if your own opinions have changed or grown. Be sure to make a journal entry while you are re-reading the pages.

Your Special Days of Celebration

The Adjustment

Depending upon your previous religious background, your first year of Craft celebrations and holidays may be a bit confusing. You may find yourself acknowledging generally accepted holidays with your family and friends right along with the private celebration of your Craft special days.

There is nothing wrong with this. Our family is a large one with many children. I am a Witch, but my husband is a Pagan and my father is a Christian. Therefore, we still celebrate the coming of Santa on December 25th, right along with Yule from December 20-23, depending upon the actual time of the solstice. Granted, some of the double holidays create a little more work, but it is well worth it!

Eventually, you may wish to drop some or all of the general popular holidays. For instance, we no longer acknowledge Lent, nor do we consider January 1st the beginning of the new year, which in our faith, begins on October 31st with our Samhain festival. It is acceptable to continue double holidays for your entire lifetime. In Witchcraft it really doesn't matter! All positive forms of celebration are accepted.

By the first Turn of the Wheel, you may find that you have missed some of your special days. I know I did. Don't worry about it. It is difficult to expect a person to totally trash how they have been living for several years and pick up a whole new set of realities, including holidays! The God and the Goddess are not going to destroy your happy home because you forgot.

They don't dispense lightening bolts to your front door if you really aren't comfortable with some of the special days, or don't feel up to celebrating others. "Shit happens," as they say, and you will not always be able to be poised at the correct astrological moment to perform a celebration for a specific holiday. Grandma may be down with the flu and you are staying with her until she is better, or your parents may have flown in from Madagascar and you have to pick them up at the airport. Imagine their surprise if you told them, "Gee, sorry folks, I'm a Witch now and I can't possibly pick you up because I will be dancing naked in my backyard under the Full Moon!" That would certainly impress them.

I personally don't recommend telling your friends and distant family members within the first year of your study of the Craft that you have taken on a new reality, unless you are absolutely sure they will not have any difficulty dealing with the subject. If you are married, more than likely your partner will discover the change in you during that first year and figure it out anyway, so it is best to deal with that hurdle first, and the rest of the world later. We will discuss that magick moment when you begin to tell people about your faith further on in this book.

During the first year of celebrating Craft holidays you may reach a period of internal disquiet. It can be upsetting to realize that not everyone in your environment will accept the celebrations of the Craft holidays, or you may feel lonely on readily accepted holidays that you no longer believe in. You may even experience anger when you realize how the rest of the world insists on shoving their holidays down your throat, and may be intolerant of your beliefs and feelings on the subject.

For instance, I can remember when my parents were horrified when prayer and other Christian religious teachings were taken out of the public school system. I did not realize at the time how restrictive having Christianity in the schools could be. Now, I certainly would not want my children participating in a religion that our family does not believe in, unless they have a choice in the matter.

It is possible that after the second Turn of the Wheel in your Craft life you will feel very uncomfortable with the holidays that are not your own. This seems most typical with the major holidays. Be wise, however, and don't voice your opinion until you discover within yourself the reason for your anger or discomfort.

Learning to honor other positive religions is part of your study. You don't have to practice them to understand them. Soon, you really won't care what they do because you will be excited about your own holidays and anticipation will twirl about you as you are preparing your own reality.

To learn your special days I recommend the purchase of the following:

1. **A Large Wall Calendar.** Although any calendar would do provided it has blocks big enough to write in, I suggest a calendar designed for magickal people that marks the quarters, cross-quarters, holidays, New and Full Moons and government holidays. Save the calendar from your local gas station for more mundane things.

2. **A Yearly Almanac.** These usually start hitting the bookstores in late August and early September. You will need this to get the accurate times for Full and New Moons, quarters, and cross-quarters. A farmer's almanac will do fine; however, there are almanacs designed for magickal people that are quite beneficial.

You may also want to carry a small date book in your purse, briefcase or back pocket — even the glove compartment of your truck or car is a good idea. Just circle the dates you wish to keep track of for quick reference. Put a star on the day that is a week before the holiday or moon so you will remember to purchase any supplies you may need.

On your wall calendar you will want to be more specific. Use the almanac to write in the appropriate times, if your calendar does not have them, for moons, quarters and cross-quarters, including any other major astrological times you may need. Of course, if you have purchased a magickal calendar, this step is not necessary. If you are unfamiliar with the Waxing and Waning Moon periods, you may want to make a notation of these spans as well. Use a highlighter to mark strings of days. For example, the three days before the Full Moon, and the three days after.

After a while you will automatically feel the coming of these days and look forward to them, just as you may have looked forward to the traditional holidays you celebrated in the past. You are building your own traditions now.

The Solar Holidays

Eight standard Craft holidays are recognized during each calendar year. They are called Sabbats, and their relationship is usually with the sun deity. This does not mean that you cannot honor the Goddess on a solar holiday. Rituals have been written in honor of both deities for many celebrations. Other deities that you feel comfortable with can be added at a later date, after careful thought on their compatibility with both the celebration and other deities involved.

The eight Sabbats represent seasonal birth, death, and rebirth. I have provided a brief description of each sabbat, along with some of the various names by which they are known. We begin with Winter Solstice, also known as Yule, because it is the first seasonal holiday that falls after the Witch's New Year (Samhain).

Yule: Yuletide, Winter Solstice

The shortest day of the year and, of course, the longest night. This is usually the 20th or 21st of December. *Yuletide* (the Teutonic version) lasts from December 20th through December 31st. It begins on "Mother Night" and ends twelve days later on "Yule Night;" hence the "Twelve Days of Christmas" tradition. In Pecti-Wita Yule falls on December 22nd and is called *Feill Fionnain.* In the Caledonii Tradition it is called *Alban Arthan* and is not considered a fire festival. A time when the waxing sun overcomes the waning sun. In some traditions, it is a time when the Holly King (representing the death aspect of the God) is overcome by the Oak King (who embodies the rebirth of the God, and is sometimes referred to as the Divine Child).

Since this is a solar festival, it is celebrated by fire and the use of the Yule log. The colors of the season, red and green, are of original Pagan descent. The act of cutting and decorating the Yule Tree and exchanging gifts are also Pagan derivatives. Wreaths of holly and fancy cookies and breads are a part of our tradition, as well. Food is prepared specially for the after-dinner Yule celebration when the tree is lighted and the Yule log is burned. A portion of the Yule log is saved to be used in lighting next year's log. This piece is kept throughout the year to protect the home.

Bayberry candles are also burned to ensure wealth and happiness throughout the following year. They can be placed on the dining table at sunset and burned until they go out by themselves. Another pair can be set upon the mantle and lit at the beginning of the Yule ceremony.

The reindeer stag is also a reminder of the horned God, so if you find yourself trying to choose a card for both Christian and Pagan friends, choose a nature scene that includes the stag — an easy way not to offend anyone! You will find that many traditional Christmas decorations have some type of Pagan ancestry or significance that can be added to your Yule holiday.

Candlemas

Also referred to as *Imbolic* (Celtic) *Imbolgc Brigantia* (February 1st; Caledonii), *Lupercus* (Strega), *Candelaria* (Mexican Craft), and *Disting* (February 14th in the Teutonic Tradition). All involve celebrations of banishing the winter season.

In October our family goes to a country market where we choose pumpkins for Samhain. We also purchase three ears of dried corn in different colors, each color representing a stage of the Goddess — Maiden, Matron and Crone. The corn is stored in our magickal cabinet until Candlemas when the three ears are tied together with spring-colored ribbons and used in the Candlemas ceremony. Hang the corn outside the house for wealth and protection until the day after the Fall Equinox, then bury it in the garden.

An easy way to remember Craft holidays is to associate them with seasons. For instance, Candlemas, Ostara and Beltane are the three spring festivals. Candlemas welcomes the change from old to new. Ostara invites the fertility energy of the earth to awaken, and Beltane represents the fertility and love energy awakening in humans. Count me stupid, but it took me a while to figure out that six of the holidays were related in groups of three.

Lavender and white candles can be burned in honor of the holiday. This is a good time to work in the house, changing tablecloths and curtains, room painting and wallpapering and fixing furniture.

Candlemas is one of those holidays that creeps up on you as you are finally breathing a sigh of relief from the steady roll of celebration from October through December.

The Candlemas Sabbat marks the time to welcome the spring. This festival is for fertility and to celebrate the things that are yet to be born, just barely waking under winter's cold shroud. This is also a good time to look over your magickal cabinet to determine what you are low on and what you may need for the coming months.

Ostara: Spring (Vernal) Equinox

In the Caledonii Tradition this holiday is known as *Alban Eiler* and represents the warrior aspect of the god. This Sabbat occurs in mid-March when night and day are of equal length. It is a celebration of balance — not really Winter but not yet Spring. This festival is considered one of fertility, and is the second in the trinity of spring celebrations. Seeds are blessed for future plantings. Eggs are colored and placed on the altar as magickal talismans. The familiar Easter Bunny is a Pagan derivative, as are baskets of flowers. The colors light green, lemon yellow and pale pink are traditional for this holiday.

This is also the time to treat yourself to a new broom if you are a woman, and a staff if you are a man. Both must be ritually consecrated. The broom is used to sweep a magick circle clean, and is given a name as you would name a familiar. A naming ceremony can also be included in your Ostara festivities.

Twisted bread and sweet cakes are prepared to be served at dusk — or better yet, prepare a family breakfast that coincides with sunrise on this day.

Beltane

Also known as *Mayday, Walburga* (Teutonic), *Rudemas* (Mexican Craft), *Festival of Tana* (Strega), and *Bealtinnc* (Caledonii). Mayday is celebrated on the first day of May, while Beltane is recognized on the 5th of May. Most celebrations mean the same thing. Beltane is the last of the three spring fertility festivals, and is when people, plants, and animals prepare for the warm months ahead. This is a time for love, union, and of course, the Maypole. I always tie in this particular Sabbat to children and faeries. It is a time of joining two halves to make a whole — the third entity.

Ribbons of bright blue, lavender, warm pink, lemon yellow and white are nice representatives of the season, but the traditional colors for Mayday are red and white, representing the blood that flows from the woman when her purity is taken. Pick a particular tree in your yard and adorn it with ribbons and bows. This particular holiday represents the Divine Union of the Lord and Lady.

House decorations on that day can include a large bowl of floating flowers and white floating candles. Baskets of fresh flowers picked moments before dawn can be hung on the front door, and the mantle can be laden with greens and flowers. Flower petals can be strewn about the circle and later swept into a pile and distributed around the perimeter of the house for protection.

Summer Solstice

Also known as Midsummer Night's Celebration, though the two do not always coincide on the astrological calendar. Pecti-Wita celebrates *Feill-Sheathain* on July 5th; the Caledonii Tradition hails in *Alban Hefin,* celebrating the kingly aspect of the god.

This is the longest day of the year. To me, this holiday represents the Sun King in all his glory. A celebration of passion and success. Some of the most powerful magick I have ever accomplished has been on this holiday. It is great for business needs or a situation where the power of male energy is needed. Sunflowers (provided you have planted them in the house in very early spring and put them out after the first frost) and any flowers of red and maize yellow or gold are excellent altar decorations. A wreath can be made for your door with red feathers (for sexuality) and yellow feathers (for prosperity) intertwined or braided with ivy. Altar candles should be of gold and red.

Money tree plants can be harvested and strung above the mantle for monetary wealth, or tied in a bunch with green ribbon, provided there has been an early planting season. If not, wait until mid-July for harvest.

Midsummer Night's Eve is also a time to commune with field and forest sprites and faeries.

Lammas

Also called *Lughnassadh* (Celtic), *Cornucopia* (Strega), *and Thingtide* (Teutonic). This is the first of the three harvest celebrations in the Craft. Lammas is celebrated on August 2nd, where Lughnassadh, a Celtic festival in honor of the Sun God, is held on the 7th. Both holidays represent the same idea. This Sabbat represents the beginning of the harvest cycle and rests on the early grain harvest as well as those fruits and vegetables that are ready to be taken.

Bread is traditionally baked for this holiday, and the altar is decorated with the first fruits of garden labor. Canning goes into full swing, and magickal cabinets are stocked with herbs before the onset of fall. Herbs for magickal use should be harvested this day. You may wish to empower some of them in your ritual.

Most of the flowers are gone; however, there are still some varieties available. An altar decorated with pots of yellow and red cockscomb is truly arresting as the tassel of the plant resembles a flame.

This is also the time to prepare your house for the fall season by replacing curtains, tablecloths, rugs, etc.

Autumn Equinox

Also referred to as *Mabon* (Celtic), *Alban Elfed* (Caledonii), and *Winter Finding* (Teutonic). Winter Finding spans from the Equinox itself until Winter Night (October 15), which is the Norse New Year. The Caledonii festival celebrates the Lord of Mysteries. This, the second harvest festival, is associated with the taking of the corn and other foods that are to be harvested at this time. Cornbread cakes and cider are an excellent addition to the festivities. The frost will hit soon, so the last of the herbs and other plants you wish to dry for winter use should be harvested now.

Depending on when the leaves turn in your area, you may wish to paraffin them and add them to your house decorations. Dip the leaves quickly in melted paraffin, and put them on wax paper. When the leaves are dry you can put them in a huge, decorative jar with a sigil of protection carved lightly on some or all of the leaves.

Colors used for candles should be brown, orange, gold or red. Altar cloths can be made of material with fall designs. River and stream stones gathered over the summer can be empowered for various purposes.

Halloween

Also known as *Samhain* (Celtic), *Shadowfest* (Strega), *Martinmas* or *Old Hallowmas* (Scottish/Celtic), this holiday is considered the Witches' New Year, representing one full turn of the seasonal year. This is the last of the three harvest Sabbats. Halloween is celebrated on October 31st, Samhain is recognized as November 7th (All Hallows Eve), and Martinmas on November 11th. All festivals stand for the same purpose.

I'll not kid you, Halloween is my favorite Sabbat. Celebrations to honor the dead are done at this ritual, along with speaking with those who have passed over; divination is heightened on this night.

It is said that on this night the veil between the worlds is weakest. Jack-o-lanterns, gourds, cider and other fares of the season can be used in ritual and family celebration. Black candles are used to ward off negativity.

I start preparing for Samhain in September. I hand-sew all the children's costumes and decorations to be hung about the house. I begin putting these decorations out faithfully on the first of October. There are Witches plastered all over the front and sides of my house, and windsocks I have made for protection depicting Halloween scenes. I hang a pentacle wreath above my wall altar decorated with ravens, little brooms and orange feathers and ribbons.

Pots of large golden-yellow mums are placed about the house, and some of the rooms are repainted for the celebration, if it is necessary.

I buy my new house broom now; it is always black. Close to Samhain, I tape a balloon on the top and stick the proverbial Witch's hat atop, and set it on my front stoop. I give this Witch a name and ask her to protect the house during our community mischief night. I started this little ritual because one year I had a skeleton on my one and only favorite rocking chair on our stoop. He was covered in fake cobwebs and spiders, and lighted for the occasion. He really did look fine! Well — too fine, I suppose, because after mischief night not only was my skeleton missing, but so was my rocking chair!

At dinner on Samhain our family sets an empty place for those who have departed who were dear to us. Since the passing of another family member last year, we have begun to set a separate table for them as they were crowding out the hungry living tummies at the main table.

·☽ ☽·

Sometimes the following holidays are called Fire Festivals, and they are also referred to as the quarters of the year:
    Yule/Winter Solstice/Yuletide/Alban Arthan
    Spring Equinox/Ostara/Easter/Alban Eiler
    Summer Solstice/Feill-Sheathain/Alban Hefin
    Fall Equinox/Mabon/Winter Finding/Alban Elfed

Cross quarters are the following Sabbats:
    Candlemas/Imbolic/Lupercus/Disting/Imbolgc Brigantia/Candelaria
    Beltane/Mayday/Walburga/Festival of Tanna/Whitsun
    Lammas/Lughnassadh/Cornucopia/Thingtide
    Samhain/Halloween/Shadowfest/Martinmas/Old Hallowmas

Performing magick on Sabbat celebrations is not a necessity. One may prefer to use them as celebratory or honorary holidays. Use of the Sabbats varies by Tradition, denomination and sect.

I suggest you get out your notebook now and write down the eight major Sabbats, when they occur on the calendar, and what day of the week they will fall on this year. After each Sabbat write a simple definition, leaving room to add information at a later date.

Esbats

Witches love their holidays, but they need days specifically set aside to do magickal work for a friend in need, to set the stage for a new endeavor, etc. These work days (and nights) are called Esbats.

Full and New Moon celebrations are usually the days and nights of an Esbat, so as to use the correct moon phase for ultimate results. This does not mean that you cannot honor the God during an Esbat (even though the moon energy is usually attributed to the Goddess). Rituals have been written for both deities. Another term for esbat is *Lunar Ritual*.

Full Moon energy is used for banishing unwanted influences in your life, protection magick, and divination. Planning, releasing and working backwards in time are done on the Full Moon as well.

It is said that the best Full Moon magick can be conjured for seven days: the three days prior to the Full Moon, the night of the Full Moon itself, and three days after the Full Moon. Sometimes the results of Full Moon magick take approximately one moon cycle to take hold and come to completion.

The New Moon is used for personal growth, healing, the blessing of a new project or venture, etc. If done correctly, success should be obtain by the first Full Moon.

Between the New and Full Moons is the period we call the Waxing Moon. This is a good time for attraction magick, especially between the New Moon and First Quarter.

The period between the Full Moon and New Moon is called the Waning Moon. This is a time for banishing and rejecting things in our lives that we no longer wish to carry around with us. Negative emotions, bad habits, diseases and ailments can successfully be banned during this time.

The three days before the New Moon is known as the dark of the moon. This is when you can't see the moon at all in the heavens. Traditionally, this is a time when no magick is performed. It is a period to give yourself a break; a time of rest. Deep meditation and vision questing can be performed now, but not for a specific magickal purpose. However, Hecate rules this time, and if her magick is needed, now is when you should use it.

Due to the rotation of the earth, there are thirteen Full Moons, and each carries a traditional name. They are:

Wolf Moon	January
Storm Moon	February
Chaste Moon	March
Seed Moon	April
Hare Moon	May
Dyad (pair) Moon	June
Mead Moon	July
Wyrt (green plant) Moon	August
Barley Moon	September
Blood Moon	October
Snow Moon	November
Oak Moon	December
Blue Moon	(variable)

In addition, the Harvest Moon is the Full Moon that falls nearest Mabon. It allowed farmers extra moonlight hours to bring in the crops. You can use it to call in favors or add extra protection.

A Blue Moon occurs when the moon with its 28-day cycle appears twice within the same calendar month, due to that month's 31-day duration.

A Blue Moon is a Goal Moon. It is here where you set specific long-term goals for yourself, and review accomplishments and failures since the last one. It is a good idea to write your goals on an index card and hang it on your bedroom mirror or by your alarm clock — some place where you will see it every morning or evening. You don't need to read it every day, just keep it visible for your subconscious to work on.

Esbats are considered working celebrations. They are times for you to raise energy, cast spells, perform healings, solve minor difficulties in your life, etc. This does not mean that you can't just have a ritual to honor a deity if things are going smoothly. Perhaps you have things well under control and your friend's problems are solved for the moment. You may well wish to spend the time honoring the Goddess; or the Lady, as she is sometimes called. You could spend the time honoring the God (or Lord) as well.

During a Full Moon Esbat, the Witch usually Draws Down the Moon. In a coven environment, this is performed by the High Priestess. In a solitary's life, he or she may do it (and should do it) to empower themselves. Much like recharging a battery, you are accepting the Divine power of the Universe within you, allowing it to strengthen and empower you. It is the act of acknowledging the power of the Lady (Moon) and drawing that energy into your body. For more on this ritual, see Chapter 16 of this book.

Summary

In the first portion of this chapter we have discussed the adjustment it may take for you to celebrate the Craft holidays. I have taken you through the eight major Sabbats:

Yule
Candlemas/Imbolic
Ostara/Spring Equinox
Beltane/Mayday
Summer Solstice/Midsummer
Lammas/Lughnassadh
Autumn Equinox/Mabon
Halloween/Samhain

I have provided you with the Americanized version of the Sabbats as well as those of other origins to show you that religious celebrations can float depending upon the Tradition, denomination or sect you are following. I have also give you a general idea of what these celebrations are for, and some information on how a Pagan family celebrates them.

There is no end to personal creativity (such as my Witch broom for Samhain) for any of these celebrations. Tailoring them to your personal needs will make them much more important to you, and therefore ensure your magickal and mundane success in life.

·☾ ☽·

The second part of this chapter covered a brief description of Esbats and moon cycles. It is now time for you to start thinking about those things in your life and circumstances that you would like to change by magickal workings.

Get out your notebook and consider the definitions for Full, New, Waxing and Waning Moons, then prioritize those items that you would like to improve or change. Place the correct moon phase beside each item on your list.

I'll bet you have a pretty big list, so review it and consider how many of these items are the direct result of one particular problem or need. This, then, is what you will want to concentrate on first.

After a time, you may find that some items on your list are no longer necessary. Just scratch them off. As you accomplish some of the things on your list, write the date beside them. We will get into accurate magickal record keeping later, but this is a good way to begin. Review this list on the Blue or Goal Moon.

Suggested Reading List

The books listed below have an excellent collection of rituals for both Sabbats and Esbats. Although this text will teach you how to write your own rituals, these books are excellent to get your creative juices flowing.

Pauline Campanelli, *Wheel of The Year.* Llewellyn Publications.

Ed Fitch, *Magickal Rites From The Crystal Well.* Llewellyn Publications.

Ed Fitch, *The Rites of Odin.* Llewellyn Publications.

Tadhg Mac Crossan, *The Sacred Cauldron: Secrets of the Druids.* Llewellyn Publications.

Herman Slater, *A Book of Pagan Rituals.* Samuel Weiser, Inc.

Starhawk, *The Spiral Dance.* Harper & Row Publishers (now known as Harper and Collins).

Marion Weinstein, *Earth Magick.* Phoenix Publishing.

Defining the All: Gods, Goddesses and Human Balance

You Mean I Get to Pick my Own Deities?

One of the most pivotal choices in Witchcraft is your choice of the deities (Gods/Goddesses) you will work with. The key thought form here is "with." The Craft is not a religion of supplication. If you intend to grovel before a God form, please stop here and throw this book away.

I am not indicating that you cannot honor or thank a deity, nor am I telling you that you cannot call upon them when you are in over your eyeballs. The common act of sniveling at their feet is unacceptable. If you truly want that type of relationship with the "higher-ups," there are plenty of well-cultured religions that will gladly open their arms to you.

The God/dess of the Craft is not interested in the sacrifice of your dignity. They are designed and function for the celebration of light and all the actions and deeds that go with it. Religion is interaction with the Divine, raising your personal vibrational sequence to accept and enjoy this union.

The Craft gives you the freedom to pick and subsequently honor your own forms of the Divine. Just as you would not call on any doctor when you are sick, you don't leaf through a book and call on any deity. As with physicians, when you need a specialist, that's what you look for, long and hard. You check references, talk to other patients, and eventually set up an appointment to interview the physician.

In the Craft, when you have a special need, you seek the deity that can assist you, much through the same format.

Why Pick Deities at All?

This is my theory; take it for what it is. I'm not saying it is right or wrong; it is, however, what I believe.

Look at the deity structure like a family tree. You know, those little projects that they have you do in the fourth or fifth grade where you trace your lineage as far back as you can scavenge from letters, Bibles, and diaries out of Grandma's attic (complete with cobwebs — very important for authenticity).

At the very top of the deity family tree is a glittering sphere of light and energy called the All. It is the essence of every living form from every plane of existence — a thing, yet a non-thing.

For a long time, the general human mind had a great deal of difficulty coping with The Force and identifying with it. The Star Wars movie saga, epitomizing both modern-day thought and future fantasy, created a simplified, understandable package for a futuristic religion. It introduced to us The Force in a manner we would comprehend. I have always found it amusing how well children accepted and understood this line of thinking from the beginning.

But most adults are still not comfortable with a non-thing that just appears to sit there and sparkle, so they rely on the images of Gods and Goddesses that appear in human, or at least partially human, form. It is that which they are most familiar with, something that at least looks like themselves.

Down we go then, to the first two branches of the tree, right below the All. Each branch is exactly the same, one on the right side of the tree and one on the left. Totally balanced in every respect to each other. They represent the God and the Goddess, or the Lord and the Lady. Separate yet equal, together they combine into the essence of the All.

These two images do not carry individual names, as they are representations of the many facets of every God and Goddess ever imagined.

To me, the Goddess represents logic, creation, intellect, diplomacy, nurturing and calm wisdom. The God represents strength, sexual passion, love of life, the fruits of earthly bounty. He is sometimes called the horned God, the consort of the Goddess. This is not to mean that he is lesser in any respect to her. He is the radiance of the sun, as she is the brilliance of the moon.

These two marvelous powers meld together into One Power — the All. Some Witches view these two entities as Earth Mother and Skyfather, making it easier to relate the male/female aspects and earth/cosmic aspects. It brings that glowing blob into perspective. Or does it?

The power of your mind melded with the power of the Universe creates magick. It brings forth the love that all humans so desperately seek, but can never seem to quite get hold of for any great length of time. To obtain what we seek, it is often necessary to climb down into the lower branches of the deity tree, where we find the deities of pantheons.

With these Gods/Goddesses, we learn to channel our energy in a specific direction for a specific purpose. To do this feat of focus, we need total concentration on something or someone we can readily visualize in our mind's eye. This is where all those other Gods and Goddesses come into play.

For instance, Selene, in the Dianic Tradition, stands for solution. If I have a minor problem to solve, I direct my energy to her. I tap into her essence and energy in a very direct manner. I can do this verbally, mentally or physically. I concentrate on her and what she means to me. I am focusing my attention on her and what I need. The second key word in this chapter, then, is "need."

All magick and celebration function around the desire for something, whether it be joy, love, security, happiness, material things or simple peace of mind. Needs can be either psychological or spiritual. The strength and focus of the desire determines the outcome.

The roots of the family tree represent you. It is from you that your beliefs and thought forms take either astral or material shape. It is for your needs that the deities were designed, and it is you who keeps them alive.

Get out your notebook now and write a few paragraphs on what you think the Goddess and the God look like in physical form. Are they both blonde; brunette? One of each?

What type of build do they have, eye color, etc.? What kind of clothing do they wear? Is there a crown, an aura? What are their personalities?

Put on some music, choose a quiet place and close your eyes. Make a fantasy in your mind about your first meeting. Don't force the conversation, just let them come and talk to you. When you are through, write the descriptions of both deities and conversations in your book. Be sure to date your entry.

The Choice of Pantheons

The Gods and Goddesses on the lower branches of the deity tree belong to a specific pantheon, therefore you would have a tree symbolizing each magickal system if you were to draw it on paper.

A pantheon is a set of human images designed to serve a specific culture of people. These images are sometimes called the Old Ones, or the Ancients. When choosing a pantheon for yourself, you must become your own detective.

I previously mentioned the procedure you would use to determine a medical specialist. Your first step would be to do a significant amount of research to determine what pantheon may suit you best. Let me make it clear that it is not necessary for every Witch to choose a pantheon. Some prefer to work with the Lord and Lady exclusively, others do not.

If your parents belong to a coven already, you will most likely have a pantheon that has been selected for the group mind. Likewise, if you work with a teacher or High Priestess, that individual will teach you what they know best and what images they are familiar with. There is nothing wrong with this as long as you keep in mind that if a particular set of images does not basically appeal to you, even thought they are well-accepted by someone else, it is more than acceptable to choose something different. The process of unification with the Divine is a very personal experience. There is no right or wrong set of images as long as those you choose reflect positive energy.

As a solitary Witch, you have the privilege to design your own pantheon and determine how you will work with it. Some examples of pantheons are: Roman, Greek, Egyptian, Celtic, Nordic, Native American, Mayan, African — just to name a few. And don't forget the Faery Tradition, either; that's an interesting one, as well.

I began with the Gods/Goddesses of the Dianic Tradition because they appealed to me the most. The five major deities are Diana (Mother of Aradia), Selene, Hecate, Kernunnos (sometimes spelled Cernunnos) and Pan. I am still very comfortable with these deities, although I have studied and tried others, and I use them in my holiday rituals.

What is important is that you pick a pantheon and stick with it while you are learning the Craft. Do not mix pantheons or interchange deities from different pantheons in the same ritual; you are likely to screw up your magickal satellite if you do. In the future, after you have thoroughly studied the different images it is possible to mix deities, but I would save that endeavor for later on. In time, you will learn who matches whom and which ones react like oil and water.

Visit your local library and the library in the biggest city near you. Hound the local Craft and metaphysical book stores. Use your networking contacts to learn more about the deities you have chosen. Ask others how they celebrate holidays, what rituals they use and what personal experiences they have had with the deities you are interested in.

A personal experience with a deity? Yup! While I was studying the Egyptian pantheon, I had an unfortunate upheaval in my life. Late one night I walked outside, just to collect some peace of mind and try to recover and calm my emotions. I sat on my porch stoop and had a good cry. (Yes, we Witches are allowed to clear out negative emotions by crying.) When I lifted my head from my arms, the most amazing sight met my eyes. In front of me was the largest shadow of a cat I have ever seen.

The shadow encompassed my own, like a protective shield. I knew that Bast had come for a visit in a manner I would understand and not fear.

My logical mind told me to determine what physical things created the shadow (as it was not that of a living cat), until I remembered that magick and spiritual attunement come to one in the most practical ways. What was important is how I felt inside and the energy I absorbed in that moment. I can honestly tell you that I have never again seen that shadow, no matter how many times I have parked my carcass on that stoop!

Visualizing and talking with the members of your chosen pantheon is the next step. As when you met the God and the Goddess, sit quietly where you know you will not be disturbed for at least half an hour, and meet each image, one at each sitting. As before, carry on a mental (or verbal) conversation with them.

Outline your reasoning for seeking them. Let them know exactly why you have thought of them above all the others. Do not force this conversation; let it drift to you.

Use your notebook for keeping accurate records of the pantheons and deities you study. You should have a separate page for each magickal system with room to spare, and each deity within that system. As you learn more about both, you can add this information in your book. Be sure to date all your entries.

When studying pantheons, keep the following questions in mind:
1. In what historical period was this pantheon at its height? What was the geographic location and where was the birth of this belief? How long was this pantheon generally accepted?
2. Approximately how many deities were involved with the pantheon? Which were considered the most important?
3. What was the culture of the people at the time? What did they eat, drink, wear? What were their occupations? Were most rich, poor, both? What was their family life like?
4. How did government affect their religion? How did the religious leaders treat the people? How did the religion affect the every day lives of the people?
5. What were the special symbols of the pantheon? Was there an alphabet or magickal language?

Write a short paragraph summing up this pantheon in your own words.

When researching deities, try to answer the following questions:
1. What pantheon or magickal system does this deity belong to?
2. What was their ranking in the pantheon, and why?
3. Describe any physical characteristics of the deity, and describe the personality type. What tools does this deity use?
4. Does this deity have a male or female counterpart?
5. What holidays does this deity relate to? (Be sure to mark your calendar if you wish to celebrate any of these.)

Write a summary of what this deity stands for in your own mind, when you would contact this essence, and why.

Now is a good time to get crafty! One way to bring the deities closer to you is to create your own deity tree. You can draw it on a poster and hang it above your altar, or you could needlepoint it, or quilt it.

As you become more involved with different deities, you can add them to the tree. It may take years for you to complete your design, but that's half the fun!

The Triple Goddess

Triads involving Gods and Goddesses are older than the Christian archetype. In the Craft, the triad is symbolized by the Maiden, Mother and Crone.

The Maiden signifies youth, the excitement of the chase, and the newness of life and magick. In human age, she would be between puberty and her twenties. She does not have a mate. Her colors are soft and light, such as white, soft pink, or light yellow.

The Mother stands for nurturing, caring, fertility; she is a woman in the prime of life and at the peak of her power. She protects her own and will ensure that justice is done, and done well. This woman is usually mated. In human age, she would be seen as a woman in her thirties to mid-forties. Her colors are warmer than that of the maiden, such as green, copper, red, light purple or royal blue.

The Crone is a being of age-old Wisdom. She is shrewd and counsels well. She cares for the Maiden and the Mother as well as the off-spring thereof. She is logical and can be terrible in her vengeance. She stands at the door to the dimension of death. In human years she is approximately 45 or older. The Crone is the most difficult of the three to place in human age. All too often I have seen women who anxiously move to the Crone stage before they should, too willing to give up the responsibilities of Mother. They do not realize the joys they are leaving behind and the heavier responsibilities they are gaining. The Crone's traditional colors are black, grey, purple, brown or midnight blue.

In a coven environment, specific women take the roles of the triple Goddess. Usually, the High Priestess is considered The Mother. A young woman of the coven would represent the Maiden, and a past High Priestess (Elder) represents the Crone.

The High Priest is usually depicted as the Consort, and his station is often the East. A young man of the coven would represent the Maiden's opposite, and a past High Priest (Elder) is the opposite of the Crone.

Because Witches believe that in the beginning there was the Mother and all things come from her, the triple Goddess role is more pronounced but is by no means more important than the role of the male.

Are the Gods and Goddesses Real?

This is not an easy question to answer, and in the end, each person will have to decide for themselves the reality of their images. Philosophically, everyone's perception of reality is an illusion.

In the Craft it is taught that thought is form. All form is energy. Therefore, any deity is as real as you think it is. Let's face it, everyone knows that you can think yourself sick, and it will manifest into physical illness if you let it.

So, if you can think a negative thing into physical reality, why can't you think up a positive reality too — like a deity, for instance?

·☾ ☽·

Earlier in the book I mentioned that we do not believe in the Christian Devil. This is true. But we do believe that evil exists in numerous forms.

One of the hardest concepts for individuals new to the Craft to accept is the visage of our God. He looks an awful lot like that nasty satan character that they have been told for years is anxious to eat their souls. To hate this concept all your life one day and to accept a facsimile of it the next is pretty hard to swallow.

Instead of giving you facts and dates, I'll make it a little more fun.

The God

At the beginning of medieval history, the general population of Europe celebrated various Pagan religions. It was normal and acceptable for them to do this as it had been done in their homelands for many, many years.

Then came the new people with their belief in one male God. They did not like the fact that everyone else did not think the same way they did. After all, they were right and everyone else was wrong — or so they said.

These people tried very hard to integrate the new religion throughout the countryside, but had little success. For one thing, this new God did not have a mate, nor did the new God stand for many of the traditional things the old God of the people did. With this new God, you weren't even allowed to have parties and enjoy yourself.

The new God's reputation was going right down the tubes. The followers of the new God brought their religion to other people by waging war. As the victors, they could impose their rules on the defeated people. These Warriors of God wore white tunics with large, blood red crosses embroidered upon them. They would leave their families for years at a time and travel to far off places to defeat the enemy and make them worship their God.

While in Persia, they came across a nasty God that was used in that country. And, wonders of wonders, he resembled the old God of the people in Europe. He was dark, half animal, with horns and a tail.

Bingo! They thought, and rubbed their hands excitedly together. Now we know how to eradicate the old religion and bring in the new.

When they got back to Europe, they told the people that the old God was really Satan because he had horns and a tail. This Satan was the fallen angel in the Bible, and of course, no one wanted to worship a fallen angel. He wasn't positive!

The people of Europe really didn't understand any of this thinking. Before the crusaders left Europe, Satan did not have a tail and horns; now, miraculously, he did. The people of the new God insisted that if the population worshiped the old God they were really bowing down to Satan, the King of Evil, and so the myth began . . .

And now, we end it!

·☾ ☽·

I wrote this story to sound rather trite on purpose. From where we sit, centuries later, it is difficult to understand how one religious doctrine could so overshadow another to the point that finding the truth is nearly impossible, because this is supposed to be the age of enlightenment.

It is a good story, though, for children, and an interesting one to tell around the fireplace. It can be used at festivals if you draw the child care tent as one of your duties! It also was written to arrest your fears if you come from a Christian background. Satan and our Lord are not the same entities, and to us, never were.

List of Goddesses

This list represents some of the more common Goddesses used in the Craft, but by no means is a representation of the number that could possibly be used.

Aphrodite: Greek; Goddess of passionate, sexual love. Aphrodite will assist you in pulling loving energy toward yourself.

Aradia: Italian; Queen of the Witches, daughter of Diana. Aradia is an extremely powerful entity and a protectress of Witches in general.

Arianrhod: Welsh; Goddess of the stars and reincarnation. Call on Arianrhod to help with past life memories and difficulties as well as for contacting the Star People.

Artemis: Greek; Goddess of the Moon.

Astarte: Greek; Fertility Goddess. Whether you wish to bear children or have a magnificent garden, Astarte will assist in your desire.

Athena: Greek; Warrior Goddess and Protectress. Someone giving you a rough time at work? Call on Athena to help you.

Bast: Egyptian; Goddess of Protection and Cats. Bast is great for vehicle travel as well as walking down a dark alley. Call on her essence in the form of a giant panther to see you through to your destination.

Brigid: Celtic; Warrior Goddess and Protectress. Brigid is also a Triple Goddess. She is strong and wise. Call on her to help protect your children in a tough situation.

Ceres: Roman; Goddess of the Harvest.

Cerridwen: Welsh; Moon and Harvest Goddess, also associated with the Dark Mother aspect of the Crone.

Demeter: Greek; Earth Mother archetype. Excellent Goddess where birthing or small children are involved.

Diana: Roman; Moon Goddess and Goddess of the Hunt. Diana is many faceted. She is a seductress (as she enchanted her brother Lucifer to beget Aradia in the form of a cat) as well as a mother figure for Witches.

Dryads: Greek; feminine spirits of the trees.

Flora: Roman; Goddess of Spring and Birth. For beautiful flowers, babies, and all bounties of Earth Mother.

Fortuna: Roman; Goddess of Fate.

Freya: Scandinavian; Moon Goddess and wife/lover of Odin. Also commander of the Valkyries.

Hathor: Egyptian; Protectress of Women in Business. A Hathor's Mirror is very important for the Witch. Hathor was cunning as well as beautiful.

Hecate: Greek; Moon Goddess as in Crone or Dark Mother.

Hera: Greek; Goddess of Marriage. If handfasting or some type of commitment is the issue, Hera is the Goddess to seek. Just remember that she has a vindictive side.

Hestia: Greek; Goddess of Home and Hearth. Building a house, remodeling, or apartment hunting. Safety in the home and the family unit.

Inanna: Sumerian; Goddess representation of the Mother.

Isis: Egyptian; represents the Complete Goddess or the Triple Goddess connotation in one being.

Kali: Hindu; Creative/Destructive Goddess. Protectress of abused women. Kali-Ma should be called if a woman is in fear of physical danger. Her power is truly awesome.

Lilith: Hebrew; Adam's first wife and said to be turned into a demoness; however, if you have ever read any of Zecharia Sitchin's work, you may change your mind. In my opinion, Lilith was a Star Woman bred with Adam. This would make her a goddess of Higher Intelligence or a representation of the Star People.

Maat: Egyptian; Goddess of Justice and Divine Order. Maat is the true balance of any situation. She plays no favorites and will dispense justice to all parties involved. Be sure your own slate is clean in the situation before you call her.

Morgan: Celtic; Goddess of Water and Magick. Morgan was said to be married to Merlin. It was from him she learned her magick. She was also doubled with The Lady of the Lake.

Muses: Greek; Goddesses of Inspiration who vary in number depending upon the pantheon used.

Nephtys: Egyptian; Goddess of Surprises, Sisters and Midwives.

Norns: Celtic; the three sisters of the Wyrd. Responsible for weaving fate — past, present, and future.

Nuit: Egyptian; Sky Mother. Often seen depicted in circular fashion cradling the stars.

Persephone: Greek; Goddess of the Underworld as well as Harvest. Daughter of Demeter.

Selene: Greek; Goddess of the Moon and Solutions. Appeal to Selene to bring a logical answer to any problem.

Valkyries: Scandinavian; women warriors who carried the souls of men slain in battle to heaven.

Venus: Roman; Goddess of Love and Romance.

Vesta: Roman; Goddess of Fire.

List of Gods

Although the Goddess plays an important part in Witchcraft, the God should not be looked upon as any less important. He is the necessary balance to obtain harmony and has his own power and expertise.

Adonis: Greek; consort of Aphrodite. Also another name for "Lord." In Phoenician his counterpart is Astarte. A vegetation God. Roman counterpart is Venus.

Anubis: Egyptian; guardian of Isis. Jackal-headed God of Protection. Call on him to protect both home and person.

Apollo: Greek and Roman; twin brother of Artemis. God of the Sun, Light and the Arts.

Apsu: Babylonian; his mate is Tiamat.

Cernunnos: Celtic; Horned God and consort of the Lady. Also Kernunnos.

Eros: Greek; God of Romance and Passionate Love.

Horus: Egyptian; Head of a Falcon and body of a man. God of the all-seeing eye and healing.

Hymen: Greek; God of Marriage and Commitment. His counterpart is Dionysus.

Lucifer: Italian; Soulmate and Brother of Diana. Father of Aradia. God of the Sun and Light.

Mithra: Persian; Sun God and bringer of Light. A soldier's God.

Odin: Scandinavian; counterpart of Freya. This is the God who hung on the Tree of Yggdrasil to obtain second sight. His familiars are the Raven and the Wolf. In his youth he is depicted as a terrible God, in his old age as a God of Wisdom and psychic sight.

Osiris: Egyptian; counterpart of Isis. Over-all God form including vegetation and after-life.

Pan: Greek; God of Nature and the Woods, Laughter and Passion. Also music and personal abandon.

Poseidon: Greek; God of the Sea. His familiars are dolphins and horses.

Ptah: Egyptian; Expert craftsman and designer. God of creative enterprise with the hands.

Shiva: Hindu; consort of Kali. God of the universal cycle of birth-death-rebirth. Shiva can be both kind and terrible.

Thor: Scandinavian; God of Sky and Thunder. A kindly God of the common people, including farmers and sailors.

Thoth: Egyptian; God of Reincarnation. Also a Moon God and favorable to science and wisdom.

Summary

This chapter reviewed the concept of religion and the deities in Witchcraft. It is assumed that while choosing your pantheon you are careful to select deities that are positive in nature to both yourself and humankind in general.

Suggested Reading List

D. J. Conway, *Ancient and Shining Ones.* Llewellyn Publications.

D. J. Conway, *Maiden, Mother, Crone.* Llewellyn Publications.

Janet and Stewart Farrar. *The Witches Goddess. The Witches God.* Phoenix
    Publishing.
    Two excellent books on the God and the Goddess including history,
names, stories, etc.

The Kybalion: Hermetic Philosophy by Three Initiates. The Yogi Publication
    Society.
    This is a must read! Theory on the All and its principles.

Charles G. Leland, *Aradia: Gospel of the Witches.* Phoenix Publishing.

Alan Richardson, *Earth God Rising.* Llewellyn Publications.

Gerald and Betty Schueler, *Egyptian Magick.* Llewellyn Publications.
    Egyptian.

J. L. Simmons, *Future Lives.* Bear & Company Publishing.
    A look at contemporary beliefs and where they are heading.

Diane Stein, *Goddess Book of Days.* Llewellyn Publications.
    A small hard-bound book, with various Goddesses listed on each day
in a date-book format.

Barbara Walker, *Woman's Ritual.* Harper & Row (now Harper and Collins).
    Presents non-secular spirituality and ideals pertaining to women.

Amber Wolfe, *In The Shadow of the Shaman.* Llewellyn Publications.
    Following the shamanistic path.

Section Two

Building Shadows

What's in a Name?

Personality Labels

We all can attest to the fact that our given name has, through the years, labeled us in some manner. First names tend to stereotype people. For instance, Jane's are plain, Buddy's are good-ole-boys, Buffy is a new breed of poodle-type-person, George works in a train station and is retired, Ariel is spacey, and Homer spends his time at the local bar after a hard day in the field.

Even more fearful is the comment, "I knew a Karen once; what a bitch!" And this one: "I've never liked any Sarah I ever met!" Those that have preceded you in someone's memory banks can cost you a new job, the sale on that house you always wanted, or a hopeful new friendship — "I'll never date a John again!"

Last names can present the same type of response. "Oh, isn't that a Jewish name?" There are times when we have wished our parents had the decency to name us something else, and times when we are extremely proud of the handles we go by.

When you enter the Craft, you are building a new extension of yourself; a new personality. This new self lives in a no-limit world, save for the restrictions you set. You are opening yourself to a brand new Universe. Achievements that your old self never dreamed of are now possible, and the personality characteristics that locked you into a single pattern are now being lifted, like a prison sentence that was removed because it did not fit the crime.

To psychologically shed the ties to the old self, most initiates wish to choose a new name to reinforce that special part of themselves that now exists and epitomizes their concept of their own interactions and skills within the

Craft. These skills and concepts are usually those that you desire to obtain, it isn't necessary to already have them.

In a coven environment, an individual may take on two different names. The first, known as the "circle" name, is used within the coven. The second, the "magickal" name, is used in ceremonial rituals where it is only known by the Goddess/God, the individual, and the individual's sponsor. The number, type, and knowledge of names does differ from Tradition to Tradition.

As a solitary, one would use the same name until such a time as he/she feels the need to change it. Some solitary Witches never change their magickal names; others use one for correspondence and writing, and a second for their private, ceremonial rituals.

There are some solitary Witches that prefer to use their given name. There is nothing wrong with this at all, it is a choice entirely up to the individual.

I suggest that you begin by choosing only one name. It will be hard enough to get to know the "new you" on a one to one basis without adding the sixteen personalities of Sybil on top of it.

Great care should be given on the choice of your name. There are no real guidelines on the handle you pick, save that it should represent the beauty of your higher self and your personal values and ideals.

Finding Your Magickal Name

Since your new name does not usually jump out and pinch you, you are going to have to look for it. Some Witches choose to take a name that is traditionally connected with magick, perhaps from a favorite legend (Beowulf), the Earth (Willow), an animal (RedStag), an element (FireHeart), etc. Names can emerge from dreams, vision questing, study of the celestial universe (StarVision) or a pantheon of Gods or Goddesses (Bridgit/Ariel/Erin).

Divination tools can also bring forth magickal names such as Magician from the Tarot, Birca from the runes, etc. Some people scry to find their names. ShadowHawk, WindSong, LaughingPanther, etc., are mystical names, integrating gifts from elements and animals combined, or the essence of two animals together. JaguarWoman is a favorite of mine.

I chose SilverRaven in the beginning, and it took much thought before I settled on it. Silver is the thread that binds the conscious to the higher self. The Raven is a bird of prophecy and a shapeshifter. However, I didn't know these things when I chose the name, hence my choice was intuitive.

As I grew in the Craft and acquired a teacher through networking, I was given a new, special name to share with others. Hence, the name I have used for quite some time — Silver RavenWolf. The Wolf is a teacher and a protector. It is also my power animal. Of course, there was much more that went into the formulation of my name, but I thought giving you the high points would help you when determining yours.

I did a great deal of thinking when I changed my name to Silver Raven-Wolf. I had been writing for Craft newsletters and contributing art work under SilverRaven, and did not want to confuse the issue or the essence of "me." You should be very careful when changing and reshaping your name in any way because you will change or reshape your magickal essence. It can even disperse your personality in a negative manner.

It also confuses the hell out of people who already know you with one name, and now you tell them another. This occurs in networking and it really is frustrating to look at a post card or letter and think, "Who is this person?" Another one that throws me is when people send me change of address cards generated by the postal service under their regular name and you only know them by their magickal one. There is nothing more irritating to have to do than go through your rolodex matching up an address, especially if you correspond with many people. My change brought the million-dollar question from many people — "Did you get married?"

If you plan to do writing or artistic work that will be published in various newsletters and journals, check around to be sure the name you have chosen is not being used by someone else. Not only is this common courtesy, it is also common sense. If you wrote an article you wouldn't want someone else to take the credit for it, and you wouldn't want to be confused with someone else's opinions (or worse).

There may be a time when you really feel the need to change your name. This could be because of personal or spiritual growth, and you would like your new name to encompass that essence. Just remember to give your friends and associates ample time to adjust to the new name. When writing, sign your old name first and place your new name underneath until you feel you can drop the first one.

When looking for your name, watch for signs around you. Learn to see, not just with your eyes, but with your heart and energy center as well. You will find that many things in the magickal universe dovetail quite neatly, if you only open yourself and accept synchronistic events.

·☾ ☽·

Take out your notebook and write the following at the top of the page, "My magickal name should stand for the following strengths . . ." Leave several blank spaces and go down to about the middle of the page and write, "This name should have the characteristics of the following deities, plants, animals, elements, personalities . . . "

Begin to answer these questions, but don't feel you have to do it all at one time. One usually doesn't come up with their name right away. Over the next few days or weeks, keep adding information to this page.

When you have chosen your name, write a statement of affirmation in your notebook, indicating why you chose the name and how. Go into detail and be sure to sign and date this entry; this time, use your magickal name.

From this point on, you should sign your magickal name on all networking correspondence.

Get used to it by writing it, saying it, and hearing it. This name should be so comfortable to you that if someone yelled at you from across the street using your magickal name, you would immediately turn, knowing that person was calling you.

Later, when you write your own dedication ceremony, remember that you will be dedicating your magickal name and bonding with it at the same time.

Meditation, Visualization and Dreaming

The study of Witchcraft is hard work if you wish to reach any level of proficiency. It is not a faith where you can dress up, go to church on Sunday, listen to the drone of the sermon and go home and forget it for the rest of the week, assured that your soul has been saved for at least the next six days.

It isn't the study where you pick up a single, all-encompassing book and find a passage, believing that by reading the words all your problems will fade away.

It is not an organization that assures you that if you give it money, you will be forgiven for cheating on your spouse or fudging on your income tax return. Even if the person who cashes your check forgives you, I doubt either your spouse or the IRS will be so charitable.

Mental Programming

To achieve excellence, you must learn to program your mind to reach your goals. The New Generation of Witches has many advantages over their ancestors: modern telecommunication systems, computers, stereos and compact disc players, and most importantly, a vast amount of information to draw from — whether it be books, magazines, video tapes, or access to individuals who are willing to share their knowledge on a first-hand basis.

Today, almost everyone is familiar with computers. Even if we don't work directly with them, society and big business has educated us with the basic principles of computerization, whether we are interested or not!

Businesses, schools, and homemakers regularly use personal computers. We know that the mechanical structure of the PC is the "hardware," and the information that one can feed into the machine via pre-packaged discs, tapes or floppies is called the "software." Once we have mastered the commands of the software, we can build, retrieve, reformat, or create information to our hearts' desire, limited only by the capabilities of the machine, the program, and our knowledge of it.

Meditation, visualization, and dreaming are the keys to understanding and functioning in the world of Witchcraft. Equating your body to the hardware of a computer (just for a moment, mind you), consider the information, or "software," you are putting into it. Like a computer, the ideas, facts, or figures you place in your mind designate what you put out — your values, judgments, feelings, etc. If you only put negative items in your mind, that is exactly what you and everyone else will get — negative feelings, judgments and values! Meditation, visualization and dreaming techniques are very important in programming your personal body/mind computer. You definitely are what you think about!

Your overall outlook on life is important not only to your physical and mental health, but it is also a vital factor in your competence as a Witch. If you are depressed, angry, or floating through life with a feeling that all things you try leave you unfulfilled, you are doing yourself little good. To be successful in any endeavor, you have to "think" success. This is why when Witches perform magick, they act and speak as if the positive outcome has already taken place. Because, in their world, it is a reality.

Do Self-help Tapes Really Work?

Our society has turned to a new era of information and service. More and more individuals are using self-help programs through seminars, tapes and video cassettes. The Far Eastern techniques of meditation and visualization that were so popular in the sixties and seventies have been over-shadowed by more Westernized versions in the eighties and nineties. Creative visualization is in — Gurus are out.

These self-help devices create a lot of capital, but are they any good? Salesmen listen to goal programming while zipping back and forth between customers, athletes enter mind-focusing programs to obtain excellence, harried secretaries and accountants listen to stress elimination tapes before drifting into an exhausted sleep each night.

When I heard my first goal achievement tape, I actually gasped. Many of the techniques and philosophical values were Craft-oriented, whether the author was aware of it or not. It sounded like I was listening to a very watered-down version of Wicca 101 — minus the God and Goddess, of course.

I have since listened to many tapes; some of them have been utter trash, some were very good. But I haven't answered the million-dollar question yet, have I? Do these tapes work, and are they beneficial to a Witch?

Yes, and yes! Self-help and other mind programming tapes and videos can be a great asset to any Witch, as long as you keep the following hints in mind:

1. Never rely solely on any book, tape, or program to wash away all your shortcomings, or depend totally on them for your personal success.

2. Different programs work differently for everyone. The results I may reap from tapes that use subliminals may not do a thing for you.

3. Do not drop over $24 for any one tape or video, or purchase an entire "set" of tapes without first using it on a trial basis.

4. If the information does not appeal to you the first few times you listen to it, do not continue — you will be wasting your time. You have got to believe in what you are doing. If you have already purchased the item, go back to it at a later date to see if it has gained any appeal. If not, give it away. Maybe someone else will benefit from it.

5. Remember, most tapes have to be listened to repeatedly in order for you to reap the benefits. If you plan to use such a program, remember you will have to stick with it in order for it to work. It takes approximately thirty days of repeated listening, preferably at the same time each day, for the programming to work efficiently.

It is easy to begin to use a self-help or mind educating program, but it may not be so easy to continue it. Things crop up in our lives, like an unexpected visit from an aunt, the demands of spouse or family, even just giving in to the plain old sleep monster. Situations arise that get you off your routine. Often we lay a guilt trip on ourselves, which promotes stubbornness, or even worse, defeat. We begin to view these programs as a chore, not a benefit to ourselves.

Hopefully, practice in anything does make almost perfect, but don't give in to self-recriminations if you miss a beat or two. Maybe you were supposed to all along.

I have found that using subliminal tapes has increased proficiency in several areas of my life when I mix them with my magickal studies. While using a tape to eliminate stress, I found astral projection came much easier. When I used a goal programming tape, I got things accomplished in half the time I normally would, with energy to spare. When writing, I used a line of tapes designed for that purpose.

What you must remember is that when things are going smoothly and you have completed the listening requirements of the tapes, you tend to forget that they exist and stick them in a drawer somewhere. Months later, you may wonder why you are not operating at peak efficiency anymore.

Just pull out the tapes and play them for a week or two. In fact, instead of putting them away, plan to play them once a week, then once a month, and take notes on your own response.

A friend of mine who runs a metaphysical bookstore told me that she used to dread the job of putting together their monthly newsletter. Now, she says, she pops in a creative writing tape, and goes to it. Before she is aware of it, the job is finished!

I used a learning acceleration tape along with various magickal spells to help my two daughters in their school work. In thirty days, my youngest daughter was getting straight A's and my eldest had pulled most of her grades up from C's to A's and B's. Both finished out the school year with above average grades in most of their subjects.

However, the next school year came and I noticed we were right back to those low grades and low self-esteem complaints you so often hear from your kids. Out came the tapes again. Like a true scientific experiment, we repeated the procedure, and it worked.

Affirmations

We all have areas in our characters that we would like to improve. Writing affirmations is another way to increase your mental and magickal proficiency. These should be kept in a notebook by themselves. Each night before you retire, you write at least two statements repeatedly, until the notebook page is full. Be sure to date each page. Continue writing the goal or affirmation until it has been reached.

For instance, people often ask my aid in overcoming procrastination. In this case, you would use a positive statement, such as "I always complete each task in a timely manner." What if you are a person who just can't say no? Perhaps acceptance was driven by the desire to feel wanted or needed, which is a sign of low self-esteem. Then a statement you could use is, "I know when to diplomatically say no." Another could be, "I am a wanted and needed person. My life is full of love," etc.

It really is hard to turn someone down when they need assistance or ask a favor from you, but sometimes it is better to tell them you simply can't do it because of previous commitments. Arm them with additional information to solve their problem if you can, and rest easy. It is far better to say no at the onset than to severely disappoint them later when you can't come through with your promise. And believe me, practicing what I preach here is not an easy task for me on this particular subject.

Taping to yourself (no kidding) is an excellent way to improve your performance. Purchase a fifteen-minute cassette tape. Write a list of five statements and record them on the tape, both sides, over and over again. Play it in the morning and at night. If you can, play it around noon as well.

The topics don't necessarily have to be normal ones. For instance, you could use the following:

"I am a skilled diviner. I have faith in myself. I instantly know what advice to give a querent in a reading. The spirit of the Tarot fills me. I am calm during a reading with strangers."

Another technique is to listen to your thoughts for 24 hours and determine how much negative programming you are using. Every time you have a negative or defeating thought, blast it with a red circle that has a slash through it. If you determine that you have a great many negative thoughts, repeat the process every day until you have your thoughts "under control."

Controlling and Directing Your Thoughts for Self-improvement

What about short-term situations? Being able to control and direct your thoughts is necessary in magick, even when you are involved in mundane situations.

For instance, last year I was invited to accompany my eight-year-old daughter on her school field trip. It was my impression (silly me) that the mothers just sat there and the teachers did all the work.

Imagine my surprise when as I boarded the bus one of the teachers handed me a list of children's names. "You are responsible for these children today," she informed me. "Learn who the children are while we are on the bus so that when we reach the caverns, you will know exactly who they are."

My first mental reaction was, "Shit, not again," because I had just taken a Junior Girl Scout troop to Lancaster and a Brownie troop to a zoo in Maryland and figured that I had more than put in my time on that score. I don't know about you, but those type of trips seem to do most people in, and we had just come back the weekend before the school outing. I had figured I could skate through this one with my bodily presence. Wrong.

I looked at the list and realized that the only child I knew on it was mine. "Nuts," I thought, "couldn't even pull one of my Scouts." I love children, but in cases like this, they have to adore you the first time around in order to control them. I wasn't in the mood to read "Child Lost in Caverns by Ditsy Mother" in the evening news.

I decided to create an aura around myself by programming my responses to the children. I shut my eyes, and for five minutes mentally affirmed to myself the type of person I wished to project to the children in my care. During the trip, while everyone else's children were running wild, my children were with me every step of the way, having a wonderful time. The bus driver actually wanted to know what my secret was, and joshed that I must have put a spell on them! Close, but not quite right — I had put a mental spell on myself!

Some Witches would tell you that this technique is walking the line as far as ethics are concerned. However, these children were my responsibility, and their protection and safety was my chief concern. I simply fulfilled my duty.

Meditation

There are many ways to meditate these days, and all kinds of procedures to follow, and not every procedure can be applied to every individual. I suggest that you try as many forms as possible until you settle with one or two.

Everyone can meditate, but not everyone can follow all forms of meditation. In teaching my children, I found the easiest way is through color association with the chakra centers — the seven energy vortexes in the body.

These vortexes are located at specific points all in a row, which makes them easy to remember. I also incorporate music, as there is nothing more boring or frustrating than asking a child to sit perfectly still in a dead quiet room. It just doesn't work.

Music is the Universal Language. Its content can be broken into mathematical formulas, and it has the ability to alter your spiritual vibrations. I always thought how amazing it was that a mathematical formula could produce unlimited "feelings" in humans, animals and plants.

The music you choose can be calming, exciting, loving, etc. It is best to find a piece you enjoy — one that is light and easy. There is a wonderful selection of music available these days in the New Age section at the record and tape stores. I do not suggest using a tape with subliminals the first time around. Give yourself a week "cold turkey" before determining if the subliminals are necessary.

If you do not care for the newer music on the market, try the classics. I do not suggest using a radio unless the music is uninterrpupted for the period of time you plan to meditate. Commercials and disc jockey blather tend to make you lose your concentration.

Pick a time of day that you will not be disturbed, and one that fits into your schedule. At first, block out only ten minutes time, then extend it as your proficiency and patience grows. When you can successfully meditate anywhere, you will know you've got the hang of it.

In the beginning, the lighting in the room should be dim — soft candlelight is excellent. Try not to wear restrictive clothing, and find a comfortable chair, but not one so soothing that you instantly fall asleep. You do not have to twist yourself into a pretzel to successfully meditate. I personally think that this is one reason why Eastern forms of meditation died quickly in popularity in the seventies; we Americans are used to the couch potato position.

Be sure that the volume of the music is not too loud. I prefer headphones because they block out all other sounds.

Begin by closing your eyes and consciously relaxing your body. Some people prefer to relax the body one part at a time, starting at the feet and working up to the top of the head. Others can consciously release tension in a few seconds. Breathe deeply — in to the count of four, out to the count of four — approximately ten times.

Let your mind slip into a semi-conscious state. Try to ignore tingles, itches, etc., but don't make a major battle out of it. Eventually your body will not protest relaxing!

Now it is time to make believe. Don't laugh! Wishes and make believe are the same as reality, it is only you who draws the line between the two.

So, make believe that you are a fountain of sparkling blue light, or a water-fall, perhaps. This light springs from the top of your head and showers down your right side, swirls around your feet and comes back up the left side. Watch this continuous flow of light from your third eye (which is located in the middle of your forehead, above the bridge of your nose). When this is fully opened, it is a powerful and natural tool.

Don't get excited if you can't "see" right away as if you are watching an inner movie. It can take up to thirty days to bring the picture in focus for some; as little as five days for others.

Do not put yourself under pressure. Many people have their imagination on a very tight leash for fear society in general will frown upon them. In the privacy of your meditation, no one will know or care about your imagination, so let it go.

Continue the fountain exercise for one full week before going further. This will give your body and mind time to adjust to a new routine and react the way you want it to. End each exercise by envisioning yourself being zipped up like a sleeping bag and counting backwards from ten to one. At one, open your eyes and instruct yourself to fully awaken.

During the second week you should follow the same procedures, but this time you will continue your meditation after you complete the fountain by opening up the chakra centers. You can envision them as tumbling balls of colored light, the opening of colored flowers (like a rose or a lotus), or as spirals of colored light. Children like to use flowers as they are easy to relate to. I prefer a colored light variation of my own creation.

Start at the crown of your head and envision a pure white ball (flower, etc.) of sparkling light. Start the ball spinning in a downward rotation, yet the ball remains in place. When you have this center set in your mind (for children the flower opens into full bloom), continue to the next chakra. This one is purple and located at the third eye area we talked about earlier. When that one is spinning and stable, move to the throat chakra, where you will find a beautiful azure blue ball. Next is the heart chakra, which can be envisioned either as bright green or warm pink. Move down to your navel and see yellow, bright as summer sunshine; then right below it, between the navel and groin, see the orange of the setting sun. The last chakra is in the groin area, and it is crimson red. There are also energy centers in the hands and feet; I let them explode all together into small, white balls of light.

The third week you will try the hardest trick. Once you have all the balls spinning, let their colors flow into one another, like a giant, colorful waterfall or fountain — hence, fountain meditation.

When you are finished, imagine a big zipper the length of your body. You must close up that zipper to shut down the chakras; never leave them open. As before, count from ten to one, then tell yourself you are fully awake. Breathe deeply. You have successfully completed the first leg of a full meditation.

Let's stop here and consider if none of this has been working for you. First, you must believe that it is going to work from the beginning. If you have any doubts, they are probably affecting your subconscious. Try writing some affirmations or taping to yourself to solve this dilemma. You may also try working the chakras from the groin area up.

Meditation may not work if you are overly tired or not in the appropriate atmosphere. There are certain times in the day where people are more in sync than others. If mornings are good for you usually, try meditating in the early hours instead of at night time.

A complete meditation is designed to accomplish something. A partial meditation, like the fountain, is structured to balance the chakras and relieve stress. When you are finished with the partial meditation, you should feel rested and relaxed, yet energized.

If you fall asleep during the exercise, do not worry too much about it. Your body is telling you that you need the rest. If this happens often, check your seating, lighting, and the time of day. Perhaps one or more could be changed to keep you from dozing off.

As you become more capable of controlling your meditation exercises, you can investigate complete meditations that incorporate creative visualization techniques to accomplish a particular goal or talent. You can use programming techniques, subliminals or visualization training.

If you are still having difficulty with meditation at this point, you should try a subliminal tape designed specifically for that purpose.

Witch, Heal Thyself

While you are working with the chakra centers you may discover that some seem to shine brighter than others on different days, or that some may have dark spots in them from time to time.

If this happens, it means that you are aware that there is an imbalance in one of the chakras. Don't get excited; they just need to be fine-tuned a little.

While doing the meditation exercise, work extra hard on the weak vortex. This can be accomplished by raising the vibrational level, or adding white light from the Universe to bring it into balance.

Another method is to make a black spot vacuum ball. Visualize a swirling ball at your feet. This ball is designed to suck up negative energy like a giant vacuum. Allow any dark spots on the chakra vortex to be swept down to this ball, where they are absorbed. When the spots are gone, sink the vacuum ball into the ground.

At the onset of physical illness, you should also use the vacuum ball. Open the chakra center that is closest to the illness, such as the throat chakra for a sore throat, and clean it out with the vacuum ball. Once the illness has physically manifested in your body, it may take several sessions throughout the day with the vacuum ball to bring the chakra into balance.

We will speak more of self-healing and the healing of others in a later chapter.

Creative Visualization

This type of training is extremely popular these days with people from all parts of society. Everyone from corporate CEO's to self-help clinics are using it, never realizing that it has always been an integral part of the Craft.

They have no inkling that this type of mind power is not new. Don't let Big Business fool you, magickal people have been incorporating creative visualization into their daily lives for a long, long time. It has only been given a different title to accommodate the mainstream.

The idea is to be able to conjure up an image of any person, place, or thing in your mind in great detail. This ability is necessary for magick and ritual, and should be practiced as much as possible to enhance your versatility. The best type of magickal practice in case of an emergency (and we all have them) is creative visualization that works almost instantaneously. This means that you can bring that visualization into actual physical form (or affect the actual physical form) as quickly as possible. In case of an emergency, it is your fear or strong emotions that will give the visualization the "punch" that is needed.

·☽ ☾·

Long before magick entered my life as a reality and not a dream, I learned this visualization technique — but I didn't know that was what it was at the time. It was taught to me in a school art class. No kidding! Here's how you do it, and master it.

Gather three objects — one that is manufactured, one from nature, and one just for fun. Do not choose an item that is complex in form or full of intricate detail. Save those challenges for later. Each object should be able to fit comfortably in your hand.

Find a place where you will not be disturbed for at least twenty minutes. (Yes, as you are learning, Witchcraft requires much solitude in the beginning.)

This is not an exercise that has to be done every day. However, the more you do it, the better you will get.

You will be drawing, writing or taping what you see, so be sure to have the appropriate tools ready. You may choose any one of these three mechanisms. Read completely through this exercise first to understand what you will be doing, and determine what method you wish to use.

Settle yourself in a comfortable chair, and if you are drawing or writing, have a sturdy surface before you for that purpose. Hold the nature object in your hand. It can be a leaf, a stone, a flower, etc. Look at it briefly, then shut your eyes and use your other senses to introduce the object into your mind.

Now, open your eyes and study the object. Pretend you are a bug (your choice of insect). Crawl all over the object with your eyes. Imagine what a bug would see if it were traversing this object. Go in and out all the nooks and crannies, see the color variations, feel the texture. When you are through, close your eyes and imagine the same object in the same way — no peeking.

Open your eyes and crawl over the object again; except this time, you will write about, draw, or speak about the object. The more detail you incorporate, the better the programming.

When you are finished being a bug, you now get to be a bird (your choice of the feathered variety, as long as it can fly — a chicken is out). Repeat the same procedure that you did with the bug; imagine what the bird sees as it flies over the object. Have the bird circle over the object as many times as is necessary to gather the information you need. Close your eyes and repeat the birds' eye view process. Then open your eyes and record your impressions.

Your final view will be from head on, at eye level. This time you get to choose an animal who can look at the object head on. Follow the same procedures as you did with the bug and the bird.

By the time you are finished, you will know that object inside and out, including upside down! My first item was a weed, and although that first exercise was done over twenty years ago, I could sit down today and draw that weed, just like I did all those years ago!

The final step in this exercise is for you to shut your eyes one more time without the object in your hand. Envision the object, and see how much your perception of it has changed.

In the days following, work with all three items. Do it more than once with the same object, or try others. When you are through with those things, try some that are more difficult. Move on to photographs and eventually, people and larger objects.

When envisioning people, it is important to feel their energy as well as their physical form. Take a trip to a place where you know there will be many people, like a mall or an amusement park. Sit on a bench and people watch, testing yourself on the time it takes for you to take in as many details of particular individuals as they walk by. When working spells and raising energy for a singular purpose in ritual, it is important that your visualization skills are better than average.

After you have worked on visualizing physical things, move on to abstract items, such as numbers. Begin with the number one and hold that image in your mind as long as possible. When it slips out of focus, move on to number two. Keep track of how far and how fast you go with the numbers. You can also use the letters of the alphabet for this exercise as well. The idea is to eventually be able to hold the focus on one number or letter until you consciously determine to let it dissolve.

What is the overall point in controlling your thought patterns? Because thought is form, and to be able to bring that thought into physical form you need the ability to focus.

Notice I haven't used the word "concentrate," because that particular idea lends to straining oneself to achieve a goal. Focus is smoother, like a camera focusing on a person, bringing the slightly fuzzy lines into clarity. No one ever thinks of a camera straining to capture an image.

Dreaming

A multitude of studies have been done concerning dreams. This is a fascinating subject because it is something that we humans all share in common, whether we remember our dreams or not. Although dreams have been scientifically categorized by many people, to me there are three types of dreams:

1. Dreams where your subconscious sorts out the events of the day, or wrestles with a problem you are consciously dealing with.
2. Dreams where you astrally project yourself into another plane or dimension. Sometimes they are just for fun, other times you are there for a purpose.
3. Prophetic dreams where you see events of a possible future. If the dreams involve yourself, you are capable of changing that future if you so desire. If it involves others that are not close to you, you will have a hell of a time convincing them to wrestle with what they believe to be fate. Prophetic dreams can also be dreams of past events that have a direct bearing on present or future circumstances.

No matter what the type, dreams are important. Sometimes it is difficult to sort out which category a dream belongs in, but that shouldn't hinder your learning to control and use your dreamtime.

Usually the most difficult hurdle is simply remembering. Everybody dreams, and everyone is capable of recalling them. You just have to determine the best method for you.

Preparation for remembering dreams is simple. First, do not choose an evening where you are overly tired, do not feel well, or have experienced a new routine throughout the day. Although days like these can bring some pretty interesting dreams, try to begin on a day that has followed a normal schedule.

Have a steno pad notebook by your bedside with a pencil or pen taped to it on a string. Be sure you have a flashlight or illumination from a night table that can be easily reached. If you can place your dream diary on the nightstand during the day, so much the better. That way you will have easy access to the things you need before you retire for the night. The act of bringing these items out each evening will help to set the routine for your recall.

If you hate to write, have a small hand-held tape recorder by your bed. Be sure to check the batteries and purchase 90-minute playing tapes if you wish to record several dreams on one tape, or 15-minute tapes if you wish to use a side a night. Be sure to label each tape with the appropriate dates.

Using a tape recorder is also convenient when dictating your impressions of the dream, or adding significant comments of things that have happened throughout the day before and after the dream(s).

Pre-recorded musical tapes accompanied by subliminals are available to enhance dreaming, and can aid you in dream recall. However, as in meditation, I suggest you try different procedures for recall before you spend your money on subliminal aids.

When you are ready to retire, check to make sure your supplies are available when you awake. Close your eyes and breathe deeply — in to the count of four — out to the count of four. Slowly relax your body. Then repeat to yourself that you will recall your dreams in full detail. Keep repeating this until your mind begins to wander and you gently drift off to sleep.

When you awaken, grab that notebook and light (if needed), and start writing! Don't worry about grammar, syntax, spelling or sentence structure; just write! At first, your recall may be sketchy at best. This is totally normal because you are asking yourself to tell your own secrets.

If you wake in the middle of the night, do not go back to sleep; instead, record your dreams. If you roll over and convince yourself you'll remember it in the morning, take my word for it, you probably won't. These midnight dreams are usually the most vivid, and much information can be gained from them. Sit up and record those dreams!

If you recall your dreams in the morning, read through them sometime during the day. Gradually, the bits and pieces you first remembered will blossom into full dream recall. There are times when you may not remember anything at all; this is natural too, because your conscious mind needs time to rest.

Do not work with dream recall every night. Three nights on and one or two off is a good method. If you do too much dream work it can lead to mental, daytime exhaustion.

But what if, by using the method already given, you still cannot remember your dreams? Try some alternative procedures.

For instance, I use the Australian Aborigine method of requesting Sister Swan to assist me to enter dreamtime. Envision a black swan and talk to her. Tell her you wish guidance into her world. You can also enlist the help of a particular power animal if you are working on a problem in which you feel the skills of that animal would be most beneficial to you. You can also call to the Angels and ask their assistance as well.

At first, I had a great deal of difficulty remembering my dreams. With four children, a husband, a parent and a dog in the house, I have little time for quality sleeping. Someone was always waking me up, jerking me from a dream or restful sleep. The shock of being constantly disturbed began to wear and tear on my system and I almost gave up, thankful for the sleep I did get, dreams or no dreams!

I finally hit upon a solution. Before I went to sleep I enlisted Sister Swan and asked her to help me recall the dreams during my morning shower, one of the few places where I am normally not disturbed (notice I said normally here).

As the rest of the family is pounding throughout the house, banging dishes, spilling cereal or burning the eggs, I relax for a short time under the hot shower — alone. There, I piece the dreams together that I have had the night before. When I'm finished, I'm ready to record my impressions.

Some Witches burn incense to enhance dream sleep, or light candles. I use a candle burning in front of a triple mirror in my bedroom, and have been amazed at the results.

Gems and crystals can also be used to enhance your dreamtime. Fluorite is said to be helpful to allow one to open the Akashic records for information. Snowflake obsidian under a pillow can give astounding results. Dried herbs sewn into satin pillows by your own hand can assist your dream recall. Lavender, rosemary and rose petals give a very restful sleep.

Interpreting Your Dreams

I do not use any dream books to interpret my dreams. I have always felt that since I create the dreams, I am the one that must figure them out. A pat explanation in a book is too unyielding for me.

Learning to interpret your dreams takes some practice. Your subconscious usually speaks to you in codes and symbols. You will have to learn what these symbols mean as they relate to you. When you are ready to attempt to interpret a particular dream, take out a piece of paper and write down all the things you recall, who was in the dream, colors, events, etc., but don't get too wordy. You are going to play a word association game with yourself.

For example, if I dream of a blue tiger, I would write down both the color blue, the word tiger, and any other things I can remember. Like night, hot, etc. Beside each word I will write the first thought that comes into my mind when I think of each one of those words. Dreams are often elaborate puzzles to be pieced together.

If you dream of total strangers in a situation, your subconscious may not want to admit the real players in a particular conscious problem, so it sets up a fictional drama for you instead. Check the cast of characters closely, you may be one of them in disguise!

A note about prescription drugs here. A friend of mine says that she, and some individuals she knows, always dream about blood under prescribed codiene. I know that after you have mastered dream recall, cold medicines sold over the counter or prescription drugs strongly affect dreaming. I do not suggest working with dream recall or dreamscaping when under the influence of any type of medication.

Dreamscaping

Stephen King and several other authors of our era have brought the reality of dreamscaping to the general public. Basically, it is the ability to control your dreams while in the dream state.

For instance, if you have a problem for which you can find no conscious solution, you can program your mind before you sleep to work out the difficulty and present you with the best alternative. Likewise, if someone is keeping information from you for whatever reason that you feel you must know, dreamscaping can bring you that knowledge.

Finally, if you consciously know you are dreaming while you are in that dream, you can control that scene, making it go where you want it to.

Tarot cards and runes are excellent devices for dream work. I have personally found the runes excellent door-openers to the unconscious during dreamtime.

Summary

Mental programming, meditation, visualization and dreaming — all are integral to performing magick and ritual as well as acquiring balance in your physical and mental life.

Having several notebooks lying around for each of these skills is rather frustrating. You may like to section off a three-ring notebook for your record keeping. As with other magickal methods, it is a good idea to go back from time to time and look over your notes and consider your progress. Especially with dreams, things may be drawn more into perspective for you at a later date.

Your Sacred Space

What Makes a Sacred Place Sacred?

I've written and read quite a few articles about sacred places and spaces, but few touch on the theories about how they get that way other than the physical items or trappings that go into them. The place you choose for working or simply communing must be a space devoid of fear. This is extremely important for the solitary Witch, because you do not have anyone, save yourself, to rely on when odd things begin to happen.

There is no one to smile weakly at or to affirm that they are feeling the same things you are. There isn't a High Priest or Priestess to nod knowingly at a physical manifestation, or to afterward discuss what has happened during a ritual.

Richard Bach once wrote, "Argue for your limitations, and they are yours." Each of us draws mental boundaries on what is and is not acceptable to occur or experience. Each one of us determines what our reality is permitted to contain.

A good example of this is the town and surrounding area of Gettysburg, Pennsylvania. Since I have always lived within an hour's traveling distance of this historical graveyard, I have been shuttled there a number of times on school, Girl Scout, and family sight-seeing trips. I was even there for a honeymoon adventure.

Each time I visited this area, my parameters on reality were different. My last visit, over three years ago, brought up some very interesting experiences and feelings simply because my boundaries of existence had again changed. Ghosts and tangible energy were now in my repertoire. Consequently, Gettysburg carries an entirely different perspective for me now.

Movies have rendered quite a bit of effect on us. Even though a scene has long been viewed and stored away, the mind adores dragging it up and laying it before us if the atmosphere seems appropriate. There is nothing more mind-blowing than to be in the middle of a ritual, alone in the house, and experience a supernatural occurrence that you were not in the least prepared for. If you are not comfortable in your sacred space or do not trust it, then whatever magickal working you are performing will most likely bomb.

A sacred space or place is not just an area in which to erect an altar and perform rituals, or simply commune with the Universe. It is a power center either of your own making, or made by the forces of the Universe, or by a drastic event in human consciousness (such as a battleground). It is a place to respect as well as a place to be respected in — whether it be a work area or a meditation sanctuary. To work in the no-limit world of the Craft you must accept that anything can happen. If you have properly prepared yourself to operate in this environment, then the experiences and lessons will reach to infinity.

For example, my best friend is not a Witch, but she does study all sorts of metaphysical and religious topics. One day out of the clear blue, she said to me, "When I pass away, you will be able to get in touch with me by sitting in my space. Right there in front of the coffee table is my power center. It is where I always sit. You will be able to reach me there if you can find no other way to contact me." And I believe her.

Physical Space

There are two types of physical sanctuaries — inside an enclosed area, or outside in the world of nature. A basic prerequisite for either place is privacy. Interruptions cause failure because you will simply not be able to focus as you should. Your attention and the direction of it is vital for your success in any magickal, ritualistic or meditative endeavor.

If you share living space with another adult, now is the time to discuss your need for privacy if you think a problem may arise in the future. There is nothing more frustrating than to attempt to perform a magickal function and have someone interrupt you because they think it is "cute" or "funny."

Solitaries who share living space with non-Craft adults in the home may find themselves in the midst of severe arguments when defending their rights to sacred space and the protection of the items therein.

The detail of your explanation for both privacy and tools will determine the extent and plans of your area. It can mean the difference between a permanent place or a temporary one. The more entrenched you become in the Craft, the more determined you become in your right to practice it.

The Indoor Sanctuary

If you are living alone, setting up an indoor sacred space with physical items does not present much of a problem as you can shut the door to that room when company comes. The more you become integrated in the Craft, the less desire you will have to keep everything locked away. A deep reverence for your faith and practices will emerge, along with a great deal of pride in what you have accomplished and believe in. This is a natural progression.

A full discussion on dealing with the outside world is covered later in this book. However, you will have to make some serious considerations now, when setting up your sacred space. I firmly believe that you should not discuss your entrance into the Craft with outsiders until you fully know and understand the belief system you have chosen.

Quickie Witches are a dime-a-dozen these days, and they rarely stay with our system longer than two to three years. In that time, they do themselves and others a disservice by rashly flaunting the little knowledge they have gained.

If you feel there will be a great deal of negativity surrounding your choice of Universal celebration, I suggest you consider creating a temporary space that can be used after everyone is sleeping, then packed up and put away before morning.

This does present a problem if you are doing a magickal working that requires certain tools to remain untouched and in the open. But these are few and far between for the new Witch, so I don't see any difficulty in erecting temporary work areas and sacred spaces.

I began with a temporary area due to both space limitations and others in the home. My first altar was a dressmaker's board laid out on my bed very late at night to ensure privacy. I am not suggesting that you practice deceit, but I am indicating that there is a way around every obstacle, if you are genuinely serious about your studies.

A Witch needs a place to work and celebrate, therefore one of your first major magickal acts will be the design, physical set-up, cleansing and consecration of the area chosen. This space should be ready to use when you take your vows of dedication. Creating your sacred space becomes a symphony of planning and movement. Your positive energy melded with the energy of the Universe will create a melodious haven for yourself; and perhaps, in time, for others as well.

Designing the Sacred Space

For indoor work (or relaxation), you should pick a place in a non-active portion of your living area. If you are fortunate enough to have an empty room, lucky you. All sorts of decorating possibilities become available to you. Most of us, however, must make do with some type of space limitation. Keep in mind that the space you choose should be large enough for you to move freely or lie down comfortably if you desire to do healing or vision questing.

Creativity in all things is the hallmark of a solitary Witch. Keep in mind that your sacred area does not need to be built on a foundation of expensive accessories. A closet, a corner, even an attic or basement (as long as you are not afraid of things that go "bump" in these places) are workable.

Once you have chosen the actual place, you should take some other design features into consideration. Shelving and storage for magickal tools, ingredients, books and files should be prepared. These things need to be in close proximity to the sacred space so that you are not running hither and yon when an emergency arises. The old motto "Be Prepared" goes for Witches, too!

Having to drag things all over the house or apartment when you are preparing for a ritual, working, or celebration is not only time consuming, but energy wasting as well. And Goddess forbid you are in the middle of a magickal endeavor only to discover that you have left the lighter or that specific tool locked up underneath the basement stairs. To make matters worse, the key is in the kitchen on the top shelf above the refrigerator and you are in your bedroom. This predicament will definitely blow a hole in your focus!

As a helpful hint, I suggest you tape a lighter under your altar. It seems to be the thing that everybody forgets at one time or another.

Plants are a wonderful consideration for inside space. Place them on shelves or hang them from the ceiling.

Your next thought should be the lighting. Will you feel comfortable only with candlelight, or would you prefer low-watt electrical lighting at first? This may sound silly, but there are people who are petrified of the dark, even with candlelight. Don't feel embarrassed about it, just address the fear. It isn't going to do you any good if in the middle of your ritual the hat tree in the corner of the living room becomes a ferocious demon because of poor illumination. If you think something is going to burst out of the closet or snatch at your bare feet from under the bed, handle it with low-wattage bulbs!

Other lighting alternatives could be large pillar candles placed about the room, the use of hurricane lamps either hung from the walls or on tables, or four-foot high taper candles set in sturdy floor sconces. If you are going to use a multitude of candles or lamps, I suggest keeping the correct gauge fire extinguisher or a bucket of water handy. Anyone can knock over a candle or lamp or get their hair too close to a flame.

An indoor or outdoor space can be concealed by a moveable partition. You can purchase or make them, and they are great for small sites that you wish to remain permanent but desire to keep cloaked from non-magickal eyes. These screens can be painted on one side with various magickal designs, and the other side can match the decor of the room or patio.

Window shades can also turn a normal room into a magickal one. Designs can be painted on the inside and rolled up during regular hours. Pull them down for instant protection or space conversion.

Repainting the room can also be a step in your space preparation. You can choose a soft color for the entire room, or get really jazzy by creating self-styled designs on two or three of the walls. Stenciling magickal borders is another terrific idea. I have black cats in both my kitchen and dining room, and a wolf pattern I created for my living room which isn't finished yet — one of these days!

Get out your notebook and begin the design of your own magickal space. List what room would be appropriate, any major structural changes you would like to make, shelving, storage, shades, lighting, etc; anything you would like to bring into form for the shell of the room. Everything does not have to be "just so" at the moment. Your space will grow with you and change as you do.

A sacred place will carry the positive energy you generate there long after a working is over. If you invite the Universe to commune with you, even in the bathroom, vestiges of that union will remain. If done often enough, it could become just a physical as the items already therein.

Outdoor Spaces

If you prefer working outdoors, and climate permits, look for a place that is totally private. This is easier said than done, as neighbors can be real detriments to magickal workings. To conceal what you are doing, you can create a rock garden enclosed by trees, shrubs or fencing. Ivy can be planted along mesh fences and trained to climb the fence to give you privacy. If you have the inclination, fountains and benches can be added for effect. Your herb garden can be planted on the outskirts, as well.

Presently, our family is working on our outdoor sanctuary that will include stone benches, a fountain and a small natural pool. We are also designing a screened area with a fireplace to give us more privacy during our holidays and workings.

Keep in mind that an outdoor sanctuary requires several years of hard labor, both in the design and in the upkeep. Start small and expand a little each season. It can also be an extremely expensive endeavor. Not only must you do the required research for magickal properties of plants, but you must also study the type of ground you have, what tools are necessary to care for the land, and what plants will prosper in your climate. Multiple trips to greenhouses and country markets are usually included during the entire process, as well as a few trips to the library!

Temporary outside places are easier to handle. Take a walk to the nearest park or wooded area. There are always areas that are willing to shelter you as you commune with the Universe — you just have to ask them first!

☽· 79 ·☾

The Heart of Power: The Altar

As you are unique in design, so should your altar be. There are several types of altars — among them are the table type, the wall altar, and the stang (or vertical altar). An altar serves three specific purposes:

1. It helps you centralize your personal power. Therefore, each item placed on it should have a specific purpose. Don't have anything there that is not needed. When the altar is dormant, you can set decorative articles on it in celebration of reverence, but don't clutter it up.

2. It can serve as a work table, like that of a master craftsman. As such, it should be large enough for comfortable crafting of tools, talismans, etc.

3. It enables you to honor the Universe and your beliefs, even when you are not physically present.

The Table Altar

The physical construction of your table altar is your choice. Witches use coffee tables, dressers, cinder blocks with two planks, desks, computer tables, etc. You can make your own altar if you are handy with woodworking tools.

The altar can be permanent or portable, and any size that is comfortable to you. There are even space-saver tables now on the market; when you fold down the side leaves, they are as small as two feet across. Most of them have wheels to enhance their portability, and can be maneuvered into small areas for storage.

The top of the altar should have enough space so you can work comfortably if you are planning to use it as a magickal work table. As a working altar, there should be enough surface space for you to place two illuminator candles or lamps safely on either side of you to provide adequate lighting.

If the altar is a permanent one, you may wish to keep the lamps or candles there at all times. You never know when you may need to use the table on short notice for helping someone.

Your altar can be decorated with magickal symbols and designs by carving, using a wood-burning tool, or painting it various color combinations.

Some Witches prefer to place the altar at the North or East points of the sacred space. This is not an absolutely necessary practice, as when you cast the magick circle around the altar area you aren't working in the present dimension anyway, and North, South, East and West are merely reference points of the material world.

The Wall Altar

In our home we have a working altar and a wall altar. The working altar is for my own personal use, but the wall altar is for the entire family to enjoy.

Wall altars are usually made of shelves, indentations or alcoves in the wall. In our case, we have set the entire wall between a door and window aside as an altar. The wall has been stenciled, has various items hanging on it (including a broom, a framed picture of the God and Goddess entwined, a large wreath of grapevines woven into a pentacle), and two double glass shelves for gems, stones, nature's gifts, a bell and small statues of Witches and priestesses cast in pewter.

Each of these things means something special to the family, whether it was gathered from the yard, picked up on a hiking trip, or purchased as a gift for one another on our holidays.

We also have a small altar in the living room that holds a stone pyramid that can be touched by the adults who enter and leave the room. Some families use the mantle above their fireplace as an altar. Candles, lamps, pictures, nature items, masks, etc., adorn these areas.

A wall altar does not take much to create. Check local craft shops for decorative wooden shelves. These are unfinished and you can paint or stain them in whatever designs you see fit.

The Stang

The stang is usually made out of the wood that is generally prevalent to your locality. It is best to research the magickal properties of your local trees and choose that which you think most appropriate.

Our family uses a pitchfork that has been handed down through the family for five generations, by accident. Yes, it made it's way back to our family by sheer luck. We purchased a house that belonged to a great uncle I had never met. While cleaning out the basement, I found the pitchfork and ordered it to the shed until I could figure out why it was in the house. I later found that it had been decorated, painted gold, and carried at the front of the town's Harvest Parade for many years by my great, great grandfather. Who, incidentally, set up a tent in the field over Harvest Weekend and drew astrological charts for the townspeople to tell their fortunes.

The stang as an altar is placed upright in the ground on the outside of the circle, guarding the entrance. Often the stang is decorated for the celebration at hand. Some traditions use only one stang to represent the God. A candle is placed "between the horns," or over the middle prong of the pitchfork. Beneath would be a mask, garlands, and in some Traditions, crossed arrows. Two stangs or pitchforks would indicate one for the God and one for the Goddess.

If you live in a rural area you could probably get away with one of these outside; in fact, if decorated lavishly over Samhain, you would probably start a fad. As an example of how yet another custom has been absorbed by mainstream culture, take the broom craze. Go in any arts and crafts store these days and you will find brooms and baskets galore to be decorated and hung on front doors, in kitchens, etc. Gee, I wonder where that idea came from?

At the foot of the stang can be placed a small table on which the cakes are set on a platter used only for ritual purposes.

Altar Items

The tools on your altar, and placement thereof, change with the season, celebration, or need. You will collect and make several special tools and decorations over the years. Some things will become standard for each ritual. Other items will be discarded or given away.

Begin by choosing an altar cloth. It should be large enough to cover the entire top surface of the altar. The color and pattern are optional. I have used everything from plain black velvet or satin to a designer sheet! For general working, the choice should be a plain color such as black, blue or dark green. For seasonal celebrations and other rites, I use a colored pattern that brings out the mood of the occasion.

On top of the altar cloth, I have a working cloth. This should be smaller, the size of a placemat, and it should be kept in mind that it will get soiled due to your various projects and rituals. You may be mixing herbs and inks, or creating other magickal items that would stain your altar cloth. If you have spent a great deal of money on the material for the altar cloth, you don't want to ruin it with an "Oops!"

All candleholders should be large enough to catch any drips, and sturdy enough that they will not easily tip if the altar gets bumped. Candle skirts, which are little rings designed to catch drips, can also be purchased if you just can't part with that favorite holder even though it spits wax everywhere.

I usually use white pillar candles or hurricane lamps for illuminators. On holidays I change the color of the pillar candles to match the season. Keep a large tablespoon on hand to bend out the wax as the pillar candles burn. This will keep the candle in good working order for quite a while, as pillar candles are usually expensive. Candle colors and uses will be discussed in depth further on in the book.

A relatively new fad in the illumination arena is the use of oil candles. Usually made of clear glass in interesting shapes and asbestos wicks, these vessels of light are like the temple candles of old. Many Traditional Witches are using these small lamps both for illumination and magick. Oils for these candles come in a variety of colors and create a striking addition to any magickal working.

Most Witches like to have a representation of a deity or deities on their altar, as well as a picture or statue of their power animal. Representations of the deity can be in the form of a statue, pictures, or even a specific colored candle or gem.

There should be room on the altar for an incense burner, holy water, cup or chalice and a pentacle. The pentacle is placed in the center of the altar space, or above if you are working on your mat.

The altar should also contain two objects, both the same design, one colored black and one white. I use them to represent balance in all things — one to repel and one to draw. Some Witches prefer the use of candles to represent this universal law.

Get out your notebook and write "My Altar" at the top of a fresh page. You should answer these questions:

1.   What type of altar do you prefer? Will you make it, buy it, or use something you already have?
2.   Where will you place your altar? Inside the house, outside, what room, which corner, etc.
3.   What will you use for altar cloths?
4.   What type of illumination will you work by?
5.   What tools and representations of the deities would you like to put on your altar?

If you plan to make many of these things, begin by listing the supplies you think you will need.

Note: There is no need to make this an expensive endeavor. Go to local flea markets, yard sales, fabric outlets, etc. In the Craft, honor doesn't come by spending lots of money. Here, money does not bring power or acceptance.

Summary

I could write an entire book on all the neat stuff you can do with your apartment, home and grounds to enhance and honor your magickal life. Making and gathering the tools, planning the space, etc., are fun parts of the Craft.

The space itself, however, should be viewed with the utmost seriousness. It's purpose is both a healing and connecting one. No one should be allowed to enter this sacred space unless you are sure they will do so with respect. This is a place for positive thoughts, not negative ones.

Stocking Your Magickal Cabinet

Choosing a Storage Area

Proper care of your magickal tools and accessories is important for the success of any magickal endeavor. If you allow someone with a culmination of negative energy to handle your tools, it will lessen or even negate their effectiveness until you cleanse and consecrate them again. Even if that individual is a trusted friend or small child, the tool can absorb emotion and energy; both are vibratory in nature. I have several small children. To prevent the misuse of my tools (because children love my treasures), I keep them locked at all times in a special cabinet that houses only my magickal supplies. Remember, people and animals will instinctively wish to touch your tools. The positive energy held there draws them like a magnet.

My cabinet is what is usually considered a bedroom wardrobe with double doors on the top half, and drawers on the bottom. It is taller than I am.

The storage area you choose should be able to hold everything except correspondence. Like a well-designed kitchen where everything is at your fingertips, your storage area should be equipped to house all your tools and accessories. You can pick up a fairly inexpensive cabinet that is either unfinished or made of light pressboard.

I don't suggest you keep things in boxes because by the time you get done rummaging through them for a particular item, the rest of your things are in shambles. If you must use boxes, get large clothing ones and place an index card on the lid listing the contents of each box. Be sure to keep the card updated as you make changes.

Filling Your Cabinet

Buying, trading, and making "goodies" for your magickal work is one of the most enjoyable areas of Witchcraft, but it is necessary that you understand the importance and the nature of these objects. Tools and accessories do not perform the magick. They do not bring thought into form by themselves. Marion Weinstein has said, "The Witch is The Magick," and she is right. Tools and accessories serve to enhance your abilities, not create them.

A good example is the crystal, an item that is magickal in character and still a mystery to most of humankind. If we believe the ancient stories of these gems, they are capable of far more than what they are used for today, even in magick. For crystals to work properly in magick, you must learn to plug them into you, like plugging a computer into an electric outlet so that you can access the software on the system. Without the connection, the computer will stare blankly at you. (However, if anyone reading this book has taught their PC to perform totally by itself, please let me know!)

The crystal becomes an extension of yourself and your energy. If it is left sitting alone in your cabinet, it is not going to decide to heal your neighbor's daughter without any help from you. They need you to assist in channeling the energy, both yours and the crystal's.

The Tradition or pantheon you have chosen may dictate some of the more specialized tools you may require. Other items, such as candles, wands, chalices, pentacles, and incense are relatively standard through the practices of the New Generation of Witches.

The guidelines for tools and accessories are simple, but important:

1. All tools and accessories should be cleansed and consecrated prior to use (even for adornment). This holds true if you have made them for yourself, they have been given to you, or you have purchased them.

2. No tool or accessory should be used for anything other than the express purpose of magick or ritual celebrations.

3. Never, ever touch someone else's tools and accessories without their permission. Likewise, never allow anyone else to touch your magickal items unless you are absolutely sure that the person's energy is synergetic with yours. The only exclusion here are the Tarot cards or some other type of divination tool that may require the energy of the querent. However, there are special cleansing guidelines for these as well.

We all know that cleanliness is important in any health care profession. Guarding against contamination is a top priority. Your tools and accessories are just as important, and you must insure the purity of their energy.

Performing magick is serious business. Your tools are an extension of you. The longer you use them, the more energy they store. After a time, you will be able to notice this by a simple touch. The tool will tingle in your hand.

I have a crystal ball that I call "She Who Sings" because she is the first tool I noticed that vibrated in such a way. This awareness through the sense of touch comes in time, much like the realization that you can type without looking at the keyboard or pad. Some of your tools will carry stronger vibrations than others, depending on how often you use them, what you use them for, and what material they are made of.

When you receive or purchase a magickal item, it is necessary to both cleanse and consecrate it. Cleansing it removes any negative residue from the piece, and consecration empowers it with positive energy in the service of the God/Goddess or other pantheon deity for an express purpose. In the next chapter, these techniques are covered in detail.

When stocking your cabinet, don't run out and buy (or order) products that are beyond the seams of your wallet. Adding to your collection is fun, but it is with wisdom that your collection grows. Simple things, like herbs you have dried yourself, or the gift of a feather from a networking brother or sister, can be far more powerful than a $75 wand that is only three inches long and uncomfortable in your hand, especially when you paid for it by eating spaghetti with no meat for a month.

I tend to agree with the thought process of the Native Americans. They feel that if you spend time making an item for ritual use, concentrating your energy and thought process on the creation of the object, you have already brought half of the magickal intention into form.

Standard Magickal Tools

The Wand

The wand serves to project your energy to a certain place, thing, person or dimension. Wands can be made of wood or copper insulated by leather.

A wooden wand should be taken from trees that are native to your locality. You will need to research the magickal properties of these trees to make the best choice. It is my belief that native trees should be used so your energy will coincide with that of the land around you. Energy patterns in different areas of the country vibrate on their own frequencies. Taking the wand from your own area will keep you in harmony with the land about you.

Special care should be taken when removing a branch from a living tree. You must first check to determine what the pruning season for that particular tree is. If you are unsure, call a local nursery. Oak, maple, and a variety of other trees are usually pruned in the fall season, so if you would like to combine the gathering of the wands with a holiday, choose Halloween or Samhain. Fruit trees, however, like peach and apple, are not pruned until colder weather. In our area, pruning begins after all the leaves have fallen from the fruit trees. This coincides with the Pennsylvania Pow-Wow belief that a wand for healing should be gathered on Christmas night, and at no other time. For followers of the Old Religion then (which is where this tradition came from in the first place), the fruit wand would be gathered at midnight on Yule.

When cutting the wand, be sure to explain to the tree why you are taking the branch. It is best to ask its permission to do so. The wand should be about 12 to 18 inches in length, relatively straight and a comfortable weight to wield. Remember to sever the aura after you have cut the physical branch, and leave an offering at the base of the tree.

All my wands are tipped with crystals, though I have seen others tipped with pine cones or knobs akin to phallic symbols. The wand I use most often was created by my father and myself as a team endeavor following instructions out of Michael G. Smith's book, *Crystal Power*. I also have a "heavy zapper" which I think is made out of cherry wood, as near as we can tell.

Not only was it a gift from a very special Witch, it is also a tool that has been handed down from Witch to Witch. Adding to its uniqueness are two feathers, one falcon and one raven, who perished in a death fall together.

As the leather/copper wand is used for general magick and healing, the zapper is used to move things quickly. Occasionally one does have to take a warrior's stance in protection and fight against mental disease.

Wands traditionally stand for communication and matters of business. So, if you wish to choose between your athame and your wand in a particular situation dealing with business or communication, you would pick the wand.

The Broom (Bossume, Bossom, Besom)

The broom can be used for decoration, magick and ritual. It is used to sweep an area clean of negative energy. "Jumping the Broom" can be added to handfastings or Mayday/Beltane celebrations, or in children's circles. The broom is basically the symbol for a female Witch and it represents her vehicle for travelling into dreamtime.

Often Witches name their brooms, because a broom can be used as a vessel to temporarily house a particular spirit or entity, acting much like an inanimate familiar. It also scares the hell out of acquaintances when you tell them, "Please, don't touch Esmerelda. She doesn't like that, you know!" Then smile and they will know you are kidding . . . maybe! Seriously, it is a marvelous instrument of protection to be hung on front and back entrances into your home.

When considering a gift for a Craft sister or brother, or for any wedding couple, decorate a broom and give as a gift with a spell tied to the handle with silver cord. They'll be talking about you for years!

Brooms are laid at the gateway to a coven circle, used to send messages to friends via astral travel, and set outside with specific instructions to make friends with your local fairy folk. Should a mist surround your broom, you will know your message has been received.

The Chalice

The chalice is a symbol of emotion and fertility. Chalices are used in dedication and initiation ceremonies, holiday rituals to honor the Gods/Goddesses, and certain spells.

There may be instances where you will use more than one chalice — one for you and one for the deity. Chalices are usually long-stemmed and made of almost any food-safe material. My initiation chalice was purchased at the local grocery store in the glassware section.

I designed my own chalice by visiting a local ceramic shop, purchasing my own greenware and glazes and firing it myself. The first firing was done on the New Moon and the second on the Full. To finish it off, I decorated it with a band of leather strung with beads and feathers.

There is no end to your creativity when you put your mind to it. Chalices can simply hold water, or something more sophisticated, like wine, cider or mead.

The type of chalice you use is totally up to you. The legend of the chalice is an old one, stemming from the times of divine sacrifice of the kings to ensure the prosperity of their people. In Craft rituals, the cup represents the female and the athame represents the male. When the athame is lowered into the cup, it symbolizes the divine union of the God and Goddess, a very moving experience indeed!

The Pentacle

The pentacle is a flat disc with a pentagram (among other possible symbols) inscribed on it. Yes, this item is taken from ceremonial magick. Its basic use is to evoke entities and protection. It can also be used to draw material gain to oneself, or hung in a room to invite protection. It stands for material things and is used in spells for calling money. The pentacle also coincides with the Native American Medicine shield or wheel, where each compass direction stands for significant elements and life forces.

My first pentacle was a wooden disc inscribed by a wood-burning tool. Other sigils can be placed on the pentacle as well, such as runes of protection, or words created through one of the many magickal alphabets. Geometric symbols are also employed.

The one I use today is from a slice of geode inscribed with the pentagram. Sigils can be added or removed by drawing them in wax. Care must be taken so that the geode slice does not split either while creating the design or while scraping it off.

This is an excellent tool for empowering jewelry and gems, as you place them in the center of the five-pointed star. Poppets for healing should be placed here, as well. The pentacle should be upright at all times while on your altar.

The Athame/Sword

The athame is used for commanding and manipulating power. This knife is usually doubled-edged and dull as it does not actually cut anything on the physical plane. It is for directing energy in a dimension where real knives are useless. Although most knives are black-handled, mine is not, and it works perfectly well for me. Some Witches prefer to use swords.

The wand and the athame are basically interchangeable; this is more a matter of style and preference than of actual reasoning.

The athame stands for intellect, right thinking, and calculation. I do not use mine very often as I look upon knives in general as potentially harmful items, even in the kitchen.

A note on knives, swords, and the law: These items are viewed as concealed weapons by most law enforcement officials, if they are found in your vehicle or on your person. This has sparked a controversial no-win scenario. Law enforcement officials do not view knives and swords as ritual items. They have the right to confiscate and not return them. Most Witches do not bring their ritual knives to festivals or outside Sabbats for fear of losing these precious items forever.

The Bolline

The bolline is the tool used for cutting things in the physical realm. It is a type of knife with a curved handle, often white. Used for harvesting herbs, wands, plants, inscribing candles, cutting cords, etc. It should not be used at a place like the dinner table, or to open a cellophane package in the kitchen. Its use is purely for magickal workings. Here is where the kitchen Witch would argue with me; many Witches use their knives to prepare food.

Their logic is that magick should be in the food served to the family, too. So, if you are ever visiting another Witch who wields his or her sacred knives in the kitchen at supper time, then cuts an astral doorway with them around midnight, don't have heart failure. He/she is doing something that is entirely acceptable to their personal magickal practice.

Incense Burner

The incense burner's function is to purify the area you are magickally working in. It can also be used to purify your home in a yearly magickal housecleaning. I do this both spring and fall as a part of celebrating the change of the seasons, or when I have had an unwanted house guest, spectral or more than lifelike. There are several kinds of burners and a variety of incense.

Incense helps the Witch reach altered states of consciousness. It is also expected to be in your home by non-magickal people who come to visit for readings. (Unfortunately, I'm not kidding here.)

Incense can be purchased in cones, sticks, cubes or raw. I like to use the raw, or powdered form, as it is sometimes called. Most of the Witches I know use raw incense set on charcoal blocks or discs. There is even self-lighting raw incense now on the market where the charcoal is not needed and the smell of its burning does not overpower the incense.

With powdered incense you can mix you own scents and include herbs, as well. Through practice, you can control the burning time by the amount you measure out. Why so practical? My husband, MindWalker, is allergic to incense and gets violent headaches when I burn it for too long. Guess you know now that we often cut our visits short to metaphysical book stores and homes where incense is overpowering! The point here is that just because a limitation of some sort or another may be imposed on you, there is always a way to work around it.

A simple spell does not require an entire cone or stick of incense to work properly. Like candles, I prefer to use virgin tools. If something is half used, I bury it or dispose of it, depending on the circumstances. Using powdered incense, for me, is cost effective.

The Cauldron

The cauldron is the symbol of the Goddess. Transformations take place when this tool is used. When you think of the cauldron, think of the legendary phoenix rising from the flames.

It can be the main point of interest in a ritual, used for developing your own oils or brews, and for divination purposes by scrying with still water, steam, or dripping wax into the water and watching the patterns as the wax expands.

It is usually made of cast iron as it needs to be able to take the heat (and keep on bubbling), and it is a tradition from the Old Religion. In the ancient days of medieval midwives, the cauldron was most likely used to heat water in preparation for the birthing of a baby or preparing the wash water with herbs for cleansing the dead. From birth to death, the cauldron was used for a variety of purposes, including remedies and medicines for healing the sick or bringing love. All people like to meld with their genetic roots; the cauldron provides a link.

Now I bet you are saying, "But we are not all related!" Ah, science is out to prove you wrong. Recent studies in DNA codes indicate that there is a definite link in females of all races in their genetic code structure. It is thought that all women can trace one DNA link back to the first woman on the planet, whose home was in the cradle of Africa.

What Else Will You Find in a Witch's Cabinet?

Not everyone's collection of magickal items will be the same. You will learn to work with what comes naturally and brings the highest rate of success. Listed below are those items that reside in my cabinet at this time. The list varies, depending upon the season, upcoming celebrations and level of skill.

Altar cloths
Amulets
Athame
Baskets
Beads (for making jewelry and talismans/amulets)
Bell
Bolline
Book of Shadows
Bowls (for holding salt, water, oils, etc.)
Candles (all colors and styles, including beeswax; I prefer to use hand-dipped tapers, and you can learn to craft candles yourself)
Candle holders (several types)
Capes and costumes
Cauldron
Chalices (ceramic and glass)
Compass
Corn (dried and powdered)
Crystals and gems
Crystal ball
Decanter (for wine and mead)
Divination tools (wide variety)
Earth
Feathers (all colors)
Felt (all colors)
Glass Bell jars with screw-on caps
Glue (various types)
Herbs, dried plants and spices
Holy water
Holy oil
Incense, bricks, burners and fire resistant plate
India ink (for writing spells on parchment)
Lighters
Magick mirror (Hathor's Mirror)
Magickal jewelry
Mortar and pestle
Musical and subliminal tapes*
Oils (various selection for dressing candles, etc.)
Parchment paper

Pens (watercolor)
Pendulum
Pentacles
Pentagrams
Pitcher
Platters
Pocket knife
Potpourri pot
Pouches
Quill pens
Rawhide, jewelry clasps, etc.
Rice
Runes
Rope (five feet for making a circle for the children)
Scales
Scissors
Sea salt
Seeds
Statues
Stencils and brushes
String
Talismans
Tarot cards (several decks)
Tobacco
Wands
Wooden boxes
Wooden spoons

Note: Many Traditions insist that the tape player for music must be left outside the magickal circle, as it is felt that the electrical energy from the tape player is disruptive to the circle of energy. I have not found this so, and have raised some astounding energy with a Walkman attached to my head.

Study

An integral part of stocking your magickal cabinet is the continued study of the principles of your tools and accessories and how they relate to you, your magick, and the Universe in general. In order for you to get the most benefit from the things you store and use, you will want to learn as much as possible about them. For instance, there are a whole gambit of skills that relate to candles, gems, crystals, colors, herbs, Tarot or other divination tools, etc. These objects have both practical and high magickal qualities. You will, no doubt, achieve excellence with either some or all of these items in this life time so that you can carry this knowledge on to the next.

How to Find Magickal Items

Magickal items and supplies are not always easy to obtain, depending upon your geographical location and budget. Learn to be a bargain shopper when using catalogs. Check references with other Craft individuals to see who has the best prices, highest quality of goods, and good customer service.

Things you find can have marvelous magickal uses. Often, if I am dealing with a difficult problem, I will either go thrift store shopping or nature walking, or perhaps take in a flea market or garage sale. Beforehand, I will request assistance from a particular deity, Angels (yes, I do believe in them and will talk about them later), or just the Universe in general. I always find (or sometimes see) something that is synchronistic to the challenge I am facing.

At one point in my life I was feeling terribly unbalanced. Things in my life appeared chaotic and unorganized; I was desperate for an answer. My husband suggested taking in the historical sites of a neighboring town. During the day we walked down the main business section of the town, moving in and out of thrift shops and old time five-and-tens (does anybody remember those?). At the last shop on the street I found a set of old decorative scales for five bucks. I knew they belonged to me. I bought them, brought them home, cleansed and consecrated them and designed The Ritual of Balance. Since that day, whenever I set up a full altar, I always place my scales there to remind me of the necessity of the many types of balance that are required in this incarnation.

Storing Tools and Accessories

How you pack and store your items is important. Wooden boxes, glass jars (the old Bell kind works great) and ceramic containers are good for herbs, incense, holy water and oils. Plastic jars are nice for "on the go," but I do not recommend them for home use. Plastic has always seemed "airy" and porous to me.

Leather pouches are excellent for all types of things, as well as natural fiber cloth (cotton or silk) for wrapping crystals, wands, runes, jewelry, divination tools and any other items that you wish to keep protected from outside energy. For this type of use, the color of the cloth should be black or blue and preferably opaque.

Have Magick, Will Travel

Becoming a magickal person does not happen overnight. Some people adapt more quickly than others in various areas. It may take some time for you to feel comfortable about carrying your tools and accessories around with you. Most people begin by choosing a piece of jewelry as a protective amulet or as a symbol of their new reality.

As you feel the "need" for different items, you may start zipping around town with quite a collection of magickal supplies. Even the most closeted Witch tends to tell at least one very close friend or family member of their Craft association, and often are called upon by that person for help. If you are so inclined as to share that knowledge, then you may want to carry a few items with you for those "out of the blue" requests.

Over the years, my husband and I have come up with some pretty interesting ideas for transporting magickal supplies. When it got to the point that my purse began to take on the identity of a magickal dump truck, I knew I had to come up with some alternatives. I have been known to carry two briefcases, one for magickal work and one for work work. Plastic boxes, especially filers with compartments and handles, work well for transportation of many items.

There are boxes that can be placed between the two bucket seats in a car, complete with writing top. My husband has a metal lock box that he keeps in his truck. We have used lap desks and tote bags, backpacks and tummy purses. But the best one of all was when I purchased a heavily lined pistol case to carry my gems and crystals in on short notice. Most of these containers are definitely obscure, and we look like any other business yuppies off to the races.

For smaller items that you wish to carry on your person, little leather or cloth pouches pinned under shirts, trouser cuffs, or undergarments work well. Pouches can also be strung about the neck, but if this is too noticeable and you are a woman, you can sew the pouch onto a garter. This works very well if the lady is going somewhere that she cannot take a purse, or wishes to keep the item close to her at all times. The garter can be of any color; however, I do not suggest using red as it is said that red is the garter color for Witch Queens only.

What is a Witch Queen? If a High Priestess' coven has successfully hived (split on agreeable terms to all concerned) three times, then she is regarded as a Queen and has the privilege of wearing the red garter. (In some Traditions it is green leather lined in blue silk. Silver buckles represent the number of hived covens.) Hiving occurs when a coven grows too large and some of its members wish to begin their own structure patterned on the original coven. It is a tradition that the new coven not contact the mother structure for a year and a day, after which the two covens merge for a celebration or festival. For fun, check your history books about Old England and the Knights of the Red Garter (or the Most Noble Order of the Red Garter, as it is known in England). I think you will find this information extremely interesting.

If you want to get truly ingenious, there are leather belts sold with zippered compartments. Army belts with canvas compartments are great for nature walking, along with those new tummy bags mentioned earlier that snap around your waist. That's a great place to carry a deck of Tarot cards and a gem or two. Coats or cloaks can be re-tailored or sewn by yourself to include hidden pockets to accommodate your needs.

Written Inventory

Keeping track of your tools and accessories is important. That way, when you give or barter an item away, you won't go looking for it a year later. It also comes in handy when you have a need and are not quite sure what you want to use to fit the desire.

And finally, it will assist you in keeping track for shopping purposes. When you run low on a particular item, you may want to make a note of it before your supply is exhausted and you have to make an extra trip instead of picking up the item on your regular rounds. Things like herbs and candles have a habit of depleting rather quickly; I have my own weakness of giving away gems for a variety of reasons and then realizing I'm out of moonstone, rose quartz or crystals before I know it.

Get yourself a clipboard and keep a list of what you have on it, as well as a sheet of paper to write the things you need to get. Hang the clipboard inside your closet or cabinet.

Summary

Take some time to consider what magickal items you would like to work with first. Can you make them yourself? Craft shops have all sorts of great things you can turn into magickal items, especially in wood, ceramics and beadwork. A burning tool, a little paint or stain, and you can make just about anything. Even if you feel you are not talented with your hands, remember that these items are for your use; they don't have to be perfect and won't be on display in a glass case in your parlor.

Collecting, exchanging, gathering and making your own magickal supplies strengthens your focus and abilities.

Cleansing, Consecrating and Charging

Well, you have designed your sacred space and begun gathering your tools. What's next? The preparation of both space and tools by cleansing, consecrating and charging (some Witches call this "empowerment").

There are three basic reasons for this process:

1. It removes any negative residue that has attached itself to the item or place.
2. It melds your positive energy with that of the Universe to bring divinity.
3. It instills this energy into the object or place for positive purposes.

The ritual act also assists in strengthening and calming your mental attitude toward yourself and your work, allowing you to focus your energy without constraint.

This chapter represents a significant step on your journey into the Craft, because it is a physical statement that you intend to change things for the better in your life. After you have cleansed, consecrated and empowered your space and tools, you are ready for the dedication ceremony and advancing into other areas of Craft study.

The Elements

In the context of magick and ritual, you will find that the four elements of Air, Fire, Water and Earth are often used. They are powerful representations of natural magick. Later, you will learn to use these forces of nature for larger magickal workings, but for now, we will concentrate on learning what they represent, where they are represented in the magick circle, and how they are used in the cleansing and consecration process.

Air: Compass point: East. Represents intellect, communication, knowledge, concentration; the ability to "know" and to understand; to unlock secrets of the dead; to contact the angels; telepathy, memory and wisdom; the hawk, the raven and the eagle; prophecy; movement, Karma and speed.

Fire: Compass point: South. Stands for energy, purification, courage, the will to dare, creativity; higher self; success and refinement; the arts and transformation; the lion, the phoenix and the dragon; loyalty and force.

Water: Compass point: West. Associated with intuition, emotions, the inner self, flowing movement, the power to dare and cleanse all things; sympathy and love; reflection; currents and tides of life; the dolphin, the swan and the crab; dreams and dreamtime.

Earth: Compass point: North. Mystery and growth, fertility, material abundance, the combined forces of nature and its bounty; birth and healing; business, industry and possessions; the bear, the stag and the wolf; conservation and nature.

On the pentacle, our sacred symbol, each point of the star represents one element. The top point of the star stands for the fifth element, that of the Spirit. It means centering, transformation, and that its limits are beyond time and space as we understand them. This element is often called "Akasha."

There are particular covens who do not recommend wearing the pentacle outside of their clothing. Their initiates are told to keep the sacred symbol close to their hearts. The reasoning is quite practical — the pentacle can store and reserve energy for use at a specific time and not be bombarded by the negativity that the symbol generates from outsiders who have no concept of its true meaning.

·☾ ☽·

(I suggest the following meditation before going further in this chapter.)

Collect four small items, one to represent each element, and locate a compass. Weather permitting, find a nice spot outside. If not, indoors will do.

Choose a spot where you will not be interrupted. If you like, you can put on music and dim the lights. Be sure you have your notebook with you, and something to write with.

Follow the basic steps for meditation listed in Chapter 8.

Find magnetic North on your compass, and face that direction. If you are seated in a chair, move the chair to face that compass point. First, close your eyes and gather impressions about that compass point. After a few minutes, write down your impressions.

Now, hold the element you chose to represent Earth and the North, and close your eyes. Open your mind and feel the impression of this element and how it relates to the compass point. Think about how it corresponds to you and the Universe. When you have finished, write down your insights in your notebook.

Take the meditation one step further. Create a positive entity in your mind that represents the element of Earth. Is it male or female, human or animal, or all of these? Write down the description of this representation and how you feel about it.

Continue through each element, facing the compass point that corresponds to that element, and finish by writing your feelings and thoughts on each one.

With the element of Spirit, focus on a golden light coming down from the heavens and filling you to the brim. When you have completed this phase, again write down the information you have gathered.

Finally, before shutting down, determine what four items you will use to cleanse and consecrate your magickal tools and space. For example, for Earth you could use sea salt, dirt, rice, corn meal, etc. For Air, a broom, hand fan, feather, incense or your own breath. The element of Water would be represented by holy water (which we will get to in a moment), water from a nearby lake or spring that has a special deity watching over it, or snow (if conditions are right). Fire would call to mind a candle flame, oil lamp, or backyard torch.

Zip up your chakra centers and read through what you have written. Refer to it when you have questions on the elements, and be sure to continue to update your elemental information.

Formula for Holy Water

Holy water can be used for a variety of magickal workings, from cleansing a room to assisting in a healing. Many Witches mix this formula and save it in glass vials or other small glass containers. Plastic is not recommended because it is a slightly porous material when compared to glass and the process used in mixing and forming the plastic is often harmful to Earth Mother.

Please follow the instructions carefully. At the end of the instructions for this formula is a spell/formula worksheet. If possible, make copies of this format to include in your notebook. You will be using it often. Although using a typewriter would make it easier to read, I suggest handwriting the information to set it firmly in place in your mind.

1 tsp of rose water (optional)
3 tbsp sea salt or Kosher salt
1 small bowl of spring water*
1 clean glass container
1 new compact mirror
1 storage bottle (small)

* *Note:* Spring water is extremely hard to come by. You may not be able to trust the bottled water, as it has been determined that many who use it are victims of false advertising, so be sure you are familiar with the spring water company. I suggest going on a small hiking trip with a large glass jar (like the type you buy family-size fruit in), and filling your jar from a running stream or other "live" body of water that is well known for "good fishing."

Cleanse and sterilize the bowl and glass container with boiling water.

Insure that you have have total privacy during preparation.

Time: Midnight during a Full Moon phase.

Place: Out of doors under the moon, or near a window that will reflect the light of the moon.

Set our your work cloth and all ingredients upon it.

Take five or six deep breaths to relieve the stress of the day.

Cast your magick circle. Hold your arms outstretched in the Goddess position (arms out at the sides like you are cradling the Universe, palms up). Say:

> *In the cloak of the midnight hour*
> *I call upon the Ancient Power*
> *I seek the presence of the Lady and Lord*
> *To bless this water that I will pour.*

At this point, you should feel the energy of Earth Mother and Skyfather move about your feet and head. Feel your own energy expand around your navel and then unite with Divinity. Take your time; no need to rush.

Add the rose water to the spring water. Pick up the bowl of water, hold it toward the light of the moon, and say:

> *In my hands I hold the essence of the Gods. I hereby cleanse and consecrate this*
> *water to Divinity that it may be used for positive acts only and may aid me in my*
> *magickal work.*

Feel the energy of the Moon Goddess pulsate down into the water. Imagine her silver light descending from the heavens and impregnating both the water and yourself. You will feel a "glowy" sensation.

Set the water down and pick up the salt. Feel the power moving in your arms as you raise the salt toward the moon. Say:

> *In my hands I hold the essence of Earth Mother, She whose bounty sustains all living creatures. I hereby consecrate this salt to Divinity that it may be used for positive acts only and may aid me in my magickal work.*

As with the water, imagine the energy of the Moon Goddess empowering the salt.

Set the salt down and pour a little into the bowl of water, and stir clockwise three times. Repeat this process twice more.

With the bowl in your left hand (receiving) and the mirror in your right (sending), reflect the light of the moon off the mirror and into the bowl. After a few moments say:

> *This liquid is now pure and dedicated to the Lord and Lady. It is free from all negativity in any time and any space.*

Set the bowl and mirror down and hold both of your hands, palms down, over (not touching) the bowl, about one inch above the water.

Let the vibrations of your body come alive. Open your third eye chakra and imagine a glowing purple light emanating from it. Form an open triangle with your hands over the water and project the light into it. In your mind, see the water change color and glow. Feel the power and energy flow from your head down through your arms and up from your feet and out from your arms simultaneously. When you feel the energy begin to dissipate, slowly lower your hands and say:

> *As I will*
> *So mote it be*
> *With the free will of all*
> *And harm to none*
> *This formula is done!*

You may ground your energy in two ways. Either place your hands physically upon the ground and feel the energy drain into Earth Mother, or imagine your energy as a force field around you, and quietly step back out of the skeleton of energy and watch it collapse in upon itself and melt into the ground.

You have just experienced your first "act of power." Transfer the water to your storage container and store it away until you are ready to cleanse and consecrate your sacred space. Be sure you clean up after yourself by putting all things away in their designated places so that you will be able to find them again when next they are needed.

·☾ ☽·

Worksheet for Spells and Formulas

Type of spell or formula: _____

Date and time made: _____

Reference: _____

Astrological phase: _____

Specific purpose: _____

List of ingredients and/or supplies needed:

_____

_____

_____

_____

_____

_____

_____

Specific location required: _____

_____

Date, time, and astrological phase when used: _____

_____

Results (include if spell or formula worked, how long it took to manifest, time limit of formula, any specific results, etc.):

_____

_____

_____

_____

_____

Deities invoked during preparation and/or use:

_____

_____

Step by step instructions for preparation and/or use:

_____

_____

_____

_____

_____

_____

_____

_____

Cleansing and Consecrating Your Sacred Space and Tools

When you feel you are ready to perform the cleansing and consecration ritual for your sacred space, you should consider extending the ritual to cleanse, consecrate and empower your tools, as well.

> For this ritual you will need:
> 1 broom
> 2 illuminator candles
> 1 chalice with holy water
> 1 lighter
> 1 silver candle
> 1 birthday candle
> 1 4" diameter pentacle
> 1 small bowl of earth
> 4 element candles (red, blue, brown, yellow)
> Incense (sage)

You will not need your wand as it should be cleansed, consecrated and empowered before you use it. During the tool cleansing portion of the ceremony, you should cleanse and consecrate, then empower the chalice and the pentacle.

After you have gathered all the necessary items (don't forget the candle holders for the candles), place everything on the altar and cover them with a black cloth until you are ready to use them. Black is the recommended color because it shields your items and helps keep the dust off.

Next, choose the date and time of your ritual. You can use an astrological calendar or simply pick the date of the next New Moon. I personally like this phase as it represents the beginning of new projects and new life paths.

As with all magickal endeavors, be sure that you will not be disturbed. Sometime during the day you choose, you should literally house clean the sacred space that you plan to dedicate, right down to washing windows and walls, mopping and vacuuming the floor, etc.

A half-hour before the ritual, go over everything in your mind, from beginning to end. Double-check items needed. You don't want to be madly flipping through this book for the right page in the middle of your ritual. If you cannot remember the sequence, put in paperclips to indicate your place and highlight the passages with a color that will show up in the light you have chosen. You don't want to break your focus.

Magick and ritual are interchangeable, and often each depends upon the other for success. If the will and emotion are strong enough, however, you can perform an entire ritual in your mind and still achieve a high level of success. This ability comes with time and practice.

Assuming you have done all of the above, go take a shower or relaxing bath with scented oil. I prefer the shower as I like to imagine a giant waterfall cleansing all psychic debris from my body before the ritual. Choose clothing that is non-restrictive — even a bathrobe will do, or you can perform the ritual skyclad. It is your choice.

When you are nearly ready to begin, place each of the element candles at the appropriate compass points. East, yellow or gold candle; South, red or orange candle; West, blue or purple candle; North, brown or green candle. Place the silver candle on the altar.

Double-check to make sure you have all you will need for this ritual. If you will be cleansing and consecrating tools, be sure they are placed on the altar or work table.

Check to make sure your privacy is ensured. If you like, you may use a rope or cord to make a nine- or five-foot circle around your altar.

Stand before your altar. Breathe deeply. Light the illuminator candles with the lighter or the birthday candle (they come in handy for this purpose).

Circle the room in a clockwise direction and light each element candle.

Pick up your broom and sweep the circle as you walk inside in a clockwise manner. Repeat:

> *Sweep, sweep, sweep this place*
> *By Powers of Air, I cleanse this space.*

Shut your eyes and feel the element of air move within the circle. Return to the altar and pick up the silver candle. Light it from the illuminator candle on the left, walk around the inside of the circle in a clockwise manner, and say:

> *Light, light, I light this place*
> *By Powers of Fire, I cleanse this space.*

Concentrate on fire energy enering and flowing around the circle. Return to the altar and pick up the chalice of holy water. As you walk clockwise inside the circle, sprinkle the water with the fingers of your right hand and say:

> *Liquid, liquid, I wash this place*
> *By Powers of Water, I cleanse this space.*

Feel the element of water flow in a clockwise direction around the circle. Return to the altar and pick up the bowl of earth. Walk clockwise around the circle, sprinkle the earth, and say:

> *Dirt, dirt, as I walk this place*
> *Powers of Earth, cleanse this space.*

Feel the element of earth bring her gifts to the circle. Return the bowl of earth to the altar and move to the center of the circle. In the Goddess position, say:

> *Spirit, Spirit, fill this place*
> *Powers of the Divine, consecrate this space!*

Feel the power of the Goddess and God enter yourself and your sacred space. Say:

> *I now direct the energy of the Universe to forever fill and bless this place.*

As when you created the holy water, feel the energy raise from your body and meld with the Universe. When the energy begins to dissipate, turn back to the altar. Lay your hands upon the altar and say:

> *This altar is dedicated to the Lord and Lady of light. May it serve me well.*

If you will not be cleansing and consecrating any tools or jewelry, you will want to end the ritual here by thanking the God and Goddess, as well as the elements, for their participation. When you are through, ground the energy you have raised either by putting your palms to the floor and feeling the sensation of being drained to Earth Mother, or back out of the energy and watch it collapse in upon itself, into Earth Mother. Then, raise your right hand over your head and in a counter-clockwise motion, circle it around the room and say:

> *The circle is open*
> *May it never be broken!*

If you plan to use this ritual to cleanse and consecrate specific items, continue with the following steps, then thank the God/dess, elements — and don't forget to ground!

Stand before the altar and pick up the first item to be consecrated. Imagine a glowing gold light from the heavens spotlighting the item. Pass the item over the incense and say:

> *I cleanse and consecrate this _____ for positive means. All negativity is*
> *removed from it in any time and space.*

Repeat this process through the remaining three elements. Pass it through the flame, sprinkle it with water and finally with the earth element.

Now, lay the item down on top of your pentacle. As you did with the water, place your palms about one inch over the item, then form a triangular opening with your hands. Imagine a silver orb in the opening of your hands. Let it glow brighter and brighter. Raise the energy from your body and gently push it out between your hands and into the silver orb. With your mind, lower the orb onto the item and let it be encompassed. When the energy dissipates, say:

By the Will of the Lord and Lady I have empowered this _____. May their bless-
ings shine upon and through it always.

> *By the Free Will of All*
> *And with harm to none*
> *As I will*
> *So shall it be done!*

Follow the closing procedures listed previously.

When you are finished, clean up the area and store away all tools and implements that you have used. Take the remaining earth and Holy Water and pour
it outside on the ground, and say:

> *I thank thee for the use of thy Power.*

After all things have been returned to their storage area and you have taken
care of the remaining water and earth, relax and go bumbling around in your
kitchen. Find something to eat and drink before you make record of the event.
The carbohydrates will also help to ground your extra energy.

·☾ ☽·

This has been the first part of the two-part dedication ceremony you will perform to begin your entrance into the Craft. You have dedicated both your space
and your tools to the Lord and Lady and the service of humankind. The second
part of your dedication will be for that of yourself.

Give yourself a breather before you complete the dedication ritual. Take a
month, even two, if you feel so inclined, before you are absolutely sure this is
the path that you wish to take in this lifetime. Only you can be the judge.

·☾ ☽·

Although the following chapter will assist you in writing accurate records of
your magickal endeavors, I have provided a ritual record sheet for your use. I
suggest you photocopy this particular form or write up your own format in
your notebook.

·☾ ☽·

Ritual Record Sheet

Type of ritual: _____

Date and time: _____

Moon phase and astrological correspondences: _____

Weather: _____

Physical health: _____

Purpose of ritual: _____

Tools and other items required: ·

_____

_____

_____

_____

_____

Deities invoked: _____

_____

Approximate length of ritual: _____

Results of ritual:

_____

_____

_____

_____

_____

Ritual composition:

_____

_____

_____

_____

_____

_____

_____

_____

_____

_____

_____

_____

_____

Summary

Cleansing and consecrating is a vital step in your magickal practices. To make something yours is to make it strong. To tie it to the positive forces of the Universe is to make any item or place clean and protected.

There are things in the universe that can not be seen and are not good. To be practical, you cannot see a germ with the naked eye, but it can kill you. There are non-physical things that are just as dangerous. When you are learning to go between the worlds, you are like a small child that does not know the dangers ahead. You are innocent but you are not unintelligent; therefore, you must learn to protect yourself against things that are unknown to you.

Cleansing and consecrating are the protective devices used by most magickal people. These are also pathways to unity with the positive forces of the Universe within yourself to make you happy, healthy and productive.

The Fine Art of Magickal Record Keeping

The Power of the Written Word

Keeping accurate records of your magickal endeavors is a high priority for any serious Witch, especially the solitary ones. Good notes, records, and even photographs are necessary unless you have been blessed with perfect recall at any given moment.

By writing down your personal history and journey into the Craft, you will be able to keep tabs on your progress. I realize that many individuals do not hold the passion for creating the written word as I do, but I do stress the necessity of accurate record keeping.

Writing improves your memory of a given situation, and helps you clarify events after they have happened. It can give you helpful insights into your own psyche at the time of an event. It will also give you the advantage of passing your discoveries and successes on to others, if you so desire, without losing any of the ingredients or steps that brought you to a particular solution or conclusion.

Notes and records also enable you to determine where you might have gone wrong or made an error. Often when we experience a failure, we are too involved at the time to see anything but that failure. These records help us step back and decide where the problem may lie, what we can do to change the outcome, and help us more fully appreciate some of the things we did not see at the time that were pivotal, but hidden.

Although some may find this cumbersome, I like to keep different books for various subjects. Some of these are mundane and others are magickal in nature.

The Personal Journal

Although far from magickal, I keep a daily/weekly journal. This helps to integrate my normal life with my magickal one. After a while, the two separate lives will meld to a large degree, and you won't even realize it. However, it is wise to keep track of the ordinary fluctuations in life, as well as the magickal ones.

For eight years I have used a large hardbound journal from an office supply store. I begin each entry with the day, date, time of entry and the weather conditions. (Surprisingly enough, this comes in very handy.) I write about the day's family happenings, the world news, and personal insights into various problems. Each passage also contains a few affirmations — statements to positively program myself. For example: "I listen to others . . . . I think before I say 'yes, no problem' . . . I am a wise and generous Witch . . . I am strong and powerful . . . I carry wisdom both in my heart and mind . . ."

Every December 31st I go back through my journal and recall the ups and downs of that year. I make three headings: Spiritual Progress, Mental Progress, and Material Progress. When I have completed my musing over that, I go back to the December 31st entry of the previous year and check on the goals I had written down for the year that has just ended.

I look to see if I have completed any of those goals, then check them off on that page with the current date. Some of the goals may no longer apply, and some I may not have accomplished yet. I transfer the uncompleted but still valid goals to the current December 31st entry. I leave a space and write a set of new goals for the coming year.

Finally, I write a brief summary of what I think and feel about my accomplishments and failures. Sometimes I have really surprised myself; other times I realize how certain areas were not up to my personal standards and need some work.

On the lighter side, this journal has settled many family squabbles and "when did I's?" along with questions like, "How long did we go through that, or have that?" Every family should have someone that keeps a journal, all magick aside.

The mundane journal also helps to keep you rooted in the world that everyone else seems to be operating in. That is why I go over it on December 31st instead of October 31st (the Witch's New Year). There are times when we, unfortunately, get so spiritual and magickal that the real world pops up to bring us down a nasty peg or two.

Please remember that although the worlds of magick and spirit are great places to spend your time in, you are here in the real world for a specific purpose. Be sure to do some normal things to keep yourself in perspective. Go to a football game, the bowling alley, or have a night out with non-magickal friends where the topics of conversation don't ever touch on the Craft. You need this balance, whether you want it or not.

The Dream Journal

Up until this time, you have been keeping all your notes in one binder. When we spoke of dreams and meditation exercises, we kept them all in the same book. If you do a great deal of studying and experimenting, you are going to have a monstrous book before too long. After reading this chapter, you may wish to purchase more than one binder for different subjects.

Although we have already covered recording your dreams, you may wish at some time to collate them into a larger volume, or separate them by subject for future reference when puzzling the meaning of current dreams. A loose-leaf notebook comes in handy for this purpose. In this way your dream journal can stay in your bedroom where it is easily in reach. If you start keeping a single volume now, it won't become unmanageable. So, on a day you are totally bored, root out your dream notes and compile them. You never know when you just might need them!

I like to read my dreams over several months later. There are times when I actually grasp the larger meanings of a few of them when looking at my life from a different vantage point — in perspective!

The Book of Shadows

The Witches' most important form of record keeping is the legendary Book of Shadows. There is some debate on whether or not every Witch has always had a Book of Shadows. There is argument that many of the Witches of the Old Religion were illiterate and therefore could not have kept written records. Perhaps that is true of medieval Witches in Europe for a particular time span; however, I don't believe this assumption is entirely true.

First, take into consideration the magickal alphabets we have recorded. For example, the runes. You could write whole books in runes if you wanted. Secondly, learning to read and write could have been a part of coven training. Since everything was secret to begin with, who is to tell us whether they actually knew how to read and write or not? Wouldn't those Witches have considered the skills of reading and writing to be powerful assets?

Let's go a step further. Perhaps, because of persecution, initiates were no longer taught to read and write for fear the information would fall into the wrong hands. Ordinary pictures could be drawn for a Witch to remember a spell or formula in a cookbook or even a family Bible.

I have also heard of scenarios where the Magistrates of the coven kept all the records. There is reference to The Man In Black, as well. Either of these men were learned enough to keep accurate records, the first of business and the community, the second of Craft business and Tradition. The Man in Black was responsible for many coven arrangements. Who knows for sure?

However magickal record keeping got its name or how it was done, to you, it will be by far the most important set of journals you will keep.

Why worry about the size of your notebook right now, or how many you will have? Because in the future, this book will become so fat and unwieldy that you will spend ten minutes looking for something, alphabetical tabs and all!

When my Book of Shadows grew beyond graceful handling, I purchased smaller additional binders for exclusive categories. I have separate binders for Rituals, Tarot, Runes, Dreams, Handwriting Analysis, etc. As I finished groups of experiments, I gathered the data together and bought a binding machine to make separate booklets with labels on the outside.

What Exactly Goes into a Book of Shadows?

This should be an accurate record of all the magickal hands-on things that you do. It should also hold research information, facts and figures on subjects such as astrology, elements, herbs, crystals, etc. It may have words of wisdom, insights you have had, and perhaps the beginning of your webweaving information.

It may also contain a list of stores and order houses where you can obtain items that you cannot make or grow yourself. Affirmations can be found there as well. And, of course, the spells and rituals you use, and their results.

My basic book consists of a three-inch binder divided into two sections, each with A-Z index tabbing. The first section contains researched information, quotes, tables, etc. The second section holds "working" information, such as rituals, spells, healing items, formulas, and other basic instructions.

On the following page I have provided you with a basic outline of the first part of my Book of Shadows. You will find that not all magickal categories are covered there. Over the years I have amassed a fairly large personal library which I use, at times, in place of this book. But the list given here will acquaint you with a number of topics and provide an indication of what types of material you may be gathering in the future.

I. Book Blessing

II. Favorite Quotes and Magickal Rules

III. Index

IV. Magickal Information

Alphabet (Magickal) Research
Astrological Correspondences
Bi-location Research
Candle Magick Research
Crystal Magick Research
Compass Point Research
Dowsing Research
Earth Magick Research
Elemental Tables
Ethics
Ghosts and Talking to the Dead
Graphology
Magickal Correspondence Tables
Moon Magick Research
Psychic Protection Research
Shamanistic Research
Symbol and Sigil Research
Telepathy Research
Vision Questing Research
Women's Spirituality Research
Astral Projection Research
Atlantean Wand Instructions
Biofeedback Research
Chakra Research
Color Magick Research
Divination Research
Druidic Research
Egyptian Magick Research
Emotions (Human) Research
Gem Research
God/Goddess Research
Herb Magick Research
Magickal Definitions
Power Research
Sensitivity Research
Spell Casting Research
Tarot Research
Time Research
Webworking Guide

At one time I tried separating the information into two books, the research into a Book of Light, and the spells and hands-on information in the Book of Shadows. Unfortunately, I was constantly trying to juggle two books.

In any magickal endeavor, accurate record keeping is important. Who knows, maybe a hundred years from now your Book of Shadows may be a Family Trad heirloom!

Summary

Your notebook has become your first Book of Shadows. On the inside cover it is customary to write a book blessing. This is done for both protection and dedication purposes of the information therein. Take some time to think about how you would like to word this blessing, then transfer it to your notebook.

If you feel the notebook you first chose is not adequate, don't delay in purchasing one that will suit your needs, and transfer the information you have already accumulated.

In this age of electronic marvels, it is feasible for you to keep your Book of Shadows stored on disc. To be safe, even if you have a hard drive, I would make two separate copies and put one in a safety deposit box. Along the same line of thinking, you should always know where your Book of Shadows is. If there is an emergency, you won't have time to crawl under the bed or unload the closet to find it.

At this point in your studies, review the list of items contained in my Book of Shadows and make a list in your notebook of things you would like to research yourself. Add your own topics as well. Consider where you would gather some of this information, and chart your plans accordingly.

Section Three

Performing Shadows

Designing and Performing Rituals

Why All this Fuss about Ritual?

The entire act of designing, implementing and completing a ritual is actually a set of various procedures and thoughts, culminating in a single magickal endeavor. From the point of determining the need to the receipt of the desired goal is ritual.

On the surface, a ritual is a tool that can be used to focus the mind and energies of the body. It can be a singular practice, or one done with several individuals. Flowing below, however, is the provision to merge your own energy with that of the Divine or Cosmic Consciousness.

There are two types of ritual — that created to honor a deity or deities, and that which is designed around a specific magickal working. Rituals for honor are usually called celebrations, and coincide with your holidays; however, they can be performed at any time. Rituals written around an act of magick, say, to bring healing to a specific individual or material wealth into the household, are working rituals.

Only one ritual does not fall neatly in to either of these two categories; that is the Self-dedication ritual because it is actually both. You are dedicating yourself in honor of the deities, but you are also working to change and better yourself and your personal environment by committing to a new way of life.

Rituals differ depending upon the season, intent, Tradition and number of people they will involve. As you are on the solitary path, you will at first be writing rituals for your personal use. Perhaps later, you will be incorporating others into these procedures for a small group ritual.

In this chapter we will concentrate on design of the generic ritual, and will end with the dedication ritual. In the chapter on spell casting we will go further in-depth about the working ritual.

Basic Outline of a Ritual for the Solitary Witch

A. Ritual Preparation
    1. Define purpose
    2. Write ritual
    3. Gather necessary tools
    4. Prepare area
    5. Prepare body
B. Open Circle
    1. Find compass North
    2. Set up Door Between the Worlds
    3. Call the Watchtowers/Elemental Quarters
C. Invocation to the Deities
    1. Align self with deity
    2. Invoke deities
D. Statement of Purpose
E. Actual Working or Act of Honor
    1. Working
        a. Complete preliminary manual or visual tasks
        b. Raise power/energy
        c. Focus power/energy
        d. Ground power/energy
    2. Honoring
        a. Complete preliminary manual or visual tasks
        b. Dedicate cakes and wine
        c. Partake of cakes and wine
F. Meditation
G. Thanking the Deities
H. Closing the Circle
    1. Mentally and verbally close the circle
    2. Physically close the circle
    3. Clean up
        a. Disposal
        b. Washing of plates and glasses
        c. Putting away tools and other implements

The above outline closely follows those rituals that are performed in a coven environment. What are the differences?

Each Tradition or coven will have their own way of doing things. However, in a coven, each compass point is represented by an individual person, sometimes called an Officer. These Officers may have specific tasks assigned to them not only in the coven hierarchy, but in different rituals as well.

For instance, the Officer of the East is generally responsible for the area preparation and ensuring that all tools enter and leave the site of the ritual. He or she may find compass point North, draw out the actual circle, and set up the Door Between the Worlds.

All Officers would participate in an initiation ceremony and hold the final vote on replacement of any Officer or the Lady, if they have left the coven. The Lady is considered the High Priestess of the coven.

In some Traditions or covens, the Lord (or High Priest, as he is often called) also functions as the Officer of the East; in others, he is a balanced participant with the Lady, and the Officer of the East is another individual.

There are Traditions and covens where each officer has appointed duties that relate to the High Holy Days or other celebrations both outside of the ritual and within the ritual itself.

The sex of the Officer may vary, as well. There are those that have ruled that a specific compass point/Officer must be of a particular sex, and there are those that fluctuate between availability of membership and, yes, skill and competence.

I have heard the comment, "I would choose so-and-so, but he/she is just not ready . . ." Often when a position is open there is a great deal of discussion that ensues to find an appropriate replacement. Why is this so important?

If the right balance and harmony is not fulfilled by the High Priest and Priestess in conjunction with their Officers, it could easily spell the disintegration of the entire coven. This can happen with a greater rate of speed than it took to build the coven environment in the first place.

In some Trad rituals, the Lady calls the Quarters, aligns herself with the deity, and invokes it/them. In other Traditions, the Officers carry their own knives and call the Quarters individually. To be responsible for calling a Quarter means that you are responsible for monitoring the energy of that element. You do not control the Quarter, but feel the energy as it moves around the circle. When dedicating the cakes and wine, the High Priestess and the High Priest together perform the task. Notice that I have not listed grounding under the honoring ritual. The actual eating of the carbohydrates of which the cakes are composed will ground the circle. However, if the Lady chooses, the act of grounding can be done as well.

In the solitary ritual, you are responsible for the entire procedure, from beginning to end. I say responsible, because you should perform any act of magick or ritual with the knowledge that you are in control of the procedures, and the results of those procedures are of your making — therefore they are your responsibility. If you screw up big-time, it is your fault and no one else's.

I feel it important to indicate some of the differences between the coven ritual and the solitary one to ease your fears that what you are doing on your own may not be legitimate. A solitary Witch can do just about any magickal act or ritual alone, save for that of the Great Rite, which does require a partner of the opposite sex to perform. Sex magick is also generally considered in this category, as well. However, the odds of a solitary Witch performing the Great Rite are minimal, and solitaries usually do not dabble in physical sex magick early on in their studies. It requires competence (which has to be gained) and a magickal partner (who has to be found — and trusted).

The Generic Ritual

Ritual Preparation

First, you need a definite purpose for holding a ritual. This purpose will determine if you are designing a celebration or a working ritual. At this time, a day and date should be chosen with any astrological correspondences that are necessary for the ritual.

Your next task is to format the ritual. Research will be required. You will have to choose deities, educate yourself more thoroughly on traditional celebrations, or perhaps consider a variety of techniques for a working ritual.

You will also need to determine what you will say and when. Will you incorporate dance, music, or drumming, or none of the above? Although I prefer a small amount of spontaneity to my rituals, I like to have some sort of skeleton to go by. Especially during your dedication ritual, you don't want to fumble; it rather takes the mood away.

Get out your notebook and copy down the following outline for ritual preparation:

Type of Ritual
Purpose of Ritual
    A. Ritual Preparation
    B. Open Circle
    C. Invocation to Deities
    D. Statement of Purpose
    E. Actual Working/Act of Honor
    F. Meditation
    G. Thanking the Deities
    H. Closing the Circle

Be sure to leave plenty of space between each category to fill in the data.

You must also determine what tools and props you will need. One consideration is what jewelry you will wear, if any; and what clothing, if any.

To dress or not to dress is purely a personal choice. It is said that Gerald Gardner was a naturist before he became outspoken about the Craft, and merely integrated his personal preference of practicing nude into his rituals. In the sixties and early seventies when free love reigned supreme, it is not surprising that this policy was acceptable in many covens. However, the nineties are upon us and the New Generation of Witches may not be quite as comfortable as our recent predecessors. Many contend that it is highly unlikely that our ancestors pranced about naked when under siege by local and national clergy. I tend to think the determination of clothing was more of the dictates of the society of the day, be it a tribal, clan, or local affair.

There are some covens today that practice skyclad, there are those that practice in fanciful garb designed by the individual, and those that practice in garb that has been decided upon by the coven hierarchy; for example, a full-length black robe.

If you wish to wear clothing, choose something that is not constricting, but not billowing in the sleeves, either. You don't wish to feel uncomfortable in the Goddess position, yet you certainly would not be joyful if your sleeve caught on fire from the illuminator candles!

There are those Witches that prefer half-robes, those that cover only to mid-thigh, or those that have slits or openings in the front or sides. Then again, you may have different styles for different rituals.

Color is important when choosing a robe. You want it to suit your mood, you want to feel that you look terrific in it, and you want it to reflect your feelings about the ritual itself.

Whether you make or purchase your robe is up to you. I personally suggest that you make it yourself, even if you are not handy with needle and thread. There are many patterns in fabric stores that lend well to whatever style you may choose. If you can't find something immediately, look under Halloween or Christmas costumes. Making it yourself allows you to be extremely creative, from the choice of fabric down to the designs you may wish to add to the robe, including trim and stenciling.

If you don't wish to brave the sewing machine, a robe can be cut from a knitted fabric that does not ravel when washed; a washing machine can become a great white shark at the most inconvenient times. Just fold the material in half and cut a hole in the center of the fold for your head. Be careful, though; what looks like your head won't fit through could put the robe down around your waist if you haven't measured properly. Material is expensive, so be careful before you do any major cutting.

If you wish to wear jewelry, have it cleansed and consecrated beforehand. Each piece should have some symbolic meaning to you. Often, a solitary Witch will choose a particular piece of jewelry to present to themselves during the dedication ritual.

This is not a selfish act, but one of total confirmation to what you are doing. If you have decided to make such a gift to yourself (I did), cleanse and consecrate the piece beforehand and lay it on a black velvet cloth or in a case, and set it upon the altar. After you have made the dedication you can work the empowerment of the piece into the ritual and complete this function.

Your list for tools and other items may look like this:
Two illuminator candles
One silver candle
Four elemental candles
One athame or wand
Broom
Pentacle
Chalice
Plate
Cakes
Drink
Bell
One red candle
One dedication gift
Four items to be placed on the altar to represent the four elements
Robe
Rope to make the magick circle
One mat or rug (to lie or kneel on should you add meditation to the ritual)

If you will be using the sacred space that you prepared earlier, most of the site cleansing and set up has already been done. Perhaps though, you have decided to work outside or in a different area. If this is the case, you will have to prepare the site. Take this into account when planning your ritual.

Lastly, on the eve of the ritual, prepare your body and mind. Take a shower or hot bath and spend a few minutes in meditation, opening the chakra centers. I prepare with "The Lesser Banishing Ritual" found in Donald Michael Kraig's book, *Modern Magick.*

Opening the Circle

Assuming compass North has been found and you have made arrangements for some type of Door Between the Worlds, you may enter the circle. Some Witches walk over a broom that has been placed in an angular position across the threshold, and then pull the broom in after them. Others merely walk into the circle and use the knife to part and close the door.

If you are using the sacred space that you have previously prepared, simply take the broom and sweep as you walk around the circle in a clockwise motion. Imagine that your broom leaves trails of positive light and energy in the clockwise movement. Return to the altar.

It is now time to charge the circle and call the Watchtowers. Another reference here is "casting the magick circle." Here is where the various rituals become diverse, depending upon the purpose and the Tradition. There are those that take all four elements and charge the circle, as was done in the cleansing and consecration ritual. Others do not do this (especially if the space is a permanent one), and merely draw the circle with their wand or athame.

Working with the Watchtowers is a matter of choice. There are those Witches that wouldn't be caught in any dimension doing this, others use Angels at the Quarters, or elements. You will have to determine which you prefer.

Beginning with East, call the Quarter. An example would be:

> *Ye Guardians of the Watchtowers of the East, I do summon, stir and call you now to witness this rite and guard this circle.*

Another line can be added with reference to what each compass point represents. For example:

> *Powers of Air, move thy cool essence about me as I journey Between the Worlds.*

Then move to the South, then West, and end at the North. At each quarter, a pentagram is drawn in the air and the guardian is verbally invoked. You should imagine that this symbol is roaring with blue flame. When you have called the Quarters, face the center of the circle and make mention that you are now Between the Worlds. In her book *Spiral Dance*, Starhawk has written the most moving piece I have over read for this purpose. It begins:

> *The Circle is Cast and we are between the worlds, beyond the bounds of time, where night and day, birth and death, joy and sorrow, meet as one.*

Although I highly recommend writing your own rituals throughout this book, this one particular passage seems to ring true above all others. I do not perform a ritual without including it.

As you call the Quarters (actually the guardians you have chosen to protect you while you are in the magick circle), a sense of growing will be about you. Do not be afraid. It is now time to do the invocation and alignment.

Invocation and Alignment with the Deities

I align myself with whatever deities I am working with. As a solitary, you are your own Priestess or Priest; therefore, you will meld your energy with that of the God/dess. When you have aligned yourself with those energies, you then invoke them, or call them to the circle.

Wording may be as follows:

> *I, _____, align myself with Isis.*

Or:
> *I am in perfect alignment with . . .*

There are those Priestesses who say:

I,_____, am (the deity) incarnate.

Which, in essence, is definitely true for the solitary practitioner. You would continue by saying something like:

In this night and in this hour I call upon the ancient power of (name of deity).

At this point in a dedication ceremony, I would read the Charge of the Goddess, which can be found in the preface of this book or written for ritual purpose in many Craft texts.

When you align yourself with the deities, light a candle for each one on the altar. For instance, if you use the God and Goddess, then light a gold and silver candle respectively. After the invocation, ring a bell once to signal the opening of your ceremony. This invites the energy of the deity into the circle.

The Statement of Purpose

The next step is to simply state your purpose, whether it be an act of honor or requesting aid for a working.

In the act of honor, you would continue by blessing the cakes and wine. Cider, ale, fruit juice or spring water could also be used. While focusing your energy on meeting with the Divine, you would slowly lower your athame into the cup and imagine the God and Goddess joining together. After this procedure has been completed, you would partake of the offering and leave one behind for the deities. This is much like a communion at a Christian church service.

You may say something like:

Oh mighty Diana, protectress of children, mother of Aradia, I have come this night to honor thy presence and to give thanksgiving for bringing my custody hearing to a successful end.

Or:

On this eve of the Samhain celebration I have come to honor those that have passed beyond the veil . . .

In a working ritual, here is where you would finish the last few stitches on that poppet, mix herbs, or create magickal writing. Then, power would be raised, focused, and grounded, depending upon the nature of the spell or working. In this case, you would state your purpose exactly:

I have come this night to bring health to Martha Jones, who has been diagnosed with pneumonia . . .

Ring the bell three times.

If you are thinking that some of the examples I have given are pretty serious, you are right. The Craft and the use of it is no game. You have the power and ability (as all humans do) to deal with life and correct those things that are unbalanced, as long as you do it with permission granted from the individual for whom you are working. We will discuss this more in detail further on in the text.

Meditation Sequence

Meditation is next. It doesn't have to be long, but it can be, if you so desire. For instance, if you have asked the deities to grant you some type of intangible gift, such as increased psychic awareness, you may want to put yourself in a meditative state to receive this energy through visualization.

The most astounding experience I have had while in this state was when my mouth was literally forced open, head thrown back, and my body filled with the gift I had requested.

Complete the meditation by closing the chakra centers, counting from ten to one, taking a deep breath, opening your eyes, and telling yourself that you are fully awake.

·☾ ☽·

Here is an example of a dedication sequence. Feel free to edit or change it to suit your needs.

> *I have cast this circle this night to perform the act of dedication of my mind, body and spirit to the Lady, Her Consort, and to the religion and science of Witchcraft.*

> *From this day forward, I will honor and respect both the Divine and myself. I will hold two perfect words in my heart: Perfect Love and Perfect Trust.*

> *I vow to honor the path I have chosen, the Divine and myself.*

Pick up your wand or athame and say:

> *I vow to hold the ideology of the Craft in my heart and my mind for the totality of this lifetime, and beyond.*

Point the wand at your feet and say:

> *Blessed be my feet, may they always walk the path of the eternal and Divine light.*

Point the wand to your knees and say:

> *Blessed be my knees as I kneel at the altar of my faith, not in supplication, but in thanksgiving.*

Point the wand to your groin and say:

> *Blessed be my womb/phallus that holds and produces the creation of the human essence. I vow to guide, protect and teach the children of the world.*

Point the wand to your chest and say:

> *Blessed be my heart that it may beat steady and true. May the warmth of my love spread throughout the galaxy.*

Point the wand to your lips and say:

> *Blessed be my lips that they shall utter truth and purity of mind and soul. May wisdom flow for the benefit of all humankind.*

Point the wand to your third eye area and say:

> *Blessed be my astral sight, that I may see through the veil of life with the truth of the Divine.*

Ring the bell seven times. Take a white cord and wrap it firmly around you hand, with the knife handle in your palm. Now say:

> *I, (your name), in the presence of the Universe, do of my own free will and mind, most solemnly swear that I will ever abide by the religion and science of The Craft. I shall neither harm my fellow human with the secrets that I learn, nor shall I flaunt my beliefs or power before them. Henceforth, from this day, I shall be reborn as (your magickal name) and shall honor, respect and cherish this oath I have taken.*

Unwind the cord and place it on the altar. Ring the bell nine times.

Hold the chalice in your left hand and pour from the decanter with your right. Dip your dedication gift into the goblet and place it on your body. Hold the chalice in both hands aloft and say:

> *With the partaking of this wine I take into my body that of the Goddess, and seal my oath . . . forever.*

Drink half of the wine and hold the half-filled goblet up to the God/dess. Say:

> *Accept this wine as my offering of thanksgiving.*

Hold the plate up and say:

> *As grain is the bounty of the Goddess, and the eating of it denotes the sacrifice of the Lord and his rebirth, I seal my oath forever as I take into my body that of the Consort!*

Thanking the Deities

Thanking the deities is important. After all, the energy of the All manifests itself in them to assist you. Your prose does not have to be overly flowery or gushy, but remembering them in thanks is appropriate.

As an example, you stand facing the altar and say:

> *I, (your magickal name), wish to thank the Lord and Lady for presiding over this dedication ritual. May we together walk within the light, forever.*

Closing the Magick Circle

Finally, you will go through the process of closing the circle. I usually hold my wand (remember, I don't care for the athame too much out of personal choice) above my head, and as I circle the room while moving my arm in a counter-clockwise motion, I say:

> *This circle is open, but never broken.*

At the same time, I envision my circle as being opened. Remember to snuff out the candles you do not wish to leave burning (do not blow them out) and prepare them for burial.

Cleaning up the Area

Clean up is now necessary. If you have not eaten during the ritual, I strongly suggest a refrigerator assault complete with plenty of carbohydrates. Dispose of any magickal residue from a working ritual. If you have cakes and wine left over, go outside and pour the wine into the ground and set out the cakes for the animals or faery folk. Wash all plates and cups, then put your tools safely away. If you feel you are carrying excess energy, send it into your tools to give them an extra boost.

Why Not Use Rituals Written by Somebody Else?

There is nothing wrong with following rituals that have already been written and performed by others. There are many fine books on the market with rituals designed for many pantheons and deities, and I encourage you to read as many of them as possible. Newsletters are also a good source for new rituals, providing the publication follows that type of instructional format.

My only advice is that if it doesn't feel right, don't do it. When you write your own rituals you bring yourself closer to the acts your physical body is performing. Also, most rituals are written for groups and must be slightly rewritten for your solitary purposes, anyway.

The Dedication Ritual

Before you take this first, yet final, step, think hard on what you are about to do. Are you willing to wash away many of your old beliefs and save only those that will further your studies in the Craft? Are you willing to honor the gods and goddesses of old, without feeling guilty or sinful? Are you willing to take responsibility for your own actions, instead of blaming your problems on everyone else? Are you willing to handle the knowledge you receive wisely, without intentionally harming another living being? Choose wisely, because you can no longer take the position of a bystander in life.

Take out your notebook now and begin planning your dedication ritual. List:

1. The date you wish to perform the ritual.
2. The time you wish to perform it.
3. The appropriate moon phase.
4. Any astrological correspondences necessary.
5. Purpose of the ritual.
6. All tools and items required for the full ritual.
7. The guardians you will use.
8. The deities you will invoke and align yourself with.

On the next page of your workbook, use your ritual planning format and begin actually writing the words you want to say in your ritual, and all physical movements you will perform during the ritual.

After you have completed any ritual and relaxed a bit, you may find yourself euphoric. This is normal; in fact, it may last several days! You may be bursting to tell someone what you have done. If you really feel the need, choose a very trusted friend, but I believe that your dedication is between yourself and the Divine, and for no one else's ears. It is a very big step that the dedicant takes. Congratulate yourself when you have completed it. It took courage to enter the world of wisdom and knowledge.

Suggested Reading List

Herman Slater, editor, *A Book of Pagan Rituals*. Samuel Weiser, Inc.

Ed Fitch, *Magickal Rites From The Crystal Well*. Llewellyn Publications.

Ed Fitch, *The Rites of Odin*. Llewellyn Publications.

Barbara G. Walker, *Women's Rituals*. Harper & Row Publishing (now Harper & Collins).

Lynn V. Andrews, *Teachings Around the Sacred Wheel.* Harper & Row
Publishing.

Scott Cunningham, *Wicca: A Guide For the Solitary Practitioner.* Llewellyn
Publications.

Starhawk, *The Spiral Dance.* Harper & Row.

Janet and Stewart Fararr, *Eight Sabbats for Witches.* Phoenix Publishing.

Webweaving

You have met your Shadows (both real and not so real). You have let some remain intact, and you have banished others. Best of all, you have built some new ones, and will continue to do so for the rest of your life. There are Shadows that you will master quickly, those that will take a tremendous amount of work and will, and those that you may not conquer in this lifetime.

·☽ ☾·

An individual can derive only so much from reading books. During the early eighties, book sales exceeded over nine billion dollars per year. Unfortunately, only a very small fraction of them were magickal in nature.

It is estimated that there are over 2500 book publishers in the United States that pump out over 60,000 books per year. It is my estimation that the average magickal person reads about three or more books per month on any given enlightened subject; if, that is, they can get their hands on them.

Magickal people also buy in bursts because of the nature of what they are learning. If one is studying the Tarot, one may buy five different books at a pop, then go back two weeks later for a few more. This usually happens once you get past the "this is how-to for beginners" part and you are interested in eating up as much advanced material as you can possible find.

To date, my personal training has been fairly balanced — 33% through books, 33% through practical application and experimentation, and 33% through webweaving (a Witchy word for networking). Oh, the 1% — well, I personally think that there is some guide up there or out there who is pulling this all together for me!

Often a book or article can be a catalyst in your spiritual growth, but nothing beats the one-to-one sharing of thoughts and practices between two human beings. Since a book cannot socialize, the next most logical step is to find a warm body that does!

Solitaries may practice by themselves, but that does not mean they live in caves without phones, or monasteries without contact with the outside world. For any human, magickal or not, interaction with our own kind is essential.

One advantage a solitary has over group-oriented magickal people is that they are not in danger of breaking any oaths when sharing information. You won't be giving away any secrets or hidden knowledge. There will be times during your networking that someone will say to you, "I am sorry, but I can't give you the answer because I would be breaking an oath to do so." If this happens, you should respect the fact that the individual has taken a vow and does not wish to break it. Simply back off and switch the subject.

The word "secret" is also double-edged. There are those people who will flaunt that they "have secrets." Tread lightly with this individual. Dimes to dollars that person doesn't know jack you-know-what and is simply trying to impress you.

Many people shy away from networking with others at first, because they feel there may be real danger in associating with strangers, even if it is only by mail. But, if done with the necessary precautions that you would use when entering almost any unfamiliar environment, you should have few difficulties.

Webweaving Guidelines

Acquire a Post Office Box

If you live in a small town or rural area, I advise that you rent a box in the next town over, or perhaps in the city in which you work. Boxes from the U.S. Postal Service require that you produce some type of "official" identification, such as a drivers' license, voter card, etc.

You must fill out your real name and address; however, you may indicate under what names mail may be delivered to you. This is where your magickal name may come in, if you choose to share it with the world. Often individuals do not wish their real names to be known due to family ties, job security, etc. Under postal laws, it is acceptable to have your mail delivered under an alias, as long as your correct name and address are on file.

I personally do not advocate having magickal mail delivered to your home, especially in the beginning. I would like to tell you that the world is full of wonderful, loving people — but I'm not a fool, and neither are you. Witches, Pagans, and other magickal people are basically gentle, caring folk. Like any society, however, there are infiltrators that do not belong or outsiders looking to make you an easy target for harassment, or, at times, worse.

Likewise, do not give out your phone number or your place of employment. If you happen to run across that rotten grape on the networking vine, you certainly don't want to give them the advantage of ruining a life that you have so carefully built.

When the Wiccan/Pagan Press Alliance (WPPA) first released its telephone number to member editors, we got very few phone calls. We were in the process of developing a phone tree for Pagans in trouble and felt that as we were becoming a trusted clearinghouse of information, Pagans should have our number. As we became larger, we got less careful with our number, which resulted in a few crank phone calls and calls at very busy times of the day (like supper). To ease this difficulty, we installed an answering machine.

At first, friends, family, Pagans, and my newspaper employer got a little frustrated, claiming they could never get hold of me. What none of them realized was the large volume of calls I was receiving each day. If I had picked up the phone every time it rang, I'd never get anything accomplished.

My point then, is to plan carefully when releasing any type of information that will intrude on your environment, whether it be home or business.

In the years I have been webweaving I can think of only four instances where I have encountered real problems. What should you do if a webweaving difficulty arises? First, determine the cause. If it is something you have done or said, correct it. If someone is attacking you unjustly through the mail, politely tell them that you are ending correspondence with them, and henceforth you will be returning all mail. If they write again, give it back to the Post Master and have it marked unaccepted. Don't even bother to read the envelope or post card and don't open it.

Now and then, a verbosely rabid individual from one of the "standard" religions may catch you in their personal mailing campaign. One's first reaction is to bombard them with your knowledge and educate them. Don't bother — trash it. These people don't want to be educated, they just want to take their frustrations out on you.

Psychic attack is a rare reality, but, as the comedian says, "It can happen!" If you feel that such a thing is happening to you, contact some of your more experienced webweaving friends. I'm not ashamed to tell you I did. Witches do take care of their own.

Another alternative to the box at the Post Office is a relatively new franchise business called Mail Boxes Etc., USA. Although the fee per box is higher than the average U. S. Postal Box, they do offer a variety of services that the postal service does not. It is sort of a one-stop shop for all your mailing needs.

They also can provide you with a suite address, hold your mail indefinitely, and have a 24-hour open door service for you to pick up your mail. You can even call them and ask if you have received any mail, or a particular piece of mail, so you don't have to make a trip only to have your box turn up empty.

Do correspond with as many people as your budget and time allows. With the increase in postal rates, you may have to be more selective with your correspondences, but I heartily urge you to build a strong web of contacts.

Contacts

Webweaving contacts often fall into the following categories:

1. Those people that merely want pen-pals and write little on spiritual developments. This is great, as long as you can afford it. These people ground us and help us to remain linked to general society.

2. Those individuals who are interested in specific skills and want to both share and learn new techniques. Topics you might hear about are divination, telepathy, or a specific Craft Tradition that is generally well known. I have found, however, that Witches do not often trade spells, unless one specifically requests it. They do like to share rituals, however.

3. Those persons who are interested in the "training" process of fellow magickal beings. A note of gentle warning here: never forget that we are all teachers as well as students. So often I hear or read, "I am desperately look for for a teacher! Please help me." When you are ready for a teacher, one will be provided for you. It may be a person, a text, or even the wind. It really isn't necessary to advertise for one.

Synchronicity plays an important role in Craft activities. All things do happen in perfect timing if you relax and let your life flow. The more stressed over an issue you become, the more likely it is that things will take longer to develop. Wisdom and knowledge are acquired when you are ready to accept and understand.

If you write to twenty people and tell them you are looking for a teacher, the first thing they will think is either that you are a sucker and try to scam you (it happens), or that you haven't gained the wisdom that you are constantly in a learning environment and the Universe will be your teacher.

Don't feel bad if you have already done this. I did it. But I was lucky enough to find two people who were patient enough to encourage me along my own learning path. I also ran into some real nut cases.

Patience is difficult, especially when you are studying something as wonderful and powerful as Witchcraft. Patience is both a posture and a practice.

Be careful of individuals who pour on the metaphysical knowledge and jargon, or give you a healthy list of credentials. It is one thing to provide simple references for safety (for example, list one or two networking contacts who can vouch for you and don't mind being contacted), it is quite another to snow a person under with ten pages of where they have been and how they have received those last twenty titles, none of which you could possibly check even if you wanted to make the effort to do so.

Most likely this person — the one with the list of titles as long as your wand — is on a self-inflicted ego trip. Don't help feed it. Learn to read between the lines or skim through the volumes of personal data you have been provided. Follow your intuition. If what they are saying to you does not ring true, either don't respond or send a polite "no thank you" letter. Those networking friends that are firmly rooted in sensibility will not use a cabinet full of titles. It simply isn't necessary.

Another group of people out there are those that are looking for mates/sexual partners and make no bones about it. To me, the Craft is not a handy-dandy dating service, although I am sure there have been wonderful alliances because of it. Usually, you will find these ads under the "Personals" columns in some newsletters, though not all Craft publications carry this type of advertisement. These inquiries are pretty straight-forward.

I always know when I'm holding one, because somewhere in the letter is the statement, "Do you look anything like the pictures you draw?"

The answer is . . . (drum roll, please) No, that's why I draw them in the first place. A psych major would tell you that they are a product of wish fulfillment. If I did look like that, I sure wouldn't be working for a living!

Seriously, though, you may get a few of these. If you are interested, just be careful. If it is the farthest thought from your mind, politely write back and say no, if the letter was a nice one. If it should have been published in a sex magazine instead of reaching your mail box, trash it.

Meeting Witches Face to Face

Before you plan to meet anyone as a result of webweaving, check them out as thoroughly as you can. Have they personally met any of your other webweaving contacts? I suggest speaking to them on the phone first before setting up a meeting if you are really serious.

When you do decide to meet, choose a public place, such as a restaurant, a library, or even a museum. Let someone in your family or one of your close friends know where you are going and why.

If you are new to the Craft, do not fashion pre-conceived ideas of whom you will meet. Quite often they will not live up to your expectations, especially if this is your first time. Also, don't fall into the trap of thinking that someone is an adept just because they have been involved in the Craft longer than you have. When someone starts spouting to me how many years they have been in the Craft before we've had a decent general conversation, I get suspicious. You can be a Girl Scout for eleven years and still get lost in the woods.

Do not attend any type of closed meetings or rituals unless you have met and feel you can trust the participants. Often you can meet like-minded individuals at your local occult or metaphysical store. Many of these places offer standard classes and good fellowship. Just don't go running off to a Full Moon ceremony in Bakker's woods just because you've never been to one, and here's your chance — even though you met this guy (or gal) night before last beside the crystal display at Shop 'n Craft.

What I'm saying is, don't put yourself in a position you won't be able to get yourself out of. Don't endanger your safety without thinking first. A huge number of people disappear in the United States each year — don't you be one of them!

Behaving Yourself When You Are Invited Out

Should you be so inclined to attend a coven or group function, please follow the rules of good etiquette that Mother taught you. Don't be horrified or insulted that I mention this, but surprisingly enough, this subject shows up in many Pagan publications. Unfortunately, it doesn't hit home until you witness bad manners first hand.

Why am I discussing this at all if this is a book about practicing solitary? Because eventually, you most likely won't be. Most people are not social hermits. If you are visiting a group of Witches, please watch what is going on around you and take your cue from the other people. Being in a circle comes with responsibility, even for a visitor.

Do try to be good. If the group does something that astounds you, don't gasp, please. I know it is a scary experience to be with a group of people who you mostly don't know, doing things you may not understand, and feeling like a third wheel. We all have experienced this. But that is no excuse for bad manners. If you are at someone's home, bring something to give the hostess, whether it be a bag of chips, a roll of paper towels, or a few candles. Remember to clean up after yourself. Your behavior also decides whether or not you will be asked back. Sometime the circle may be at your house.

Designing the Introduction Letter

When first writing to any individual, whether it be answering an ad, requesting information, or contacting an editor of a press, make your first impression polite and one page only. As with all correspondence, you should indicate the date you wrote the letter, the time and your return address on the letter itself. A remark of the weather or astrological phase or holiday is interesting. To some people it may mean nothing; to others, a great deal.

Remember to place the correspondent's address on your letter. For instance, if you are writing to me, you would place my entire address on the letter. This ensures proper placement in its envelope when it comes time for you to mail it. If you become a rabid letter writer, as I did, this keeps you from getting things mixed up.

If you have read about the person in a particular publication, please tell them so. Include the name of the publication, issue number and date. Why? Because if they have their name posted for whatever reason, they have probably paid money for the ad. By telling them where you heard of them they will know how successful their ad has been.

Above all, be straight-forward in your writing. Save the theatrical prose for a different endeavor. In the beginning keep the personal information to a minimum. One of the most amusing letters I have ever received contained the sentence, "I am much like you; I am a warlock." I'm sorry, but I laughed my sides out on that one because the individual was drawing a conclusion about me and telling me, without knowing it, that they didn't know diddly about the Craft.

First of all, I'm a she, not a he. And secondly, there is no such thing as a

Warlock in the Craft. A male Witch is just that, a male Witch. Either that person got me confused with the old television show, or they mixed their magickal systems somewhere along the line. And believe me, there are times when I really wished I could twitch my nose, making my dishes wash themselves and my laundry float to where it belongs instead of piled on the basement floor!

Include a self-addressed stamped envelope, or SASE for short. This is a courtesy you should always extend. If you have developed a high volume of webweaving by running a press for a non-profit organization or what have you, it is really insulting to receive a request for information or for help for a predicament, and the writer has not had the decency to enclose an SASE. The people at the receiving end of your letter may be paying for postage to help you out of their family budget.

On the same note, don't let anyone take advantage of you in the same way. In the beginning you may feel you are doing your spiritual duty, but when it starts affecting your regular expenses, you are only hurting yourself.

If you have requested and received specific information, please send off a thank you note to the individual who answered your correspondence. A simple thank you is not very difficult for one to say, and means a great deal to the person who has tried to assist you. It also lets them know that there is no problem with the mail and that you have received what you asked for. A simple post card will suffice. I usually add, "This is a letter you can trash when you are through reading." When high volumes of mail are involved, they will kiss you a hundred times over!

As the Director of the Wiccan/Pagan Press Alliance, I can tell you that editors of presses, journals and newsletters in the Pagan community work long and tiring hours for little pay (if any) to serve their subscribers. There is nothing more frustrating than receiving a letter for help, sitting down at the typewriter and writing for over two hours to assist that person, and then never hearing from them. You haven't the foggiest idea if they even received your letter.

Another pet peeve of mine is to receive a note, scrawled in one or two lines with barely discernible writing on a torn scrap of paper, looking like yesterday's grocery list that ran through the washer. Editors are professionals and they should be treated as such. Besides, if they can't read your note, do you expect to receive what you asked for?

Webweaving Files

If you plan on extensive webweaving, start some type of filing system early on. Put each individual's name or organization on a manilla file folder along with the address, date, and method of first contact. Later on, you can add pertinent information on the front of the folder, such as birthday, type of correspondence they are interested in, family members or animals that they are fond of, etc. This comes in very handy if you become well-acquainted. To remember their birthday or some other special occasion will mean a lot to them.

If you have placed an ad in one of the various newsletters, keep track of the number and type of responses you receive from each ad. This will enable you to determine if you have wisely spent your money and what type of contacts you have received from that press or newsletter. Add a department number to your address that corresponds to the press you are using. For example, if you place an ad in *Llewellyn's New Worlds,* then use Department LNW under your P. O. Box number. When the letter comes in, you will know exactly where it came from.

Webweaving can be rewarding and enlightening for any magickal person, solitary or coven-oriented alike. Many people you correspond with will become a type of extended family to you — there when you need them, full of happiness, hope and envelopes full of caring for many years to come.

Workshops

Many Pagan organizations, occult shops, and metaphysical stores offer a variety of workshops and classes. Some are good, some are mediocre, and some are downright not worthy of your money. Here are some things you should consider before you open your purse or wallet and count out that hard-earned cash.

Local Workshops

Visit the store on several occasions before you sign up for any course. Since this is local, it shouldn't be a problem. Get a feel for the place and the owner to determine whether or not you would be interested in what they have to offer.

Some stores offer free classes with a donation passed around afterwards to cover the expenses of the speaker or trainer. Give what you can afford. If you have spent an hour and a half there and learned a lot, $5 to $10 is acceptable, depending upon the cost of living for that area.

Some courses are on-going, so if you are on a tight budget, pace yourself. Other stores set their schedules up in advance with detailed course construction, or have arranged to bring someone in from another part of the state or country. In these instances, they will usually set a price for the course and ask for early sign-up and a deposit.

Do not feel embarrassed to request a detailed outline about the course, or a press release about the instructor or speaker. Will all the materials be provided under the fee you are paying? There are some stores that will goad you into the class, and you will find yourself paying out the you-know-what to purchase the "needed materials" to get the "full benefit" of the class. These shop owners push particular products and books before, during, and after the classes. My advice is: don't take any extra cash with you that you are desperately going to need before the next paycheck. If you have to think about a purchase and come back for it, chances are you will decide that you really didn't need that $50 crystal after all.

If you do decide to attend a pre-paid class or workshop, please remember to consider group etiquette. MindWalker and I have been to workshops where one or two unhappy people used the entire class time telling the group about their experiences or problems. Not all speakers are capable of shutting these people up, especially if they are on the road for the first time. This doesn't mean they don't have wonderful information to give you, it just means that they are learning — unfortunately, at your expense.

Also, if you are more knowledgeable on the subject than the instructor, or at least you think you are, don't interrupt and show off your expertise. It spoils it for everyone else and you end up looking like the ass, not the instructor.

If you find the course was a waste of your time, sit back instead and observe. You can learn a great deal from the reactions of the other participants. It may have been an unfortunate expense (and you will know better next time) but you won't be wasting your time.

When the event is over, tell the shop owner and the instructor, speaker, etc., what you thought about the class. Often they will give you a review form. Use it! Give them both good and bad impressions, but don't make it one-sided; nothing is totally terrible or completely perfect. This gives the shop owner and the speaker a chance to review their own work later and pinpoint where they can make improvements.

Don't hog the instructor as soon as the group breaks. If you really think you have something to discuss in depth with them, arrange to contact them either by phone or through correspondence. There is nothing more irritating to the poor soul who just wants to say thank you and buzz out the door, if someone is there blubbering big time for over twenty minutes. It can put a damper on everyone's whole afternoon or evening.

Out-of-town Workshops

Again, request a detailed outline about the course and ask for a press release package on all speakers and instructors. Again, will all course materials be provided with your fee? Are your room or any meals covered under the initial fee? If not, is there a discount provided for these items if you stay at the place of the seminar (assuming, of course, there are accommodations there)? Is the site of the seminar or workshop easily accessible for the type of transportation you have chosen? What kind of area is it in?

Once you have made the decision to go, consider the following:

1. Do you have an adequate budget to cover all expenses, even emergency ones?
2. Will the hotel accept your credit card or personal check if you do run into trouble?
3. Is there a friend who may want to attend with you? It is nice to have someone along who is willing to share the expenses and share the fun.
4. If there is an emergency that requires the cancellation of your plans, can your money be refunded?
5. Will there be a ritual held? Do you need special garb?

6. Is one of your networking friends near by that you could possibly stay with, or at least spend some time with while you are on your trip?

7. If you have any writing or photographic expertise, contact a few Pagan newsletters and ask them if they would like a review of the seminar or workshop for publication. Many editors cannot attend many of these functions and will welcome your expertise.

Courses

Educational courses are events that last from six to twelve weeks, or longer. They meet regularly, have a paid instructor, and promise some type of enlightenment (whether it be skill or knowledge). They can be held at a metaphysical/occult bookstore, a college campus, or some other community establishment. At times, they are offered at someone's home.

Ask for a copy of the syllabus to ensure that you are going to like what you are paying for. Check out the teacher's references by speaking to individuals who either know the instructor, or who have taken the course before you.

If you can, meet the teacher in person first. Do you like their personality? Do you feel that they will be able to present the course in a manner you will understand? There is no sense paying good money for something or someone you are not interested in. If something happens that you cannot attend the course or must drop out, what is their policy on catch-ups and refunds? If you must sign a document, read it, including the fine print.

Please keep in mind that your instructor or teacher is not God, nor do they usually aspire to that particular pedestal, nor are they there to be bashed on their own ideals. Give respect, and you will receive respect.

Excellent friendships and a wealth of knowledge can await you at these various functions. Just remember to keep your wits about you, and have a good time!

Festivals

When you feel you are ready to take the plunge into a totally magickal environment, it is time to go to a festival! There are many held throughout the United States and Canada during the year. They usually last from three days to one week, and several fall on or near our solar holidays.

Once you are on the mailing lists of several magickal presses and newsletters, you will receive announcements of gatherings or they will be advertised within the body of the press. An excellent resource to find out what is happening near you is the Calendar of Events, published by Larry Cornett, 9527 Blake Lane Loop, Apartment 102, Fairfax, VA 22031. This press is $2 per issue, and is published six times per year.

Most festivals require payment in advance (and give you a discount if you do so) and have a limited number of spaces available. However, some do allow you to pay at the gate. Unfortunately, the fee is usually astounding (sorry guys, especially if you can only make it for one day). The desire to spend your money quickly dissolves. I realize that this is done to keep a high volume of people from drifting though the festival grounds, but it does prevent some people from participating due to family responsibilities, job considerations and travel expenses. Some of the larger festivals run programs to help pay for expenses of Pagans who cannot afford to attend by working out some type of services for stay system. Check this out; don't be ashamed to lend a helping hand.

The Rules

There are rules involved when you participate in a festival and questions you should ask before, during and after you attend.

Are accommodations provided? If so, what? Should you bring camping gear? How extensive in your packing should you get?

Are children permitted? What facilities have been provided for their care, if any, and what rules must you follow to ensure their safety?

Some festivals provide child care during specified hours, but not the entire day or evening. Are you prepared to take that responsibility in the off hours? I know this statement sounds stupid, of course you know your children are your own responsibility, but you would be surprised at the number of parents that allow their children (including the little ones) to run free, without discipline or care in the festival environment. Most of the individuals who attend are extremely tolerant of children and will go out of their way to ensure their safety and happiness; a different atmosphere from the local amusement park where you don't know who the hell is roaming around with Goddess knows what on their minds. However, that is no excuse for letting them blunder into a private ritual with you nowhere to be seen. And no, this advice is not coming out of the mouth of a spinster. I've got four children, and I know what they are capable of.

Does the festival allow pets? If so, what are the rules governing them?

Do you need to bring your own food and cooking gear? What type of clothing is required? What is the weather there usually like, if you are travelling a long distance?

Perhaps there will be a ritual where you may wear your favorite magick apparel. Is nudity permitted? If it is, prepare yourself to see it if you are not used to it. This may also influence your decision whether or not to take your children with you.

As long as I live I will never forget the first festival I attended in Maryland where skyclad was acceptable. MindWalker and I took some friends with us. Not long after we arrived and signed in, we took a walk down Merchants' Row. MindWalker and my friend's boyfriend were walking behind us and we were yapping madly about all the wonderful things at the stands.

My friend dropped something and I bent over to pick it up. Behind me, MindWalker was laughing and I could vaguely hear him saying, "Wait until she sees this!"

Now, what you must understand is that I am from Pennsylvania — the twilight zone of rural America where wearing clothes in public is a prerequisite to living there. It is not a topic one finds up for discussion.

Imagine now, I am on my knees, picking up whatever it was, and as I slowly raise my eyes, I see male legs encased in fur chaps. Okay, I think, not unusual, I had seen other people in costume. No big deal. Naturally, my eyeballs keep travelling upwards as I am rising. At mid-crouch position, I stop dead. I think my eyeballs have just popped from their sockets. My friend has noticed too, and I heard a sharp intake of breath. One of us, I'm not sure which, said, "Oh, my God!"

Which is exactly what this young fellow was dressed to portray, right up to a fantastic horned headdress, with nothing between that and the chaps!

By this time, our two men were practically rolling on the ground behind us in the throes of tear-running laughter, and my face was redder than a sunset in Florida. However, I must certainly admit it is a fond memory of the God.

Most festival sites have a medical area, but be sure to check that out. What type of services are available?

Other questions you may have are, can you get ice? Is there refrigeration available? Are there showers? Are there cabins or dorms? Are they co-ed? (Many of them are.)

Check out the surrounding area in relation to the festival site. Is there a town nearby where you can purchase food on the way in, instead of lugging it from New York to Tennessee? Before you go, get yourself a map of the state and be sure you know what routes to take if you are driving. Mark off any sites that you may like to visit while you are in the area, or friends you would like to see. Before you enter the festival site, drive around the nearest town and determine where the pharmacy and hospital are. If you are not the camping type, or you discover you do not like the festival, see what kind of alternative accommodations are in the area (such as a motel/hotel of good reputation). You may also look to see what restaurants are in the area, as well. Maybe on the day you leave the festival you would like to relax and be waited on before your journey home. Locate the nearest gas station for fuel-up, and, of course, garage capabilities should you have car trouble, Goddess forbid.

Make sure you have read the rules about alcohol, drugs and weapons. Aside from what one usually thinks of as a weapon, be sure to ask if ritual implements such as athames or swords are acceptable. It is a little disconcerting to be at a festival where there is someone walking around with a knife that could easily carve a dinosaur strapped neatly to their thigh. Especially if the grip has finger holes.

A few festivals allow alcohol in moderation. However, if you think you are going to party, party, party, you may be sadly disappointed. Most festivals are attended by magickally-filled people who do not desire the use of drugs or alcohol.

Also, if you are a smoker, please be polite. Many festival people do not smoke. Be sure you put your ashes out well and stick the butts in your pocket.

If you drop them on the ground, someone is probably going to tell you about it. Conversely, if you are a non-smoker, don't infringe your beliefs on the polite smoker, either. After all, maybe they have never driven drunk in their life, and you have. Keep the motto: to each his (or her) own.

If you plan to take a non-magickal partner or friend with you, please explain the rules before you are in the car a hundred miles from home. There have been some instances where non-magickal partners/mates and/or friends have caused real problems because they have been drunk, disorderly or violent.

I will never forget one High Priest from a Northeastern group who told me not one, but two stories about violence he had witnessed at festivals because individuals had been either uninformed about procedures or drunk. Granted, these two instances occurred once in the ten-plus years that the individual had been attending festivals on a regular basis, and you should never fear attending a festival just because it can happen. The odds are you will never encounter such an event yourself. However, choose your companions wisely. Gatherings are safer than city streets. Vendors can leave their wares out unattended and no one will touch them through the entire gathering.

Many covens and organizations will have a banner staked or posted by their tents or cabins. Although this is not a prerequisite, you may wish to design one to take with you. Even solitaries can have a personal crest.

Merchants' Row

Most festivals have a Merchants' Row where vendors can display their products. You will find everything from tools and clothing to literature and body painting. If you are a magickal craftperson, you may wish to make arrangements to set up in this area, complete with your camping gear. Have business cards prepared to exchange with others and to hand out to potential customers. Even if you cannot have your own place on the row, you can still do business and network.

Merchants' Row is a wonderful place. People are willing to talk to you about all sorts of things from mundane to magickal. Many items are high quality and lots of them you can't find in the department stores.

There are only two possible drawbacks to Merchants' Row. First, you never seem to have enough money with you; second, there are some festivals that limit what the merchants can sell to you. Usually this happens at the smaller gatherings.

There are a few festival committees who forbid competition. I think that this is ludicrous and an example of bad Pagan business. I had a friend who couldn't sell her crystals at a particular festival because there was another woman there selling hers at lower quality and higher price. Absurd!

Other festival committees control the number of vendor types, meaning they don't want an over-abundance of leather workers and no jewelry makers. This is sound business sense when the space available for merchants is limited. These usually work on a first-come, first-serve basis.

If you would like to be on Merchants' Row, write months ahead of time to reserve your space, make the deposit (if required), and thoroughly check out the rules.

Merchants' Row usually closes up around supper time and does not re-open until the following day, as these people join in the evenings' festivities.

Main Circle Events

Most festivals have one or more evenings of main circle events where everyone participates, no matter the Tradition, sect or magickal style.

The main event, which is usually scheduled at the mid-point of the festival, has been planned in advance by the festival committee. You will encounter varied traditions throughout your stay; try to take advantage of as many invitations to join in their celebrations as you can.

Leaving the Festival Site

When you are preparing to leave, clean up your camping/bunk area and leave it better than you found it. If you can, find some of the people who were responsible for the festival events and thank them for their hard work. When you get home, be sure to write them a note extending your thanks and telling them what you liked about the gathering. This will assist them in planning future festivals.

Festivals are a wonderful place to meet people, raise your vibrational level, and find answers to questions that perhaps you have been looking for for a long time. The week after attending a festival you may feel wired and accomplish many things due to the interaction with such intense magickal energy. Often, one wishes one could return as soon as they have reached home!

Summary

Webweaving, workshops and festivals can be truly rewarding experiences. Remember to plan well, check out all your sources, and above all, be courteous in your exchanges.

Being a solitary Witch may be a lonely endeavor at times. There will be instances when you feel the need to be with your own kind, either for support or just for companionship. You may often look at the world around you and think, "If only they knew what they were missing!" I know I have.

Divination vs. Fortune Telling

Skill or Gift?

I heard a psychic once on a local radio show tell the entire Harrisburg area that divination was a "special gift," not a skill. She told the people of this capital city that only a chosen few were given the privilege of seeing into the future.

Bah, humbug! The announcer later went on to say that you could see this woman, in person, for a private consultation at a local hotel. Fee: $50. In my mind she was fleecing the public in exchange for a reading and a little common sense on the pretense that only her special, gifted self could assist those who wished to part with their money.

Don't get me wrong. There is nothing inappropriate about paying for a service rendered, as long as you are not paying for something delivered under false pretenses. It is my firm belief that divination is a skill and an art, not a "gift." There is nothing that irritates me more than someone who spouts their prowess at this art in the guise of "I'm gifted, yes me, me, me!"

There are individuals who are more open or sensitive to universal information. There are others who have never had a precognitive experience. But once the blocks are removed, there is no reason why every single person cannot tap into the collective unconscious and learn to divine; if not for others, at least for themselves.

Fortune Telling

The idea of fortune telling usually conjures up visions of a dark, sloe-eyed, pleasantly plump female with tons of bangles and bracelets dripping from her body. She exudes mystery, naughtiness, and has the best set of half-revealed breasts this side of the Mississippi. To delve further into her personality, she is not exactly the type you would base your life decisions on, because she does not precisely appear to be of the trustworthy sort.

Today, we often see reports of swindlers and charlatans who are in the market to steal sizeable amounts from unwitting clients. I myself have been to women who have said, "Give me eighty dolla' and I will burn candle for you. My seester will fashion it by her own lovely hands and we will pray for you under the light of the Full Moon!" Baloney!

One woman in particular was a real character. After every sentence she would say, "You understan' ?" She also told me that there was a woman in my family unit who had cast an evil spell on me and it would cost me a pretty penny to remove it. I flatly told her I was the only woman alive in the immediate or extended family unit. She flawlessly went on to a different angle.

But there are lots of good readers around. Many occult shops have an individual who is quite capable of giving a good reading. Naturally, some are better than others. if the proprietor feels they are not sufficiently skilled to read you, often they will give you the name of a dependable individual who can.

New Age shops have jumped on the band wagon, too. I have seen more Medicine card decks floating around those types of shops than I could count. I am not picking on the Medicine cards, incidentally; I love them. I just find it very amusing that they have taken the place of the Tarot in the more Christian-based stores. Often the prices in these stores are not too salty. However, if they are, I would check references first.

Why should you seek another reader when you plan to acquire the skill yourself? The same reason a psychiatrist must seek the help of another in his/her field — balance, and an unemotional, uninvolved opinion. Most times you will not feel the need to seek another reader's assistance, but every now and then it is a good idea to have someone who can read for you. There are times when our emotions will totally confuse and muddy a reading when we do it for ourselves. Perhaps you could make an arrangement to trade services with another reader or Witch.

Divining

There are many types of tools that can be used for divining purposes. Some of the more well-known divinatory tools are listed here.

Cartomancy: Divination or fortune telling with cards. These can be the Tarot, Rune cards, the Cartouche (an Egyptian symbolism system) playing cards, Karma cards, Medicine cards (which use animal symbolism), the new Phoenix deck for past life readings, Star + Gate (an exceptional psychological tool that is excellent for magickal and non-magickal people), The Celtic Tree Oracle (based on plants and trees), etc.

Crystal gazing: Sometimes referred to as **scrying** where the vehicle used is a crystal ball, a bowl of inked water, or a magick mirror.

Dowsing: Divination by the use of a pendulum, forked stick or metal rod. Excellent for yes and no questions. A pendulum can be fashioned from fishing line with a small weight, or it can be a necklace with a crystal ball on the end. Dowsing is rather exciting because you can design your own charts for answers, and it is really a very flexible tool.

Numerology: Divination by the use of numbers and calculations thereof. Anything from your birth date to dream analysis can be used. Tarologists and astrologists often will use numerology to give a more complete reading.

Palmistry: Divination by the examination of an individual's hands.

Runes: Divination by the use of stones or ceramic squares inscribed with the magickal alphabet of the Germanic, Scandinavian, or Norse symbols. Runes are excellent for dream analysis, spells, talismans, as well as general divination.

Graphology: The study of an individual's script or handwriting. This is extremely useful in webweaving and also adds to any other reading you may be doing.

Geomancy: Divination by use of marks in the earth. **Astrological geomancy:** divination combining astrology and inner consciousness, wherein a set of random dots are correlated to a type of astrological chart.

Other vehicles are tea leaves, and the I-Ching. The I-Ching is a divination vehicle using three coins or chips. Once tossed, a linear pattern is determined by the right or wrong side up of each coin. Coins are tossed several times to determine a single pattern. The interpretations are listed by pattern in any I-Ching text.

You may use American money, foreign money, I-Ching coins that can be located in some metaphysical shops, poker chips or wooden discs the size of a quarter or half-dollar. Standard I-Ching coins are usually made of metal with a square hole in the center of each coin. One side is elaborately decorated, the other is not. The I-Ching is an extremely suitable oracle for business questions. It also works well for those individuals whose religion forbids things like the Tarot, but accepts the tool of another culture. The basis for this is that it is so foreign, it can't be possibly be harmful. I didn't say this was a realistic assumption, just one that exists.

Another interesting form of divination is fire scrying, as mentioned in Dion Fortune's book *The Sea Priestess*, where one gazes into the embers as you would a crystal ball. This is an excellent oracle for the winter months, and nice to incorporate into the Samhain or Yule celebrations. Caldron scrying, too, is of the same nature, wherein one gazes upon the steam rising from a pot of selected herbs and spices.

·☾ ☽·

Almost all of the divination tools listed can be used in the performance of magick. Tarot cards and runes are two of the most popular vehicles and will be discussed in the following chapter. If the tool comes from a particular culture, as the runes do, you should have a general understanding of that magickal system before using the tool for magick.

Learning to use at least one divinatory tool is important for any Witch. This tool should be consulted before any magickal working, either for yourself or for another. It is a protection check to keep from the accidental performance of black magick.

For instance, one of the first spells I cast was for my husband. It was during the beginning of buck-hunting season in our area. As I have mentioned before, we have a large family, so the meat he brings home goes on the table, not on my wall (unless, of course, the children get rowdy and have a food fight!).

Anyway, I cast a spell to have my husband see the biggest buck in the forest. I assumed that he would be able to bring it in because he's an excellent shot.

Wrong. He did see the grand-daddy of all bucks, but as he was finishing a bodily function he had the wrong weapon in his hand when the deer appeared. Subsequently, he came home that year without the deer.

I did more than one thing wrong. First, I didn't use any type of divinatory vehicle for the outcome of the spell. Had I done so, I would have seen that something was amiss and gone back over what I wanted to do. Second, I assumed. Assumptions have no place in spell casting. Everything must be planned out to the littlest detail.

I should also have contacted the power animal for the buck indicating the specifics of what I planned to do and why. Then, I should have requested the sacrifice for the need and honored the animal through some type of gift exchange. Live and learn.

The Scope of a Divination Tool

Before you begin readings for other people, you should be aware of what a divinatory tool can and cannot do for you. So often people think that because you can see what they cannot, you can see everything — which is simply not the case and puts everybody, including yourself, in a dangerous position.

Naturally, some readers are better at interpretation than others. Some are very good at the fortune telling angle, meaning things like pipes breaking, house purchases, affairs, etc. Other readers do better on the more spiritual and mental side of things; helping to get people out of the blues by finding the trigger, or assisting in planning a career, or past life readings to help in sorting out today's circumstances.

There are readers who do both quite well. You will find people who listen to their spirit guide while they are reading and relay that information to the querent (the person you are reading for).

I have found that the information sought is usually there, and if a mistake is made it is on the part of the reader in the interpretation. The cards never lie. Determining if a mistake has been made is not easy. Readers are usually 85% accurate. Why not 100%?

First of all, the future fluctuates with every decision made by the querent. The vehicle will show what will most likely happen if the path of the person being read for remains the same. The key phrase here is "most likely."

Secondly, your interpretations are based on your own experiences in this life time and in others. Since no two souls process data in the same manner, there is room for error. If you are reading for another person, get them actively involved in the reading. The more they participate, the better the reading.

A divination tool allows you to observe a situation that is currently facing you through a basic format or structure in which you can see what is really happening. Divination allows you to bring things into a more defined perspective, to take a more logical stance with a problem or question.

A divinatory tool can not and does not stand for a fixed or fated future. The future is based on choices of the past and present, which fluctuate with the passage of each decision we make. The tools can show us mini-scenarios of what will most likely happen if we stay on the chosen path at the time of the reading. The tool can give you information on what you may need to do to avoid an unpleasant situation, or make one a little more acceptable than what it would have been before.

A tool can also act as a mirror. If you are extremely upset over a situation, you may only get mud. An emotionally charged problem often reflects back what you want to believe, not what actually is so.

If you are extremely tired, distraught, or ill, do not attempt a reading until you have balanced your emotions and physical well-being.

Do You Believe?

One of the most difficult hurdles to get over in using a divinatory tool is not the meanings assigned to each card or stone, but the belief in your ability to relate and interpret the message. Often our own self-doubt completely obscures our readings when we first try our hands at divination.

You must believe and trust in yourself. The tool will enable you to expand as long as you have faith in your own abilities. After a while, you will be amazed that you no longer need to rush for your notes or flip through countless books to get it "just right." It will come to you easily and quietly.

Even experienced readers are not right all of the time, and neither will you be. Don't fret over failures, just keep practicing. Perhaps it is the will of the querent — they may not really want to know the truth.

Where does Divinatory Information come From?

Different readers believe different things. For instance, one friend of mine believes that the spirit lies within the oracle itself, yet also surrounds it. Other believe that they are plugging into the Collective Unconscious and accessing the information much like a satellite dish. No matter where you determine the information comes from, you believe it. If not, a divinatory education will be long and hard for you.

Choosing the Correct Tool for You

Since there are so many oracles to choose from, you must pick those that first appeal to you. Settle on only one or two to start. Unless you have a real knack for one tool in particular, all oracles require study and concentration. Therefore, practice is important. If you determine that the Tarot, for instance, is too involved for you at this time, move on to something else, like Cartouche, which contains fewer cards. Perhaps you prefer the rune stones, or the I-Ching. It is entirely up to you.

Reading for Others

There are two kinds of readings, those for magickal people and those for "once-borns" (a term Breid Foxsong, publisher of *Sacred Hart,* uses). Once-borns belong to other religions that do not believe in reincarnation or magick. Reading for a magickal person is easier, in that they are more willing to accept your methods and thought forms.

A once-born, however, is not so trusting. Their lack of education in magickal matters is a detriment to the reader until he/she learns to handle the psychological safety mechanisms they exert upon the reader. The once-born is less likely to believe you, more likely to "test" you, and generally does not really want to know the truth as the reader sees it. Please do not assume that I am trying to dump a lot of negativity here about non-magickal people. I'm not saying they are worse than anyone else. What I am trying to explain is that they see readings, and the purpose of them, differently than you do.

Never get trapped in a game of "Let's Test the Fortune Teller," unless you think you can handle it. Do not read at parties, large gatherings, or other numerously peopled events where there are many once-borns (especially ones you do not know and do not know you) until you have the confidence of steel. It is no fun sitting in the middle of ten people who are trying to gang up on you.

There are those people, magickal and non, that will lie to you the entire time. This can be very disconcerting if you are the trusting sort or new to doing outside readings. In time, you will be able to recognize the truth or fiction of their replies.

For example, if you draw the trump card Death in the background portion of a reading and ask the querent if there has been a major change recently in their life, and they adamantly deny it, they are pulling your pentacle. It took me a long time to learn this lesson. I would get some readings where everything cooked along wonderfully, and others where every card was a lesson in anxiety (on my part).

A trump card means basically the same thing, no matter how you read the nuances. If you think you are being toyed with, pull out all the trump cards and shuffle them. (Or you can keep a separate deck just for this purpose so you don't have to destroy the reading in front of you.) Have the querent pull out one of these cards from your extended right hand.

That card will usually tell you exactly what's afoot. Now you must make the decision to either pack it up and call it a day with this person, or continue if you think the deception is subconscious on their part.

I suggest you always read for the querent in private. Never tell the person they are going to die, or that a family member is going to expire. There are a specific set of cards to indicate physical death and they have to be beside each other in the same category. Temper your readings with comments such as, "There could be a real difficulty arising in the future regarding . . . " or, "What type of safety measures have you taken recently with your property? It might be a wise idea to check broken windows or latches as the cold winter is coming on," etc. You could also say, "There is risk of losing a physical item that is valuable to you. Have you taken the necessary precautions with your home or vehicle (etc)? Have you taken the time to list the contents of your house or property lately and filed this list with your insurance people?"

If they get excited and say, "Why should I do that? Is something terrible going to happen?" You should counter, "If you change your present path by securing your possessions, probably not. Besides, even if I am wrong, you will benefit from my error in the long run anyway," and list normal everyday reasons why they should keep such a list in the first place.

Never word your sentences as if something is positively so. Say, "maybe," "perhaps," or "there is a chance" when dealing with things in the future. A reader has tremendous power over another individual's mind during a reading. It is possible they can consciously make something bad happen because you said it would. There have been numerous articles in the papers on suicides, accidents, etc., in connection to a previous visit to a card reader or other divinatory type person. Who are you to control another person's life by telling them that they are going to die in the next 24 hours? They just might take you up on it.

When a once-born seeks the consultation of a reader for the first time, it is usually because they are merely curious, or they have a terrible problem and all other avenues of solution have been exhausted in their own minds. You are then the proverbial last cookie in the box because their friends and family are so sick of hearing about the problem that they come to you for new ears to pound on.

Also, what type of person you are draws particular people. Most of my readings are for people who are really in trouble and are ready to seek the mental or spiritual sides of their nature. I don't often get general reads. And when I do, I'm pleasantly surprised.

Recording Your Readings

Keeping a good record of your readings is important for two reasons. First, when you are learning a divinatory system you need to be able to go back and check what symbols were where, when, and how in relation to what actually occurred later on.

For example, in the Tarot there are many meanings for each card, but eventually, these cards will have specific meanings of their own for you. Not every reader sees the same thing in a deck of cards or group of stones.

If you would draw the ace of Wands in a Tarot spread, the Empress, and the three of Pentacles, to me, you've got a definite physical pregnancy on the way. But that is what it means to me in my experience of handling the cards, it may not boil down to that for you.

Another example: in one reading for a gentleman, four knights in a row came up. This was a long-distance reading (LDR) and I later discovered that he had left his wife that very evening, decided to quit his job, moved into a new apartment, and replaced his old girlfriend with a new one. All in one fell swoop. Talk about big-time Karma!

Secondly, if you are using the divinatory tool for magickal purposes, you will want to repeat the process if the results were favorable. Then, too, you should have an accurate record of the steps you took to achieve the same result at a later date. In your Book of Shadows (remember your notebook?) you may want to set aside a specific portion for recording your readings.

How Do You Begin to Divine?

If you have never used a divination tool more than to play with it, you should realize your conscious decision to enter into serious study. I began by writing a ritual to show my desire to divine and to ask for assistance from the God and Goddess.

If you have chosen a particular tool, you should purchase or make it before the evening of the ritual. You may also choose a particular deity that is known for its psychic or divining abilities to incorporate into the ritual. During the ritual, you should cleanse and consecrate the tool. You may dedicate it to a specific deity, as well. Near the end of the ritual there needs to be time provided for the "entering" of the knowledge and "removal" of self-imposed blockages. This would come in the form of meditation or quiet time.

Once a year, close to the date of the original ritual, perform it again to assist in building your capabilities.

Reading Props: Do You Need Them?

There are those readers that can slap out their divination tool at any time and at any place and perform an excellent reading. Others can do it, but prefer a specific place or time. There are also readers who feel they must use a specific routine in order to reach peak efficiency.

As you study your divination tool you will develop specific patterns — the lighting of a candle, the use of a special cloth, the placement of particular gems or crystals, etc. Have-tools-will-travel is decidedly up to you. Readers may perform almost an entire mental ritual before they begin, or simply take a moment or two of quiet meditation.

When at home, I prefer to keep the tools I use most often in a basket along with a piece of moonstone and the cloth I lay my cards upon. For on the go, I have designed a wrap-around book-type affair out of black satin with a tie ribbon. In it I keep a set of rune cards and a set of Tarot, a pendulum, a candle and a small reading cloth. It sounds like a monstrous thing to carry, but it folds up very small.

Taking Care of Your Divinatory Tools

Because oracles are often handled by many people, you should be sure to cleanse and consecrate them when necessary. This means when you first get them, and when you have had a particularly negative client or one with a great deal of misfortune. You should also cleanse the tool after a day of heavy readings, or at least once a week, if you don't do that many.

To cleanse a divinatory tool is simple. Let it sit for a few hours in sunlight or moonlight and finish off with a few drops of holy oil or water.

Keep your tools in some type of covering. Black keeps out the negativity. If you use stones, cards, or coins you may want a throwing or divining cloth to set on the surface of the table or floor. You can make your own out of beautiful material, add fringes, embroider designs, etc.

The size of the reading cloth depends primarily on the scope of your readings. If you do large card spreads or use two divinatory vehicles, you may want a cloth that covers most of the table top.

Combining Divination Tools

Readers often combine divination tools for a more accurate or extended reading. For instance, one could use a Celtic Cross spread with a Tarot deck and flesh out the reading by using a star spread with the Cartouche, or a line spread with runes. Using two vehicles helps to validate certain points and clarify others. If you are more inclined to scrying, you may want to lay out a simple Tarot spread after the visualization or create your own chart and use the pendulum. A rune reading may give excellent information, but more in-depth advice could be added from the I-Ching. A sample combination reading is provided for you at the end of this chapter.

Long Distance Readings

LDR's, or long-distance readings, are performed when the person you are reading for is not physically present. Perhaps a webweaving friend has written to you for help, and you wish to assist them by doing a reading. One way to do this is to wrap the divination tool in the letter or envelope for a few minutes, imagining the energy flowing into the cards or other tool used.

LDR's can be very accurate. Most once-borns are not aware that you have this capability, and I suggest not volunteering the information unless you are ready for an onslaught of phone calls at strange hours.

Use your better judgement when you feel the need to "check up" on someone. LDR's are considered by some as an invasion of privacy, but my opinion has always been that if they are tied to my life in some way, I have the right to know why.

For example, a friend's marriage was on the rocks; although she knew some of the reasons, she was unsure of others. There were things happening that simply did not make sense, and she could find nothing to validate her feelings. We read the cards to determine what was hidden in her life, and we found nothing, at first. The only indication of anything was the eight of Wands — swift messages, etc. We decided to read her husband's cards using his significator card and the eight of Wands on top, then laid out the rest of the spread.

Well, what do you know . . . there was another woman abed. My friend and her husband are still married, but I understand he has never been able to figure out how she knew about that other woman and the details of the relationship. He does, however, hold more respect for his wife and her capability of both understanding and resolving things unseen!

Graphology

Graphology, the study of an individual's handwriting, and LDR's go hand in hand when providing service from a written document. When I began reading for prisoners I discovered that their handwriting was not the same as other webweaving letters I had received. They had particular characteristics that were definitely different. This lead me to the study of graphology. I gave myself a crash course and have been practicing it ever since.

Graphology enables you to flesh out a reading. You can tell the general personality of the individual and can pinpoint areas where they may need counseling or self-improvement that may not show up in a reading. After all, the divinatory tool usually shows you what is the most prominent concern at the time of the reading and may not always answer the exact question posed.

In graphology, you can even tell what a person thinks not only about themselves, but about a particular subject, as well. People put their feelings in their handwriting. A letter could contain many statements on how well things are going in their lives, and the handwriting for each subject will reflect that feeling. Therefore, you know it is genuine.

Let them mention, however, the name of a person they have been having difficulties with, and you can tell, just by that name, their general feelings about that person or subject, even if they don't express those emotions to you.

Most graphology texts teach you to view the handwriting as a whole, which is fine for a general overview of the person and their emotional state. However, most of the books do not tell you to look at the subject of each paragraph closely to see how that person reacts to that particular subject or line of thinking. You can actually tell what a person thinks of you by the way they address an envelope to you and how they write your name.

Astrological Correspondences

Using the study of astrology in an LDR can be important as well. By knowing a person's birth date and other correspondences, you can get a general idea of how they react to life situations in general. When you are working in an advisory capacity, this information can be invaluable because most people don't understand the forces under which they operate. If you can help them by education about their own make-up, they will be better for it.

Length of Readings

When teaching yourself to divine, keep your readings short and simple until you are familiar with the tool. Extended readings take a long time, sometimes up to two to three hours. They also take up a lot of your energy. After an extended reading, you should relax and meditate, take a long hot bath or shower and do a mental cleansing. Then, change your environment. Go to the park, the museum, the grocery store, whatever.

If you invite people into your home for readings, keep them isolated in one room if you can. You should cleanse and consecrate the room in the beginning, after a particularly negative reading, etc. Cleanse the room at the end of each day.

You may also wish to place pieces of rose quartz around to balance the room with loving energy, or perhaps a piece or two of onyx or smokey quartz to repel negativity, or a piece of amethyst to absorb the negativity and cleanse it. Some readers wear particular jewelry to protect themselves, and cleanse it regularly with running water, moonlight or sunlight.

When you read for another person, you should always shield yourself with the blue egg so that you will not be affected by their energy. Get used to saying to yourself, "shields up!"

Keep face-to-face readings relatively short. Use about fifteen to twenty minutes for the actual reading and the remainder of the hour for discussion. LDR's done by yourself can last as long as you feel physically and mentally bright.

Dependence

Although it is wise to consult your divination tool when a difficulty arises, before doing a magickal purpose, or just to check things out for the immediate future, one should never depend solely upon the information received. Rather, the information given should be balanced with other considerations at the time. You should not allow the divination tool to control every decision you make.

Nor should you allow a client, friend, or querent to become dependent on either yourself or your divination skills. A once-born will get "hooked" before a magickal person, because they are totally unfamiliar with the intricacies of magick and divination. Phone calls in the middle of the night, a knock on the door during the supper hour, or an insistence that they must see you immediately may herald dependence. Although this does wonders for the reader's ego, it will spell disaster in the long run.

One of the best ways to control seeker dependence is to be totally honest during a reading. Never act mysterious about the outcome of a situation if you do not know the answer. Simply say, "I don't know." The fact that you are human and fallible will slip through, and although you will still be considered a good reader, you are not setting yourself up for unsavory circumstances.

Close once-born friends are usually the first to hover on the "dependence" line. Do not offer to read for them every time you see them. If they really want a reading, make them ask.

Payment for Readings

There may come a time when you feel that you have reached a level of proficiency where you may ask for payment for your services. Since most magickal people can either divine for themselves or have a friend who is willing to do it for them for free or barter, you won't get many requests from them.

Your basic clientele will come from the once-born population. Before charging for your services, check the laws in your state to be sure that you will not be breaking any if you advertise and perform readings. Some states, such as Pennsylvania and Connecticut, have Fortune Telling Laws, where it is against the law to offer such magickal services for advertised sale. You can ask for a donation, or advertise like the singing telegram, "For entertainment purposes only."

The state of Virginia allows such psychic counseling services to exist; however, at this writing an individual must a purchase a license for an exorbitant amount of money (in the thousands). Not too many people can afford that, unless we are doctors or lawyers on the side!

Since we have determined that once-borns who desire readings are either curious or really in trouble, you should set your fee somewhere in between. You don't want to charge so low that you get really rude and low-caliber clients. As terrible as this may sound, people tend to think that if you charge too little, your services must not be worth anything. Nor, do you want to block out those who are really in trouble and might not be able to pay a high fee. Remember, the Witch pledges to serve. You are not serving anyone except yourself if you charge high fees.

I have one friend who tells people to pay them what they think is fair or reasonable. I did this a few times and got burned — badly. I spent three hours with a woman, doing readings and instructing her on rituals and protection spells. Had she been a sister Witch, I would have charged her nothing, as that is part of my oath. But, she was a once-born and I spent a great deal of time and energy answering her questions as well as giving her some supplies.

When she left, she gave me $10. If you are thinking that's all she could afford — wrong. She owned several properties and had a high-paying, full-time job. I haven't seen her since.

You don't want to offer your services for free, either, because you will be taken advantage of; or on the other hand, as I mentioned before, people will think you are not any good. The American public is a funny animal. They think the more they pay (as long as they think it is reasonable), it is worth it.

Inside the magickal community, I have found that you are not taken advantage of if you wish to advertise free readings. I have advertised them for years, and I receive maybe one or two a month at the most.

So where does that leave you? Check around your area. See what others are charging and for what specific services. Go ahead and visit them as a client. You don't have to tell them you are a Witch or studying yourself unless you want to. Later, take advantage of all the readings you have investigated and settle on an amount that is comfortable to you.

Readers in my area charge the price of a good haircut or lower-range permanent. Like a new 'do, a reading is a personal pick-me-up and a fun form of maintenance.

Using an Astral Guide

As you progress in your readings you may wish to contact an astral guide for further assistance. I do not often tell once-borns that I am using a guide. They already think I'm rather flaky; why add insult to injury?

Further on in the text I will be giving instructions on how to contact your personal guide. Guides can come in handy when you are really stuck. There have been times when I have looked at a card layout and not been able to make heads nor tails of it. The first time I lost my cool, gathered them up and told the querent to shuffle again, and we got most of the same cards back. The second time I closed my eyes and called on my guide, the reading went smoothly.

I often tell people to write down what they think is important during a reading, or bring a tape recorder. It is a fact that I do not remember the content of most readings. The information comes, I let it out, and that's the end of it. It doesn't stop to rest in the memory part of my brain.

Later, they may call me and say, "Do you remember when you said . . . ?" The answer is no. I feel that it is not my information to use, it is theirs. They are to do with it what they will.

When you get rolling in a reading, people will not remember everything you said, either. They tend to concentrate only on the parts that seem relevant at the time and may not absorb the rest of the information you have given them. So be prepared when you do remember a point later on, and they don't!

What Happens If You Get Really Stuck?

Every once in a while you be reading along and you will hit a massive block. The cards present at that position will not make any sense at all. Earlier, I indicated that you can try to work through this failure by contacting your guide. If that works, fine, just continue your reading. But what do you do if absolutely nothing comes?

There is a little saying we use often at our house. It goes, "Sit back. Relax. And just chill!" Take a deep breath. If the querent has not noticed you are stuck, skip that particular card and keep going. Maybe it will make sense further on. If the querent has noticed you are squirming, just be honest. "This doesn't make sense, let's come back to it later." Or, "I'd like to use this to draw further information from. We will come back to it." Then do another spread with this card as the significator. You can also tell the querent what this card means to you and ask them how they think it fits into the reading.

Summary

In this chapter we have determined that divination is a necessary skill to develop not only for magickal purposes, but for daily living and planning for your future. Earlier, you learned that you are responsible for your own future — not the next door neighbor, a co-worker, or a family member. You are in control; therefore, you need a map (divinatory tool) to help you evade some of the hazards on the way. The key word for this chapter is "practice!"

·☽ ☾·

The remaining pages in this chapter contain a few exercises and divinatory tables for your use. The tables only highlight information on each divinatory tool. If you would like to study one of these tools in-depth, refer to the suggested reading list or visit your local metaphysical book shop for further texts.

The Tarot

You will need a deck of cleansed and consecrated Tarot cards, and the simple interpretation table at the end of this exercise. Be sure you have chosen a deck that is appealing to you. You will also need a cloth to lay the cards on.

This shuts out any negativity that may be on the surface of the table or floor. On the practical side, it keeps the cards from picking up potato chip oil or spaghetti sauce.

Place a piece of moonstone or clear quartz crystal by the cloth and set a silver candle nearby where it will cast its light on the cards.

In this exercise you will be using only the Major Arcana, so separate them now. Remember, the Major Arcana are the trump cards, numbered from 0-21.

Sit quietly and open the chakra centers. Either aloud or in your mind, ask the Spirit of Divination (or perhaps a favorite deity known for psychic prowess) to assist you.

Think of a simple question.

Shuffle until you feel the energy from your hands pouring into the cards. Imagine them pulsing with blue light. When you are ready, cut the deck into three piles. I used to shuffle them endlessly, worrying that I would stop before they were just right. This isn't necessary. No matter how or when you stop, it will be right.

Pick up the pile that is the farthest to your right and put them on the pile that is farthest to your left, then put the combined piles on top of the pile in the middle. They are all now in one pile.

From the top, deal out only three cards to represent past, present, and future. With the interpretations you have learned, determine the meaning of the cards.

Put the cards back together and reshuffle the deck. Never force the cards or do tricks with them; save that for poker night. Think of a situation that has already passed; an issue where you already know the outcome. Follow the same procedure for cutting the cards, then lay out the top three cards. How close do they come to what actually happened? Do you notice a combination pattern?

I use the Tarot right side up only. It is a personal choice based on the premise that there are 78 cards in the deck with a multitude of meanings and combinations. To invert and distort the meanings is rather senseless.

Continue to work on this type of exercise until you feel your confidence growing and are ready to branch out into larger, more detailed spreads.

·☾ ☽·

Another way to gain helpful insights into the Tarot system itself is to imagine meeting each one of the characters in the cards. Start with the Major Arcana.

Go into a meditative state and meet each one like you were meeting a person. Ask them about their lives, how they feel on different issues, etc. When you have finished your meditation, write down your impressions and keep them with your Tarot notes. This will take a while to do because of the number of cards in the Tarot deck. If you persevere, you will be rewarded.

Tarot Divinitory Meanings: Major Arcana

The Fool: The beginning of a new cycle or enterprise; a matter that is unexpected or unplanned; moving in a different direction; heading toward an unknown future; look before you leap; use hidden talents.

The Magician: Master of self; readiness to put plans into action; great power and energy at your disposal; time to use your skills.

The Priestess: Awareness of planes of existence; hidden forces with new solutions; feminine balance and occult learning; utilize leadership potential; matriarchal thought.

The Empress: Financial and emotional security; motherly or womanly love; good fortune and happiness; epitome of a female partner; pregnancy.

The Emperor: Reason over emotion; government, politics, system; command and authority; patriarchal thought; the need to be famous.

The Priest: Conformity and tradition; going with the flow because everyone else is; dealing in a facade; Karma.

The Lovers: A choice between opposites; a decision that will affect several people; second sight; love versus practicality.

The Chariot: Balance through movement; bringing two opposing points under control; self control; vehicular movement.

Strength: Victory over difficulty; successful end to a tiresome event; spiritual strength; sharp and incisive mental action.

The Wheel: Rotation of any situation or life event; tidal movement; steady and even turn of events; upward mobility.

The Hermit: Introspection and spiritual enlightenment; planning and evaluating the next move; seeking a higher intelligence; meeting a physical teacher.

Justice: Legalities, contracts, agreements; what you sow so shall ye reap; think before you act; the Goddess will balance the situation.

The Hanged Man: Thoughts, ideas or projects in suspension; stuck between a rock and a hard place; obtaining second sight.

Death: Radical, unplanned change; old ripped away to prepare for the new; illusions swept instantly away; a new life path.

Temperance: Ability to adapt to new circumstances; action as a result of higher self or guide information; mature love; control through wisdom; the art of mixing and matching.

The Devil/Pan: Binding by thought, word, or deed; unbridled lust or deep passion; charismatic but untrustworthy person; fate through human frailties.

The Tower: A breakdown in a situation; seeing a situation as it really is; unexpected setbacks or repercussions; danger; fate.

The Star: Faith, confidence and hope; positive influences; ability to cut through illusion; new life with wider choices.

The Moon: Dreams, intuition, vision questing; imagination; emotionally charged circumstances; being pulled in two different directions; psychic work or magickal work; possibility of deception.

The Sun: Joy and happiness; well earned rewards; new and creative environment; good news on its way.

Judgment: Project or situation nearing completion; final decision has yet to be made; awakening at the end of a long process; ending may not be what is expected; the past comes back to haunt you.

The World: End of a cycle in a situation; scenario has played itself completely out; no loose ends left; satisfactory conclusion; possibility to explore new avenues.

Timing and the Tarot

Timing in predicting the future is extremely difficult, no matter the vehicle. Before using the divination tool you should set in your mind what the time period for the reading will be. Will it be tomorrow, two weeks, six months, etc.?

There are several ways to tell timing with the Tarot. First, you can use the number on the card. For instance, The ace of Cups would stand for one hour, day, week or month. The World (usually number 21 in the deck) would be 21 hours, days, months, or weeks.

If you wish to work with seasons, Wands stand for spring, Cups stand for summer, Swords stand for fall, and Pentacles stand for winter. In a seasonal reading, aces stand for the week at the beginning of the season (e.g., ace of Wands represents the week of Spring Equinox). Twos stand for the week after, threes stand for the week after that, etc. Kings indicate that the matter was completed last year at this time, and Queens tell you that the matter was concluded in the previous season.

Card combinations also lend to timing. The more matching numbers you have (e.g., four kings, three aces, etc.) the faster the outcome. Combinations also have their own interpretation.

Aces:	4	Fast-moving forces at work; don't be blind-sided.
	3	Success is insured at a fast pace.
	2	Change afoot, such as job or home.

Twos:	4	Quick reorganization and possible shake-up.
	3	Conversations that bring quick conclusions, including gossip.

Threes:	4	Strong finish and excellent rewards.
	3	A lie is close by (look for the moon as a giveaway).

Fours:	4	A strong foundation has been built at a fast rate. Are there any cracks?

Fives:	4	A large confrontation will hit fast and leave you either spinning or running for cover.

Sixes:	4	An attitude adjustment will hit home.

Sevens:	4	Grief comes quickly; hang on and flow with it.

Eights:	4	Quick communication (for good or bad, check surrounding cards).
	3	Pack your bags, you're soon bound for a trip.

Nines:	4	The end is fast approaching; hope you are ready.

Tens:	4	Something will be bought or sold quickly; remember to read the fine print.

Pages:	4	New ideas will hit soon; hang on for a creative burst.

Knights:	4	Swift action in the matter. Be careful what you wish for.

The Meaning of Numbers

Not only can the number on the card indicate a time period, it can also tell you something about the situation.

One:	This is the beginning.
Two:	This is the direction or first meeting point.
Three:	This is where details grow and the idea solidifies.
Four:	This is where roots are put down in order to build.
Five:	First challenge or glitch in the situation.
Six:	This is where the issue changes and grows in order to continue.

Seven:	Variety is now added to expand the idea or project.
Eight:	This is the evaluation period.
Nine:	A moving forward to near completion.
Tens:	Completion of the cycle, project, or issue.
Pages:	Risk and messages.
Knights:	Movement and direction.

Now that I have given you all this information, don't have heart failure if you can't remember it. If you are supposed to, you will; if you are not, you won't. Keep more in mind the design of the card, the position it is in and what strikes you first. Your brain is capable of filtering the correct interpretation to you.

The Silver Spread

One of the most popular spreads is called the Celtic Cross and is usually provided on the information sheet enclosed with each new Tarot deck. The silver spread uses this as a base for a more in-depth reading. In review, the basic Celtic Cross includes eleven out of the 78 cards provided in the deck.

For this particular procedure, you will need a second divination vehicle, whether it be rune stones, rune cards, the Cartouche, Medicine cards, etc.

Position 1: The significator card. This can be one of two choices. You may pick a face card that most closely represents the querent, or it can be a card from a previous reading that you want more surrounding information on. A face card does not have to be chosen for the significator. Go through the deck and choose the one you feel most represents the individual you are reading for.

Position 2: Right over top position 1. This is where the querent is right now.

Position 3: What crosses the querent. What stands in their way, keeps them from going forward or making a positive decision. Something that the querent is concerned about.

Position 4: What is on the querent's conscious mind. Something that has just happened or is happening now. Can be an event or a frame of mind.

Position 5: What is hidden or under the surface in the querent's mind. Something that is either constantly at the back of their minds, or something that the querent refuses to acknowledge that could be helpful to them in dealing with the present situation.

Position 6: What is directly ahead of the querent, within a very short period of time. What sets the stage for the completion of the events in the reading. This is the trigger card.

Position 7: What is in the past that bears directly on the present situation. What lies at the bottom of the experience or conflict. This is the first card you would wish to magickally change, should you not like the outcome of the reading.

Position 8: The event or person that firmly entrenches the outcome of the reading. The second important factor in the situation. This is the second card you would wish to magickally change should you not like the outcome of the reading.

Position 9: How other people in your sphere of influence are being affected by your decisions or situation. How they see you which affects their treatment of you. Their general impression of you and your actions.

Position 10: Where you will be in the future as a result of your actions or thoughts. What you should be careful of or look forward to. This is the third card you should magickally change, should you not like the outcome of the reading.

Position 11: The culmination of the reading and general overview of the situation and, how, at this point, the situation will travel. This is the fourth card you would magickally change, should you not like the outcome of the reading. This is also the card to be checked, should you perform the magick, to see if you have swayed the outcome of the situation.

Shuffle and cut deck.

Lay out the entire Celtic Cross. Keep the remainder of the deck on the table.

View layout, and check for percentage of suits, percentage of Major Arcana, odd or unusual combinations.

Read each position in order. If the card at the position in question is perfectly clear, go to the next position. If the card is unclear, or you wish further information, take a card from the deck and lay it beside the position card. If still unclear, pull another card. You may pull one more card, but do not pull more than you can handle in a linear story. If, while adding to a position, the card is a Major Arcana card, stop. If it still is not clear, save that position for a reading on its own after you have continued this sequence.

Continue to the next position and read that one in the same manner, until the spread is done.

Take out the second divination vehicle, shuffle (or whatever) and place one card (stone) of that vehicle on top of each position. Use that second vehicle to double-check your original assumptions. Sometimes it will merely affirm what you have been saying, other times it will add depth to the interpretation.

At the end of the reading, if there is still question on a particular position, set that card in Position 1, and reshuffle and cut the deck of the original divination tool. Read the circumstances around that position as you would in a general read.

You will not find this technique in any other book that I am aware of. I designed it for myself because none of the many spreads I have studied gave me exactly what I wanted. Because it satisfies me doesn't mean that you will be comfortable with it. You may wish to design your own spread and procedure, which is perfectly acceptable.

Remember your modification principles when reading the Tarot. Wands are opposite Cups, and Swords are opposite Pentacles. If a Wand is surrounded by Cups, its meaning will be lessened or even negated. If a Sword is surrounded by Pentacles, its meaning will be lessened or negated.

Remember to record your readings as often as possible and write down particular patterns that indicate specific situations or events, such as divorce or separation, pregnancy or birth, weddings or engagements, new job within a company, new jobs without, etc.

Quick People Check

Sometimes a situation involving another person may totally baffle you. In essence, you can't see the forest for the proverbial trees. To check on what area of the person is affecting you, and how, use the following technique.

Shuffle the deck.

Take a small cut off the top — say about ten cards. Turn that stack over. The card on top tells you what that person is feeling.

Take another cut, and turn over. The top card here tells you what they are thinking, which is often different that what they are feeling.

The next cut tells you how they see the situation as a whole.

The final cut informs you what they are planning to do about it.

The Runes

Every Witch will tell you that there is a particular vehicle that has brought them great spiritual progress. For me it was the runes, even though I am not as proficient at them as I am the Tarot and Cartouche. The awakening was by accident.

One of the best known books on the subject of the runes is *The Book of Runes* by Ralph Blum. Although I began my first experiments with the use of this particular text, Blum's use of the Christian religious system really bothered me. The interpretations the author gave, though basically sound, did not seem to fit the magickal alphabet. I felt that much was lost.

Months later I received *Leaves of Yggdrasil* from a fellow editor because he was too busy to review the book and asked me to do it for him. I was fairly busy at the time, but agreed. Freya Aswynn, the author of *Leaves,* brought me a whole new world of magick and understanding with her text.

To read the runes you will either need to purchase rune cards, make tiles, or buy rune stones. Runes can be made from pebbles found in a river bed painted with white symbols, or you can buy unfired ceramic tiles, cut them with a small hand saw (while they are still in greenware form) in one-inch by one-inch squares. After firing they can be inscribed with ceramic paint, fired again, then glazed if you wish; or simply use acrylic paints after the first firing and the second is not necessary. You can also make runes out of wooden tiles, if you prefer.

The tiles are kept in a bag and drawn one at a time, Some individuals throw them all onto a specially embroidered or printed cloth. Although I have made the cloth, this method does not appeal to me.

You will also need a silver or white candle, a plain cloth to lay the tiles or cards on, and of course a quiet place.

Runes are extremely versatile. You can use Tarot spreads as a pattern for interpreting your runes, or you can draw only one to seek a quick answer. A quick read can be done with three, naming your positions as past, present and future; or as in Blum's book, background, challenge and outcome.

Think of the questions before you draw the runes from the bag. I prefer the rune cards, and shuffle them the same way as the Tarot.

When I do use the stones, I borrow the holder from a Scrabble game to set them up on, as I often pull a few while answering correspondence and share what they say with the person I am writing to. It works well because my desks (yes, plural) are a mess with papers and books, and the tiles kept flipping everywhere. I spent more time than it was worth moving the type-writer or keypad to find them.

As with the Tarot, I imagine energy surrounding the cards or stones before I actually draw them. Write your conclusions in your notebook.

When you have finished the reading, put all the runes back into the pouch and shake it up. Draw one rune for the express purpose of using it in dream-time. Formulate a question in your mind where you feel assistance is needed in your life.

Draw the rune, check the meaning, and write it down on a slip of paper. Then draw the character on the paper under the meaning.

Put it under your pillow before you go to sleep or leave it in your hand. I have even drawn the rune on my hand before going to bed. Before I fall asleep I open the chakra centers, meditate, and drift off to sleep. In the morning I usu-ally have the answer to my question, either through a dream or just simply by "knowing."

If you wish to use the runes during dreamtime, take a break every three days if you find yourself in intensive study with them. If you do not, by the end of the week your messages may be garbled and you will feel tired during the daylight hours.

Runes are great for LDR's in which you wish to offer help but not go into an extended dissertation.

Runes Divinatory Meanings

ᚠ	Fehu	Good Fortune. Wealth. Luck. Creative Energy.
ᚢ	Uruz	Strength. Higher Self. Determination. Health.
ᚦ	Thurisaz	True Will. Matter of Form. Chaos. Conflict.
ᚨ	Ansuz	Wisdom. Occult. Power. Revenge. Healing.
ᚱ	Raido	Defense. Take Control. Journey. Decisions.
ᚲ	Kenaz	Knowledge. Learning. Quest. Hereditary Knowledge.
ᚷ	Gebo	Agreements. Settlements and Union. Boundaries.
ᚹ	Wunjo	Blessings. Controlling Will. Success. Fertility.
ᚺ	Hagalaz	Drastic Change. Disruptive Forces.
ᚾ	Nauthiz	Need. Future. Victory. Opportunity. Defense.
ᛁ	Isa	Standstill. Defense to delay. Crysallis.
ᛃ	Jera	Gentle gestation and change. Cycle. Time.
ᛇ	Eiwaz	Outgoing. Dynamic. GO! Hunting. Evolution.
ᛈ	Pertho	Secret. Discovery of Hidden. History.
ᛉ	Algiz	Protection. Shield. Help. Rainbow Conductor.
ᛋ	Sowulo	Healing. Strength. Centering. Luck.
ᛏ	Teiwaz	Justice. Legal Matters. Dedication. Bravery.
ᛒ	Berkana	Women's mysteries. Birth Process. Emotional Stability.
ᛖ	Ehwaz	Shapeshifter. Telepathic Links. Adjustment.
ᛗ	Mannuz	Communication. Cooperation. Legal Affairs.
ᛚ	Laguz	Occult. Sex. Influence. Movement.
ᛝ	Inguz	Astral. Vessel. Grounded. Progression. Fertility.
ᛟ	Othila	Centering. Grounding. Invoking. Values. Family. Kundalini.
ᛞ	Dagas	Rendered invisible. Catalyst. Between the Worlds.

Cauldron Gazing

For this exercise you will need a hot plate, small black metal pot (or cauldron, if you have found one), water, and the following herbs: frankincense, orris root, and myrrh, and two silver or white candles placed on either side of the pot.

Relax and bring the pot to a simmering boil, where the steam is not rolling, but gently wafting. Light the candles and cast a magick circle.

Open the chakra centers and let your mind go completely blank as you watch the steam. Do not be upset if you do not see a motion picture before you. Often a visualization will come first as a feeling, rather than an actual picture.

Bring your mind into focus on a specific question and verbalize it aloud if you wish. Do not strain while looking at the steam, merely relax and accept what you will see.

When you are finished, close the circle, extinguish the candles, and take the remainder of the water outside. Offer it to Earth Mother and pour it on the ground. Come inside and eat starchy food to ground yourself.

Suggested Reading List

Freya Aswynn, *Leaves of Yggdrasil.* Llewellyn Publications.

P. M. H. Atwater, *The Magickal Language of the Runes.* Bear and Company.

Barbara J. Bishop, *Numerology: Universal Vibrations of Numbers.* Llewellyn Publications.

D. Jason Cooper, *Using the Runes.* The Aquarian Press.

Melita Denning and Osborne Phillips, *The Magick of the Tarot.* Llewellyn Publications.

Gail Fairfield, *Choice Centered Tarot.* Newcastle Publishing.

Sasha Fenton, *The Fortune-Teller's Workbook.* Llewellyn Publications.

Sasha Fenton, *Tarot in Action.* The Aquarian Press.

William Hewitt, *Tea Leaf Reading.* Llewellyn Publications.

Murry Hope, *The Way of the Cartouche.* St. Martin's Press.

Palmer, Ho and O'Brien, *The Fortune Teller's I-Ching.* Ballentine Books.

Emily Peach, *The Tarot Workbook*. The Aquarian Press.

Ellen Cannon Reed, *The Witches Tarot*. Llewellyn Publications.

Jeraldine Saunders, *Signs of Love*. Llewellyn Publications.

Schwei & Peska, *Astrological Geomancy*. Llewellyn Publications.

Juliet Sharman-Burke, *The Complete Book of Tarot*. St. Martin's Press.

Donald Tyson, *How To Make and Use a Magick Mirror*. Llewellyn Publications.

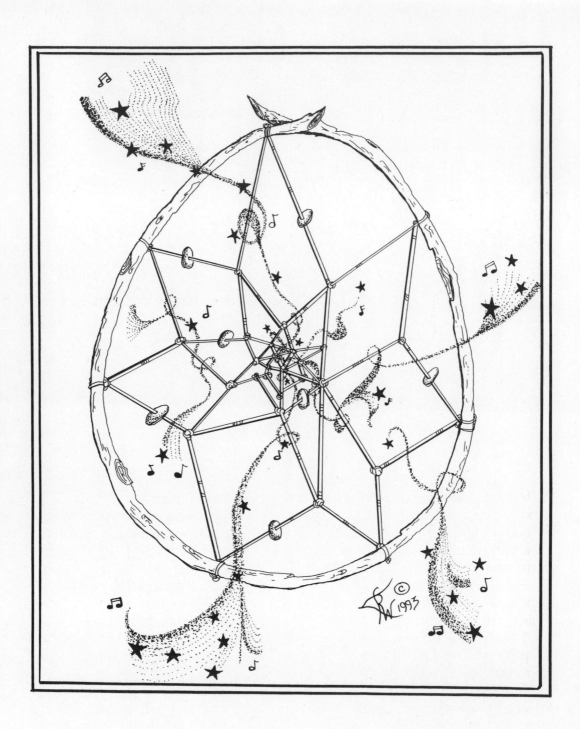

Spell Casting, Working Rituals and Drawing Down the Moon

Putting Practice into Form

At this point in your studies, you have learned the basics for performing a working ritual and a spell. You have studied creative visualization, meditation, divination, and the raising and grounding of your personal power. You have gathered all those neat tools, studied other books (hopefully), and become acquainted with one or more deity systems.

Now, all you need is courage — the drive and determination to practice magick, when and where it is appropriate, and to learn from your mistakes (which will be many) and your successes (which will depend entirely on you).

Practicing solitary magick is much like running your own business. What you put into it you get out of it, only after you have worked your behind off to get it there.

You must be persistent, believe in yourself and have a well-rounded ego that can inflate upon command to instill belief in yourself when the chips are down. You must be committed and willing to sacrifice particular elements of yourself — over and over and over again. This is how you learn and grow, by adapting and accepting change.

It takes guts and faith to practice real magick by yourself . . . alone in a candlelit space . . . and expect it to work. Many people come to this stage of the Craft, try a few spells, get high off Drawing Down the Moon, meet a few other Witches, and determine that this is not the way they wish to be.

They are afraid of fantasy and their own imaginations. The first time something backfires or simply doesn't work, they are ready to throw in the wand and trash the system. At this point you really haven't practiced Witchcraft. You have set the stage, gathered the props and prepared them, said your opening lines in a dedication ceremony, but you haven't performed the play.

From the first time you Draw Down the Moon to perform a working ritual, you will be practicing the art of Witchcraft. Up to now you have experimented with various areas of study, but you've not really put them all together to reach a specific goal, other than education.

Are you ready? Then, I believe the saying is, "Onward and Upward!"

Energy in Spells and Rituals

Energy is something you can feel. You may tingle, pulse, or grow warm while raising energy. Some people are strong "energy pushers," and others are not. This doesn't mean that if you can belt out an explosion of energy you are better than those who allow their energy to flow smoothly from their bodies.

Before you raise your energy you have to ground and center. "Grounding" is putting psychological roots into Earth Mother and stabilizing yourself; "centering" is pulling your essence in to your navel area to promote a calm and steady state. If you do not ground and center, woe unto you, my friend.

You cannot work at peak efficiency all the time, however. If you are overly tired, sick, or stressed out, you may have a heck of a time raising the cone of power. If possible, save your working for another day.

Don't feel bad or consider yourself a failure if you cannot raise energy right away. It will come in time; everyone is capable of raising energy, once they get the hang of it.

Energy and Alcohol

This is a tough one. To be absolutely honest, you should not be doing any magick if you are drunk or hung over. In fact, your body should be clear of alcohol for at least 24 hours before performing magick. Partying and magick do not go hand in hand.

Are most Witches non-drinkers? No, we have merely changed with the times. Campaigns (such as ones by Mothers Against Drunk Driving) have alerted the public to the fact that drinking is serious and can be a deadly business. Also, the Witch population is growing and must accomodate recovered alcoholics, young people, the physically challenged, etc. We must respect the needs of others.

Energy and Drugs

Rather than get into a massive argument here, let's be logical. In the United States, a drug that is illegal has no place in a Craft circle. Illegal substancess can get you jail time. Listen to Mother Silver here; if you are taking cocaine, crack, pills, etc., to get up and to go to bed, you need medical help. Get it. Drugs and magick are simply not good working partners.

With prescription drugs, use your best judgment. If the over-the-counter cold medicine leaves you feeling like part of you is floating near the ceiling, don't do magick because you are not in control.

·☽ ☾·

When you become a Witch, you are letting yourself and the world know that you are responsible for your own actions. Those people that abuse drugs and alcohol can't be real Witches because they are relying on self-denial to get them through life, and are not taking responsibility for what they are doing to their bodies, their families, and the Universe in general.

The Spell

I know this is what you have all been waiting for, the good part, right? The magickal stuff. Well, everything about a Witch's life is magickal, from the forest he/she walks through to the city streets; from the people he/she meets and helps or defends against . . . it is all magick!

Simple spell casting is not so "simple." It truly is an art in itself. It is the practice of working magick — changing thought into some type of emotional or physical form — by your own will, using specific words in conjunction with a magickal tool or entity. A successful spell is one that accomplishes the desired end without harming anyone in the process. Sometimes, this is not as easy as it sounds.

Spells are tricky little buggers, and you have to plan them carefully. Don't expect to just stand in front of a candle, whisper some mumbo-jumbo, and have everything turn out just peachy. If you do, and it does, you were damned lucky!

It is not that spells must be elaborate, but is imperative that they are specific. Remember the buck in the forest I told you about earlier?

Another prime example that almost everyone flubs up on is asking for money to pay all your bills. You may wind up with a mailbox full of old bills that you forgot about, or hoped forgot about you. I did.

The spell alone, without its partner, the working ritual, can be very effective for many needs — for example, charming a bedtime snack for a child for pleasant dreams.

Composing the Spell

Spells should be written, and the wording considered with great care. Your requests and statements should somehow connect with a specific set of deities, or the Universe in general.

A spell does not need to rhyme, but a good beat is helpful when trying to remember it if you plan to use it often. When chanting or dancing, a rhyming spell adds to the magickal working.

It is important to ask for the "essence" of a thing, if you are talking about something three dimensional. For example, if you want a computer, like I did, you would ask for the computer that is perfect for you, the brand name or better. But it wasn't as easy as that. It took me two years to get my computer, and it also took a lot of hard work to bring it into form, spell or no spell.

There are some spells that border on magickal rituals. A money spell may require that you burn seven candles, one a day for seven days, at the same time each day. This is very close to a ritual, if not a mini one.

There are spells that have time deadlines on them, like Cinderella's pumpkin (no kidding), and must be renewed for continued effect.

Many Witches have a particular way in which they begin and end their spells and rituals. Usually, it is something they have come up with through trial and error, and have found it works for them. Perhaps it is a particular rhyme or phrase wherein the beat helps them to raise their vibratory note. For example:

> In this night and in this hour
> I call upon the Ancient Power
> O Goddess Bride and Consort Bright
> I ask thee now to bring your Light!

In my mind, with the light travels the energy of the All. From there, I will begin aligning myself with the particular deities I need, and asking their assistance in what I plan to do. The same procedure would be followed in a working ritual. Above all, you must be specific. Therefore, you would continue with something like this:

> I have a need that must be met. I ask thee (name of deity) that I obtain the perfect (whatever it is) for (whatever the reason is).

> I ask the Universe to lend the power of all the correct astrological correspondences, so they may enter this circle now, to obtain my desire.

> Therefore, I specifically draw toward myself the (desire) without affecting the free will of all, and harming none.

> I now proclaim this spell is done. The (desire) is mine!

I also now add a new sentence — a line that has been said belonged to Sybil Leek — to this standard formula:

In no way will this spell reverse, or place upon me any curse!

As I will, so mote it be!

I always add a thank you to the deity I have called, even in a simple spell.

All types of items can be used in simple spells such as colored candles, colored cords, beads, gems, crystals, bottles, ink and parchment, colored felt, poppets, etc. You should practice writing the spell before you begin the working or cast the magick circle. Write several until you think you've got the hang of it. Mistakes can be costly.

Quarter Spells

Although Solstices and Equinoxes are primarily observed in celebration, they are usually credited to the seasonal cycles of the Witch and her/his Craft. Each cycle has its own type of magick. These cycles are called Elemental Tides.

From March 21 to June 20 is the Tide of Planting (or beginnings). From June 21 to September 22 is the Tide of Harvest (or culmination). September 23 to December 20 is the Tide of Planning (or calculation) and from December 21st to March 20 is the Tide of Destruction (or replacement).

Most quarter spells will take an entire quarter to come to fruition and should be used in long-term goal planning. A few quarter spells are cast to function during the upcoming quarter, such as money spells. You can tell if a quarter money spell was not given enough "oomph" at the time of the working because it tends to fizzle three to four weeks before the close of the quarter. If cast properly, you may not even notice its imminent termination, unless, of course, you forget to renew it!

A spell I perform every quarter is burning money. Yes, I actually set the almighty dollar aflame. I have a special metal dish I reserve for burning spells, and I do a rotation, clockwise, nine times, chanting:

Saturn, Jupiter and the Sun
Golden God come join the fun
Silver Priestess dance with me
Bring this quarter much money!

It is simple, but it works!

Astrological Correspondences

At first glance, astrological correspondences and their use in spells and work-ing rituals boggle the mind. All of us are familiar with the astrological sign we were born under, usually referred to as the sun sign. Mine is Virgo.

But by taking a closer look at our own sign in relation to the heavenly bod-ies, we can delve deeper into our own make-up and determine the most auspi-cious moments to perform spells for long-term purposes.

Short-term spells are also affected by the signs and planets. Their move-ment in the skies can assist us when casting a spell for a job, to bring love or even tell when to send a letter asking for assistance.

Astrological correspondences are important to a new Witch. By the correct use of planetary hours, days, and moon phases, a beginning Witch has a far greater chance of obtaining what he/she desires than if they did not use these tools. Once you have trained yourself to the point where you have complete control of your power, successful spell casting and working rituals can be achieved at almost any time.

If you do not know the correct astrological correspondences to use and you are in a hurry, you should incorporate your spell into a working where under the protection of the magick circle, you can request that the correct astro-logical correspondences be used for you magickal practice, as I have done in the example given earlier in this chapter. Please check the suggested reading list at the back of this chapter to find the books that contain the astrological information you need.

Many Witches will tell you that "you don't really need that stuff." They are right, in most cases; you don't if your height of need matches your emo-tion and you are focused on what you want. I say this because I cast spells for years without worrying about astrological correspondences, but I have had a better success rate since I began incorporating them into my workings.

Performing Magick for Others

It is not wise to perform grey magick (a term used to label doing magick for others) without the consent of all individuals involved. "Grey magick" is a tongue-in-cheek way of presenting this thought form, even though no label really applies.

Before performing all spells one should consult their divinatory vehicle not only to examine the outcome of your work, but to glean any extra informa-tion you should be aware of. You don't want to hurt another person that you know is involved in the situation, just as you would not wish to harm a person that is involved but you may not know about.

For example, you wouldn't want to cast a spell for money and have your spouse or parents drop dead. (Well, I hope you wouldn't want that!) You would have gained the money you wanted through inheritance or insurance, and lost something irreplaceable — a human life. The bottom line here is to be very careful what you wish for, it really may come true.

If you want Harry to fall in love with you, it is not ethical to "put a spell on Harry." Instead, you should practice magick to bring the type of love you wish to you. If Harry is the right one, he'll be there. If not, you've saved yourself a lot of time and trouble.

I knew a woman who put a spell on her boyfriend so that he would love her and no other. They were married, had several children, and he became so obsessive of her that the relationship deteriorated into mental and physical abuse upon herself. Maybe this would have happened to her anyway; it is not an uncommon occurrence. However, maybe it wouldn't have, or at least, not to the degree she suffered.

You may or may not believe that her spell caused all or part of the damage. If she had checked her divinatory tool first and proceeded to draw the "essence" of the desire toward her, she most likely would not have messed with him at all.

Even practicing magick with another's consent can present problems, especially in a love spell, and especially if the target is a once-born who says, "Sure, go ahead!" (pant, pant). You are gambling with their ignorance of magick and the power that can be manifested.

The most bizarre story I ever heard was of a once-born and his Witch mistress (who was single at the time). So enamored were they with each other that he consented to allow her to practice magick on him to heighten his desire for her. What could it hurt, right?

Oh my! Well, something went very wrong and he wound up divorcing his wife, leaving his Witch mistress, and moving in with another once-born! The real twist to this sad story, however, is that for years they were still linked psychically, much in the manner of twins.

Now, this may be a case of real soulmates that precariously dabbled with the unknown, or it could simply be the result of one hell of a spell. Regardless of the answer, a great deal of pain was inflicted upon all parties involved — proof that a love spell gone bad can result in the most horrendous circumstances. The entire mess could have been avoided if the Witch had done her homework and used her divination tool, which she later admitted she did not.

Unfortunately, we are not all perfectly adjusted to life all the time; therefore things like astrological correspondences, colors, props, gems, crystals, stones, and divination tools reinforce and provide a double-check in our magickal practices.

In planning your first spells, I suggest you primarily work with the moon and her magick. Try simple things; small things. The moon is an extremely powerful heavenly body and much can be learned from her.

Moon Magick and Spell Casting

Earlier in this text we discussed New, Full and the Dark of the Moon. The prime consideration in any spell or working should be the moon phase, unless there is something stupendous happening in the heavens or you are working under emergency conditions. From the day of the New and Full Moons is usually the most powerful times for these phases. There are those who practice magick who feel that three days before and three days after the event are the strongest.

Remember that the New Moon is for bringing things toward you, starting new ventures, etc. The Full Moon is to banish, cure or be rid of unwanted influences or habits. Having the culmination of either cycle close to a real need is better than having none at all.

Astrologists will tell you that the first step you make in a situation is more important then where the ending of the venture may fall. Many times, things begun at the New Moon will culminate at the Full — such as a spell for money, an object, a job, etc. Things that last longer, like procuring real estate, should be started at the New Moon but naturally will take several months to culminate.

Because of the full surface of the moon's illumination by the sun during the Full Moon phase, things in one's life may be clearer and more focused. This is a time to solve mysteries and search for hidden knowledge. Using the Full Moon for divinatory purposes is an ancient practice. It's light has the power to unveil even the deepest, darkest secrets.

The culmination of any exchange should be done on the Full Moon as well. If you must sign important papers and have the leisure to choose a date, choose the day after the Full Moon when she is in transition to the new cycle yet her surface is fully illuminated, just like your new venture.

Many Witches do not practice magick on the Dark of the Moon, the three days before the New Moon cycle. It is considered a time of unrest and a kind of void. Cursings, if necessary, are done on the Dark of the Moon, calling on Hecate or Maat to render justice.

Most deity systems contain a God or Goddess that has a particular connection with the moon itself, or a moon phase. If you are comfortable with their personalities, you should incorporate one of them for assistance. For instance, one could use Diana for the New Moon, Selene for the Full Moon, and Hecate for the Dark of the Moon.

Drawing Down the Moon

The practice of drawing down the Full Moon's energy and essence into oneself and using that power is called "Drawing Down the Moon." When accomplished, you will feel a heightened trance state combined with a power surge that radiates through your body.

One should Draw Down the Moon during a ritual in the protection of the magickal circle. However, I have gone for midnight walks with my familiar, stopped along the sidewalk and completed the procedure there, as well.

Drawing Down the Moon is often done at an Esbat, when there is serious work to be done. You do not have to incorporate the "drawing" process into every Esbat, but what Witch doesn't have things to accomplish, even little ones? However, if you wish to take a break and just enjoy the power of the moon, a simple ritual honoring the moon or the Goddess (as She is often symbolized by the moon) is certainly no crime.

There are Witches who use their wands or athame when Drawing Down the Moon. To do this, first open the chakras. Then form the Goddess Position with your arms, with the wand in the right hand. Slowly raise your arms directly above you and clasp both hands on the wand or athame. Point it at the Moon. Say:

> *I now draw the power of the Moon Priestess into myself, merging with Her power, the pure essence of the Goddess.*

Raise your vibratory rate and allow the power of the moon to enter the wand. You will feel it. Now, bring the wand down slowly with both hands and point the tip directly at your heart. Envision the surging of blue-silver light entering your body, coursing through and around your entire physical and astral being. When the energy begins to ebb, bring your arms down at your sides. You have just raised your own cone of power.

You are now empowered by the Goddess of the Moon. Use this enhanced ability wisely.

If your next step is to do a "working," leave the wand/athame in your right hand (to send). If you will not be doing any type of spell casting, leave the wand/athame in your left (receiving) hand and go into a meditative state to absorb the energy.

When you have finished either function, ground your power by either stepping out of it, or placing your hands physically upon the ground.

When you are Drawing Down the Moon you cannot be concentrating on anything else. I have read some beautiful poetry and rituals that have the Priestess or solitary Witch spouting glorious sentences while in the process of Drawing Down the Moon. Forget it. Your mouth won't be flapping if you do it right.

The Working Ritual

Is just what it says. You have something particular to accomplish wherein you feel a full ritual is needed. Writing a ritual for work is the same as when you wrote one for cleansing and consecrating your space, or performing your dedication. It will follow the same opening and closing procedures. The real difference is where you would have performed the dedication before, you will now be practicing a different kind of magickal endeavor — most likely a spell of some kind.

Working rituals are like bringing out "the big guns." They are used for controlling and banishing an inbred problem or addiction, healings, beginning a business, obtaining a home; just about anything you can think of.

Once performed, they should be forgotten, just like a simple spell. If you brood over a problem or need it will only make things worse, not better, and not allow things to manifest properly.

In working rituals you should leave some time before you actually cast the spell to meditate and build your energy by opening your chakra centers and increasing your vibrational rate. After casting the spell, you may wish to add a few affirmations that indicate that what you need is already in place.

When a Spell or Working Ritual Does Not Work

This is where record keeping is important. If something does not manifest in the way you desired, you have to go back and discern where you may have made an error. How were you feeling? What was your mental attitude? Were you interrupted? Unfocused? Were you trying to influence another in an unethical manner? Did you perhaps feel before you started that you did not deserve what you were asking for? You must remember that the world is here for everyone to enjoy and its bounties belong to you. Everyone is entitled to anything, as long as it doesn't hurt anyone. There is plenty to go around.

What if you have gone over and over your notes and cannot figure what happened? This is especially frustrating if you have performed a spell at someone else's request. You followed your records to the letter, perhaps it is a working that you have done often, and suddenly — zip — nothing. Perhaps the person who requested the spell is actually blocking it. This does happen. For whatever reason, they do not want to bring about the change requested. It isn't that you are being blocked by "evil forces," your work has actually been frozen by the very person who asked for your help in the first place.

Successful Magick

When your desire has manifested itself, make record of it and how it came to you. Often, we are not expecting the results as they come. This is because we are from the Samantha/Star Trek generations where we assume that matter will appear in the twitch of a nose, the nod of a head, or the beam of tiny light particles glittering before us. Often, the most ordinary occurrences are really the magick, and always were.

Magickal Alphabets

Spells cast with magickal alphabets, such as the runes, are very powerful and easy to do. There is little worry for supplies (like running out of an herb) and few props are required. After all correspondences are checked, a piece of virgin paper and black india ink are used. Although many Witches prefer the use

English	Theban	Malachim	Egyptian Hieroglyphs	Greek	Phoenician
A				A	
B				B	
C				Γ	
D				Δ	
E				E	
F				Φ	
G				Γ	
H				H	
I				I	
J				I	
K				K	
L				Λ	
M				M	
N				N	
O				O	
P				Π	
Q				θ	
R				P	
S				Σ	
T				T	
U				Y	
V				Y	
W				Y	
X				Ξ	
Y				Y	
Z				Z	

of a marker or pen, I stick by the "dip in the ink" method. Graphic supply stores sell crow quill pens and india ink under $5, so the expense won't be great. It also lasts a long time.

A spell is carefully worded in English first, to be sure you have composed it properly. Then, select a magickal alphabet that you feel comfortable with and translate, letter for letter, onto the paper with the india ink. Some alphabets do not have your standard 26 letters, so you may have to use phonetics to complete your work.

When you have finished, do a working ritual and burn the spell in a dish that you will reserve only for that purpose. Write down the results in your journal or Book of Shadows.

Why use an alphabet that you are not familiar with? Because you aren't familiar with it. It lends more mystery to the spell. Any spell written or spoken in a foreign language will pack a good wallop because you are repeating or writing on "faith," which is very powerful indeed!

Runes can also be "fitted" together to provide strong talismans, protection, health and wealth. These are called binding runes, and are usually in groups of two, three or four, attached by common lines. The rune in the center of the drawing is actually the binding rune.

For example, if you wished safe astral travel you would use Raido, which stands for travel, Ehwaz for the vehicle, and Hagalaz for Hel, the realm in which you may want to go. The final rune, Kenaz, would be the binding rune for one's own inner guidance while passing through other realities or in altered states of consciousness (from *Trees of Yggdrasil* by Freya Aswynn).

Using Props and Reinforcers in Magick

Many spells call for the use of herbs, candles, crystals, gems, stones, the Tarot, runes, etc. You can use them during the ritual, such as candles and the Tarot, or keep them as reinforcers after the spell has been cast and the ritual completed. Such an example would be a talisman that you plan to carry with you.

If you plan to use a particular object over and over again, once the spell has come to a successful completion and your desire has been met, you should cleanse and consecrate it for the next time you choose to use it.

Spells and Days of the Week

Each day of the week is ruled both by an astrological sign and a planetary correspondence. Checking the appropriate day to cast a spell is just as necessary as preparing for the right planetary hour and other astrological correspondences. Each day is also associated with an Angel, colors and gemstones. A correspondence chart has been provided for you in the back of this chapter.

Therefore, if you wished to cast a spell for love, you would check the chart and come up with the following:

Romantic Love

Day   First Friday after New Moon
Colors   Pink/white
Gemstones   Rose quartz (for romance); moonstone (energy exchange)
Plants   Ivy (for fidelity) and pink roses (romance)

For a little passion you could throw in a red rose, cock's comb, or ruby. Even one red candle and one pink one would work well.

If you wish to stop idle gossip, you would use the following:

Day   First Saturday after Full Moon
Color   Black
Gemstones   Jet and amethyst
Plants   Hemlock and myrrh

Remember, correspondences are just what the name indicates. They are things or ideas that "correspond" to a magickal endeavor you wish to perform.

Breaking a Spell

If a spell has backfired (and sometimes they do) and it continues, you must break it. Choose the first Saturday after a Full Moon or the Full Moon itself. Use one white candle and one black candle for balance. Your props should be of a protective nature; therefore you would use amethyst, Apache tears or smokey quartz for gemstones. Write a spell to undo what you have done, and be specific. For example:

> *On the Eve of ____*
> *I cast a spell and*
> *the effects I created*
> *I must now quell.*
> *Specifically, ____.*
> *May this spell be lifted*
> *and I now be gifted*
> *Specifically with ____.*

Be assured that a spell does not last longer than thirty days, unless you have put a time limit on it, or performed it during special astrological correspondences that have imbued it with a time limit of its own.

Correspondences

Day	Planet	Sign	Angel	Color
Sunday	Sun	Leo	Michael	Gold Yellow
Monday	Moon	Cancer	Gabriel	Silver White
Tuesday	Mars	Aries Scorpio	Samuel	Red
Wednesday	Mercury Chiron	Virgo Gemini	Raphael	Orange Light blue Grey
Thursday	Jupiter	Sagittarius Pisces	Sachiel	Purple Royal blue
Friday	Venus	Libra Taurus	Ariel	Green Pink
Saturday	Saturn	Capricorn Aquarius	Cassiel	Black

Table

Plant	Stone	Intention	Element
Marigold	Carnelian	Health	Fire
Heliotrope	Citrine	Success	
Sunflower	Tiger eye	Career	
Buttercup	Amber	Ambition	
Cedar	Quartz crystal	Goals	
Beech/oak	Red agate	Personal finances	
Night flowers	Moonstone	Psychic pursuits	Water
Willow/orris root	Aquamarine	Psychology	
Birch	Pearl	Dreams/astral travel	
Motherwort	Quartz crystal	Imagination	
Vervain	Fluorite	Women's mysteries	
White rose/iris	Geodes	Reincarnation	
Red rose	Carnelian	Passion	Fire/Water
Cock's comb	Bloodstone	Partnerships	
Pine	Ruby	Courage	
Thyme/daisy	Garnet	Swift movement	
Pepper	Pink tourmaline	Energy	
Fern	Aventurine	Wisdom	Earth
Lavender	Bloodstone	Healing	
Hazel	Hematite	Communication	
Cherry	Moss agate	Intelligence	
Periwinkle	Sodalite	Memory/education	
Cinnamon	Sugilite	Business/logic	Fire/Water
Beech	Amethyst	Gambling	
Buttercup	Turquoise	Social matters	
Coltsfoot	Lapis lazuli	Political power	
Oak	Sapphire	Material wealth	
Pink rose	Rose quartz	Romantic love	Earth/Air
Ivy	Moonstone	Friendships	
Birch/heather	Pink tourmaline	Beauty	
Clematis	Peridot	Soulmates	
Sage/violet	Emerald	Artistic ability	
Water lily	Jade	Harmony	
Myrrh/moss	Jet	Binding	All
Hemlock	Smokey quartz	Protection	
Wolfsbane	Amethyst	Neutralization	
Coltsfoot	Black onyx	Karma	
Nightshade	Snowflake obsidian	Death	
Fir	Lava/pumice	Manifestation	

Summary

Magickal workings can be both beneficial for yourself and those who request assistance. You are now beginning to build solid Craft skills that you will use throughout your life. Once you have reached this point, you can drop it, but you will never forget it. And, whether you want to admit it or not, it will always move within your subconscious. Once you have allowed the Power of the Goddess to enter your being, it cannot be eradicated.

Somewhere around this time, you will begin to worry about the ethics of what you are doing. This is good. Not consciously thinking about ethics can lead to nasty setbacks. I wish you Goddess speed as you move forward into your next step on your journey into Witchcraft.

Suggested Reading List

Llewellyn titles to assist you in your calculations:

The Daily Planetary Guide

The Moon Sign Book

The Sun Sign Book

The Magickal Almanac

Additional titles for educational purposes:

Ray L. Malbrough, *Charms, Spells, and Formulas.* Llewellyn Publications.

Valerie Worth, *The Crone's Book of Words.* Llewellyn Publications.

Mark and Elizabeth Prophet, *The Science of the Spoken Word.* Summit University Press.

Janet and Stewart Farrar, *Spells and How They Work.* Phoenix Publishing.

Frater U. D., *Practical Sigil Magic.* Llewellyn Publications.

Color, Candle and Sympathetic Magick

To Gel a Spell

Colors, candles and sympathetic items (such as a lock of hair, a photograph of an individual, or a representation of something) are the "glue" that binds your words, intent, and power together. A spell using these items tends to be more cohesive, lends to a better atmosphere, and allows you to focus on something physical. Our creative visualization may be excellent, but our minds and bodies have been trained for years to interact with the physical environment. There is nothing wrong with using that reality.

Just think of it! All species that interact in this particular physical plane must be very special indeed to be able to manifest and interpret physical reality, when in essence, there is none — just tiny bits of unseen energy that coalesce to make our world acceptable to us. In that regard, we bring matter into form every single second of our physical lives, unconsciously. Spells are just a conscious way of doing what already comes naturally to us!

Why Can't We Use Creative Visualization All the Time?

Although quite powerful, creative visualization does not work all the time. This is due mostly to the boundaries we have previously set for ourselves. You cannot one day believe that the only way you can get a new set of living room furniture is by buying it, and tomorrow fully believe that you can conjure it up out of thin air, or at least put that $1000 for it in the bank account.

See? Our conscious minds race ahead to the way we usually acquire things — the process that we are used to in obtaining our desires. The human mind, no matter how open to change or belief, has developed unconscious blocks to prevent us from slipping entirely away from what we have diligently been told, learned, analyzed and come to this plane with. Much like Pavlov's dog, the mind must be retrained with persistence to obtain completely new outlooks. We are creatures of habit.

Some people may experience more success with non-physical spells (such as making themselves better people, gaining a sense of humor, controlling negative energy, etc.) in the beginning, than with those that are performed for physical items (such as a typewriter, dictation unit, new clothes, a car, etc.). Since we do not fully understand the human mind or the laws that govern this Universe, it is easier to accept a change in our own personalities because we don't understand how that works, anyway.

When dealing with something physical, your mind will try to second-guess a spell or other working of magick. Questions like, "Where could it possibly come from?" pop up right away. Your mind will forget the spell and concentrate on where the physical items will come from, such as a particular store, a friend, the junkyard, etc. It will try to decide where the physical item is located before you actually get your hands on it.

Your mind, then, is defeating the purpose of the spell, and will work against it. This is why almost all instruction books tell you to do it and forget it. If you don't, a stalemate is created and you lose.

I also believe there is a second reason; I call it the "filter system." This theory rests more on creative visualization that has not been totally thought out by the Witch. For instance, how many times have you heard the old cliche, "If looks could kill . . . ?" Since human emotion can be controlled only to a point (we are not all sweetness and light), and human anger, frustration, and sadness are a natural part of a healthy mind, there must be some type of filter system that controls all negative emotions normally. If there weren't, we'd all be dead.

In my theory, the filter system counteracts and negates many of these ordinary emotions, or at least takes the edge off them. I'm not saying that looks cannot kill, because they can, if there is enough trained intent behind them, but unconscious negativity is controlled by some type of intelligent barrier. There are names for this block. Some people call them Angels, guides or power animals. These will be discussed more later in this book.

The third reason for failure is fate. Not fate as an indiscriminate bundle of events, where one thinks that everything in life is destined and nothing is spontaneous, but fate as in before you reached this plane of existence you yourself chose particular events or circumstances to occur. I believe that some (not all) opportunities are fated to happen at specific points on our life path, and that we have previously planned them ourselves as a trigger to reach a particular goal.

Color

Color results from our interpretation of different kinds and waves of light. Although there are an infinite number of colors, they can be broken down into seven secondary colors: red, orange, green, yellow, blue, indigo, and violet. In turn, these seven colors can be factored down to the three primary colors — red, green, and yellow. Combined, the primary colors (when dealing with light only) factor down to white, or what we interpret as white. Black, by the way is not really a color, but the absence of color — the direct opposite of light.

Light is vibratory. Each color vibrates at a different rate of speed. For example, red is the fastest vibrating color, and is a stimulatory color to the human interpretation process. Violet is the lowest vibrating color, and tends to calm the nervous system. The various vibratory waves of light can be utilized by the human brain for healing, meditation, and magick.

Using color in your work falls under the heading of practical magick, as it is the employment of an element — that of light. It is not immediately danger-ous and you are not dealing with a host of unknown factors, unless you get in to the use of the various kinds of light, such as ultraviolet.

Each color stands for a particular principle or set of principles and values. The following list of colors and their related properties can be used for both color and candle magick.

Color and Candle Correspondences

Red
Energy, Strength, Passion, Courage, Element of Fire, Career Goals, Fast Action, Lust, Blood of the Moon, Vibrancy, Driving Force, Love, Survival.

Orange
Business Goals, Property Deals, Ambition, Career Goals, General Success, Justice, Legal Matters, Selling, Action.

Copper
Passion, Money Goals, Professional Growth, Fertility in Business, Career Maneuvers.

Gold
Wealth, The God, Promote Winning, Safety and Power of the Male, Happiness, Playful Humor.

Yellow
The Sun, Intelligence, Accelerated Learning, Memory, Logical Imagination, Breaking Mental Blocks, Selling Yourself.

Pink
Romantic Love, Planetary Good Will, Healing of Emotions, Peace, Affection, Romance, Partnerships of Emotional Maturity, Caring, Nurturing.

Green Earth Mother, Physical Healing, Monetary Success, Abundance, Fertility, Tree and Plant Magick, Growth, Element of Earth, Personal Goals.

Blue Good Fortune, Opening Blocked Communication, Wisdom, Protection, Spiritual Inspiration, Calm, Reassurance, Gently Moving, Element of Water, Creativity.

Purple Influencing People in High Places, Third Eye, Psychic Ability, Spiritual Power, Self Assurance, Hidden Knowledge.

Silver Telepathy, Clairvoyance, Clairaudience, Psychometry, Intuition, Dreams, Astral Energies, Female Power, Communication, The Goddess.

Brown Influence Friendships, Special Favors.

Black Protection, Repelling Negativity, Binding, Shapeshifting.

White Spirituality, The Goddess, Peace, Higher Self, Purity, Virginity (as in the woman's mind is owned by no man), a substitute for any other color.

How Effective Is Color Magick?

Very! You can use colors to create the proper environment and bring success, happiness, wealth, and love into your life. You can use colors in healing by applying them to particular parts of the body. The chakras can be opened, balanced, or healed using colors.

Energy in Color

All color is energy. When you interact with color you interact with energy. Remember the red power tie of the eighties? Although now a rather amusing joke among corporate executives, the power tie did have its purpose — to promote the feeling of power, strength, intimidation and energetic pursuits. The eye, subjected to various colors over a period of time, passes images to the brain. An electro-chemical process results in both physical and mental change.

If you are visiting someone who is emotionally upset, wear a predominance of white, beige, blue or cream. If you are planning an intimate evening, pink or peach. Pink is also a good color to wear when mending broken emotional bridges between two people, whether they have happened on the job or in your personal life.

Do you wish to go unnoticed? Wear light grey. Would you rather present a regal appearance? Indigo, lavender or a soft violet will promote this attitude. Black gives an aura of the "untouchable." This is why this non-color is so exciting to many of the members of the male species. A woman in black denotes mystery and a definite challenge; the thrill of the chase. A lady in red? Passion, of course!

If you don't think colors affect how people act toward you, try it out. You will be a believer.

Prisms

Many people scoff at the use of those pretty prisms that come in all shapes and sizes (and keep going up in price). Since they are not genuine crystal but manufactured lead crystal, many magickal people feel they have no value. Wrong.

Prisms create rainbows of colors in dots, triangles, bands, etc. Your body absorbs colors it is lacking. Yes, your body requires different vibrations of light to survive. A prism can be just as magickal in nature as that of any gem or stone because of its properties of refracting light to create color. Every Witch should have a prism in their cabinet or bag to assist in any type of healing.

The Aura

Although we will deal with this topic more in-depth in the chapter on healing, I would like to mention that the aura is the energy patterns that emanate from the seven elements of the body — solid, liquid, gaseous, ethereal, astral, mental and spiritual bodies. The colors present in the aura tell us the disposition of an individual. Few people are adept at first in ascertaining the colors; however, with practice, you will first "feel" the colors, and then advance to seeing them.

A person who is feeling and expending great amounts of caring energy will have a pink aura. One who is very spiritual in nature will have a blue one. Strength and courage are reflected by red, etc. The aura is primarily affected by the emotional state of the individual and therefore fluctuates with feelings and deep-seated emotions.

To exercise this ability in seeing auras, keep a record in your notebook for the next three weeks. Every time you see a person you know, jot down what color aura you think that person had at the time. Choose the color at your first glance of the person, then weigh their emotions and body language to determine if you were correct.

Home Color Exercise

Take a piece of paper and go to your closet and dresser drawers. Which color is predominate? Write down how many pieces of clothing you have in each color. Now, match what you have to the color correspondence chart provided.

Are there any colors on the list that you do not own? Consider why. Determine what colors you would like to have more of. A complete outfit isn't necessary. A woman could choose scarves, vests or perhaps a sweater. A man could add colors through ties, vests, sweaters or jackets.

Next, equate the outfits you do own to the attributes you would like to project. For instance, if you were in a very loving mood, what would you wear? How about a passionate one? If you felt the need to go unnoticed, what would you choose? Consider an unpleasant situation that you know you may have to deal with. What would you wear then?

Now that you have matched the colors to make-believe scenarios, put them into action and keep a record of the results. An easy way to do this is to tack a chart on your closet door. Monday — business meeting — blue — result. You will be surprised how much colors affect your life!

Candle Magick

Candle burning is an ancient art. Not only does it create a provocative atmosphere, the candle itself is symbolic in color and shape. Some Witches make their own candles to add additional power to the taper. Since it is created by the Witch, it holds the essence of that person. You can purchase books and kits at hobby or craft shops if you wish to experiment in this art. A nice taper candle usually takes 35 dips.

When purchasing candles, try to find a shop in your area that hand-dips them. Factory candles are more expensive and burn faster. Beeswax candles, although usually higher in price, are extremely powerful as they come directly from nature and her industry.

You should stock your magickal cabinet with at least two candles of each color on the correspondence list provided, as well as ten black candles and ten white candles. White is the universal color, and it comes in handy when you run out of a specific color. Black candles are hard to come by in some areas of the country (especially rural), except around the Halloween season.

There is nothing more frustrating to realize that you have run out of black candles and a friend is in desperate need of repelling negativity. Although there are other ways to master this difficulty, candle magick is quick, easy, and inexpensive. Plus, it works just about every time!

Dressing Candles

All candles, whether store-bought or hand-made, must be dressed before they are used. This is the cleansing and consecration of the candle.

For this process you will need some type of oil. Some Witches use "specialty" oils, such as Lucky Oil, or Love Oil. These oils are made of herbs, flowers, and, of course, oils from certain plants as well as olive or saffron oil. Animal oil is not usually used because of both environmental concerns and the impurities that may complicate it from the slaughter.

Names such as "Lucky" or "Love" are given by the supplier of the oil, and are usually made up themselves. To my knowledge there is no standard formula for "Lucky Oil" or "Love Oil."

You can make the oils yourself, or you can purchase them through occult shops or catalogs. Many Witches make their own oils for sale or barter. You should be able to locate several through your networking contacts. If, however, you have none of these things available, you can always use plain olive or saffron oil. Corn oil is good, too, if you desire some type of fertility or harvest in your life. All oils must be consecrated to the God/Goddess or to the All before use.

If you wish to draw something toward you, rub the oil on the candle in a downward motion from the top of the candle to the middle. Stop. Now rub from the bottom up to the middle with the oil, as well.

If you are repelling something from you, reverse the process by rubbing from the middle to the ends. Never go in a back and forth motion as this negates the entire process.

When you have completed the process, dab some of the remaining oil on your third eye, and then in the middle of your breastbone. Speak words of power over the candle, such as:

I cleanse and consecrate this taper in the name of the God and the Goddess. May it burn in strength in the service of Light.

Continue by stating the purpose of the candle.

When inscribing a candle, use the same directional procedure. To bring things toward you, write from the top to the middle, then from the bottom to the middle of the candle. If you are repelling something, reverse the procedure. The athame is used to carve the inscription.

Just How Good Is Candle Magick?

Candle magick is extremely powerful and very practical. I had a friend who one holiday season realized that there was not enough money to buy gifts for her several children. Although she had been careful to budget her money (I don't want you to get the impression that she was unstable), she forgot to pay her school taxes and found herself with both an empty bank account and a bare wallet two weeks before Yule.

Since money was at a premium, she purchased one green pillar candle, gazed at the flame, called upon the Ancient Gods, and visualized many presents under the Yule Tree for her children. The third day, she received a commission for some work for $100. This was great, but with several children, not enough. She persisted.

The fifth day she received four bags of food, three bags of clothing, two bags of toys and a gift certificate for $100 from some old friends. The seventh day she received a $100 check for a job she had done over a month before, but hadn't gotten paid for. On the ninth day, her husband's stocks soared and they received a check for $300. She stopped the ritual and thanked the Gods. After the holiday season, while everyone else was paying off seasonal bills, she was free and clear of any burden.

Even though she had finished the ritual when she felt her family was well taken care of, the day before Yule she received a check for another $100. This she kept for after the holidays to tide the family over in food until the next paycheck came in. So, if you had any previous doubts about lighting only one candle for a big job, put them aside!

Variety

Candle magick can be the sole focus of a spell, or it can be used in combination with other tools. Candles are also used on major holidays and Esbats. For a Full Moon ritual, one would use white or silver candles. Candles in the shape of the moon can be added to the ritual, too.

For a working ritual and to bring yourself in line with the elements, you may wish to have a candle of each color corresponding to an element. Use green or brown candles for Earth, blue or purple for Water, red or orange for Fire, and white or silver for Air. To represent the God, the candle color would be red or gold. To represent the Goddess, it would be white or silver. You could also think in terms of Skyfather (blue) and Earth Mother (green). There are many possibilities. The representation must be important and comfortable to you. It must make perfect sense in your logical mind.

For choosing colors for particular needs, refer to the color list provided. You can use these in combination, or alone. Experiment and see which colors work best for specific needs.

Any ritual or spell can contain several types of candles. Perhaps you will have illumination candles on the altar, and a silver candle to represent the Goddess on an Esbat. If you are planning a working on that evening that will include magick for obtaining love, you would add a red candle, as well. This would be the focus candle. To assist, you may add a candle for the day of the week.

I would like to add one final note here about color and human reaction. I've heard comments such as, "So and so says that every time she uses a pink candle, the spell goes awry." This may very well be true for that person, but it doesn't necessarily mean it will be true for you. You will have to experiment.

Lighting, Extinguishing and Disposing of Candles

Light all illumination candles, deity candles, daily candles, and focused candles with either a lighter or birthday candle. Do not use matches as the sulphur is not compatible to your working. You may even use a simple white candle designed for this purpose with inscriptions or magickal symbols.

To extinguish a candle, do not pinch it, as you pinch out the desire; and do not blow it out, as you blow the desire away from yourself. Use a candle snuffer (which is inexpensive), or wave your hand over the top of the candle to create enough draft to extinguish it.

If you plan to use the candle again, store it carefully. If the spell was one that calls for a virgin candle, bury it off your property, if possible, for spells involving the movement of things away from you, and on the property if you wish to draw something toward you.

Keep candle drippings when performing all rituals, save those where you are repelling something. You can add drippings to healing pouches (if the spell was for a healing), remelt them on a talisman consecrated and empowered during that same ritual, or keep them simply in the bottom of purse or coat pocket for good luck, fertility, romance and fortune.

If you wish to construct a dream pillow for prophetic dreams, throw in some of the candle wax from a Full Moon ritual along with the herbs you have selected. The old adage "waste not, want not" carries a double meaning in magick!

Candles and Sympathetic Magick

Candles molded into shapes are considered sympathetic magick. Our ancestors at some point placed animal head-dresses on their heads and animal skins on their backs to ask their spirits for good hunting. This is also a type of sympathetic magick; using a like object to reach our intent.

To assist you in finding a familiar, burn a candle of the animal you desire. For a hunter in buck season, burn a candle for a male deer. In both these instances, you would be contacting the animals' collective unconscious to request their assistance.

Fertility spells can be cast with a phallus-shaped candle. Healing spells can be performed with human-shaped candles (pick up those skull-shaped candles around Halloween). White ones are great for healing; black ones for reversing spells or warding off negativity.

Sympathetic magick mixed with candle magick is very strong stuff. I once purchased a candle of Sister Spider, because I felt I needed the protection of that particular cosmic link. Although the spell was successful in the long run, the first morning after the spell I woke up literally covered with spider bites! My error was to ask for the most powerful protection the spider could give me, without adding a protective clause for myself! I should have added something like, "In no way will this spell cause me to suffer any adverse effects!"

In that way, Sister Spider would have had to think of another way to instill her power. However, the spell was successful and the danger I faced passed, leaving me safe, but itchy!

Another type of candle/sympathetic magick is to inscribe runes, names, or other magickal symbols directly on the candle before burning. If you are in a real hurry and need results pronto, take a hat pin (yes, they are still around but you have to look for them) and stick it as close as you can to the top of the candle without breaking it. As you are inserting the pin, say:

When this candle burns to the pin, the process of (name the desire) will begin.

Insert a second pin close to the first, and say:

> *When this candle burns to this pin, the process of (name desire) will come to a successful completion, and end.*

Of course you may have to re-word the spell, but you get the idea.

Candle and color magick are considered "sympathetic magick" — wherein like attracts like. The color red, for example, attracts passion, courage and strength. A candle of that color or any color acts in the same fashion.

Other items commonly used in sympathetic magick are locks of hair, photographs, personal effects of a particular individual, and poppets (dolls). Because these items have a psychic link to the person they have been taken from (the dolls are made with the link), they are very powerful. These things can be used in healing rituals or for drawing good fortune to that person, and aid in eliminating bad habits.

Using Personal Effects in Magick

What are the best personal effects to use when employing magickal practices for another individual? A photograph, something that the person carries with them often (for instance, a favorite bracelet or a tie), a lock of hair, and yes, a drop of blood.

Why bother? If you want to forge a strong link from your magick to the person, you would use personal effects. These items have a psychic and physical link to the individual that has given them to you. These things can be used in healing rituals, drawing good fortune to that person, and aid in eliminating bad habits.

Sympathetic magick employed for someone other than yourself should not be done without that person's permission. There are situations where sympathetic magick involving personal effects or poppets filled with them in combination with herbs are used.

Sometimes, you may only have a letter requesting your help. I often put the letter in a colored envelope matching the need, or I have hand-sewn felt pockets out of various colors and color combinations to place the letter in to assist me in helping that person.

Tattwas

The men and women involved in the Hermetic Order of the Golden Dawn contributed much to our knowledge of the occult today. The Order first appeared in London in 1877 and introduced a revival of esoteric practice involving astrology, alchemy, the chakras, the Qabalah, and the attwas (or tattwas). The symbols, originally from Sanskrit and Hindu philosophy, relate to planes of existence, the elements, colors, and the seasons. They can be used singular or in combination in meditation and magick.

To make a tattwa envelope you will need:
    An 18" long and 12" wide piece of white felt
    3 white velcro circles
    One small piece each of black, blue, red, and yellow felt
    One small piece of silver material
    Corresponding thread for sewing the colors

Fold the bottom of the white felt up about six inches. Sew on the right and left sides to make the envelope ends. Attach the velcro circles so the pocket will be securely closed when flap is folded over. Cut the tattwa shapes in their corresponding colors from the table. Sew or glue them to the front flap of the bag. When you have finished, do a ritual of balance and consecrate the bag. Empower it so that it will neutralize all the negative energy of whatever it contains or is placed within it.

If you receive something of a disturbing nature, such as a letter, photo, or jewelry that carries unbalanced or negative energy, place it within the packet for 24 hours to balance the energies of the situation. When you have taken care of the problem, air the envelope in strong sunlight for ten minutes. Small envelopes can also be made of black and white for balancing pictures and little items. These envelopes can also carry the tattwa symbolism, either in unison or separately. (I would like to indicate here that the original idea for the colored felt envelopes came from Ray Buckland's book, *Practical Color Magick*.)

The following table is a list of correspondences for the five tattwas (although through serious study you will discover that there are seven).

Symbol	Tattwa	Quality	Color	Season	Qabalah
	Akasa	Spirit	Black	Flowing	The Crown
	Vayu	Air	Blue	Autumn	Emanation
	Tejas	Fire	Red	Spring	Creation
	Apas	Water	Silver	Summer	Formation
	Prithivi	Earth	Yellow	Winter	Action

Doll/Poppet Magick

It took me a long time to employ doll magick as I associated it with incredible power — which is accurate, but my reasoning was from a different perspective than you might think. My respect of this power was absolutely genuine, not borne of Hollywood horror pictures — rather its roots were in a true story told to me almost seventeen years ago.

A very close friend of mine was in a bad domestic situation. It was especially bad for her because her injuries from spousal abuse mixed with the aftereffects of the polio virus rendered her unable to walk. The injuries came from constant beatings by her husband. She was in the middle of a terrible divorce, yet he refused to move out of the house they were both living in. She couldn't leave the house because she had several children; and, of course, she couldn't walk.

You must understand that the actual events took place several years before I heard this story. So, you will have to remember that the laws of the state she lived in at the time were not very conducive to abused wives. The husband was permitted to remain within the home until the final decree, even though it was alleged that he had been abusive toward her.

My friend was desperate with a big "D." When her father travelled to Haiti during the summer of her divorce, she begged him to bring her back two Voodoun dolls. Such a time he had finding these dolls! A native finally took him to an nearly unpopulated area of the island and there, for a price, he acquired the dolls — one male and one female — made of bark. When her father returned to the States he gave his daughter what he thought was a simple box of souvenirs, albeit unusual.

Things in the home grew progressively worse. Finally, seated at the dining room table, my friend began to play with the dolls. Her husband was upstairs, shouting abuses over a fight that they had just finished. Frustrated at being bound to such horrific circumstances, she grabbed a pin and a piece of his soiled handkerchief, tied the cloth around the male doll's leg, and raised the pin.

As the abuses continued pouring from upstairs, hatred and fear merged together into a powerful psychic situation. She raised the pin, but could not bring herself to stab the doll in the heart so she stuck it in the leg instead, chanting the words "mumbo-jumbo, mumbo-jumbo" over and over again.

On the surface, this story is actually funny, and the first time I heard it, I was literally in tears of laughter as she acted out what had happened long ago. A grown woman pounding a doll up and down on the top of the dining room table, chanting words of nonsense because she hasn't the vaguest idea about magick or Voodoun, but is desperate enough to try something she really thought was silly.

When she was through, she tossed the doll up the stairs and it landed at his feet. He laughed and kicked it back down the stairs. He got ready for evening shift work and left the house. He didn't come home when his shift was over, but since that was usual (he had a girlfriend), my friend did not worry about it until the following day. Finally, she called his parents who told her he was in the hospital with a terrible affliction. His leg was full of open, running sores.

Aghast, my friend took the two dolls, rolled them up in a towel, and had her son hide them in the attic — where they still are today.

I never forgot that story, so it was with great trepidation and respect that I began using poppet magick. I have shared this story with you in an effort to explain just how powerful magick is when mixed with uncontrollable emotions. Truly unique is the knowledge that my friend was not involved in magick and never has been, save for this remarkable experience.

Making a Poppet

Dolls can be made of wood, cloth, clay or even paper. They should have a basic human shape of either male or female, depending upon the sex of the person for whom it is to be used. The doll itself is useless; the effort is combined with an act of ritual.

The doll can be stuffed with batting, tissue, even straw. Other items placed within the doll would be herbs, personal effects (such as a lock of hair) and small gems. Therefore, your knowledge of these items is important.

In cases of a real emergency, poppets can be drawn with colored pencil on a plain piece of white paper and the ritual taken from there. In a binding situation, you would roll the doll up and bind it with black thread.

After the doll has been made, wrap it in white cloth until the ritual is performed. During the ritual, you will cleanse and consecrate the doll. It is at this point where the psychic link is begun. To seal this act, you would say:

> *Though separate you were,*
> *Now you are one*
> *The link of unison has now begun.*

Poppets should not be destroyed. If they have been used with the permission of the person they represent, they should be given to that person for safekeeping. If it is yours, store it in white cloth in your cabinet. If it has been done for a child, give it to the parents or keep it yourself. If it was a doll made for binding, it should be buried.

Spells to Bind

The first order of business in any binding spell is to carefully consider why you wish to employ it. Perhaps you would be better served to heighten your own protection by learning to strengthen your psychic shield, clearing your home or work place of negative energy, or casting a spell to positively remove yourself from the situation by better education, a new place to live, or a promotion.

If you are in physical danger, you should remove yourself immediately from that scenario. If you feel for some reason that you cannot do this on your own, ask a friend, a trusted neighbor, a family member or an organization in your home town that has been designed to help those who are in trouble. Often we subject ourselves to the most horrible dangers because we feel that in some way we deserve them. Never fall prey to that kind of self-ridiculing thought form.

Once you have removed yourself from physical danger, you must think clearly about the next step to be taken. Use both the legal system and magick, not one or the other alone.

A binding spell is the act of grasping the negative energy that is propelling a person or thing and stopping it. In this way, you are negating the unhealthy energy. The most important thing to remember when conducting a binding spell is that you must control your own violent emotions of hatred or fear. The binding spell is for protection only, not for harm. This is not easy. The Goddess to be employed is Aradia, Queen of Witches. Be sure you are honest in your intentions. The symbol of Aradia is the red garter.

If you desire justice, which often we do, then call upon Maat, she who balances the scales. However, you must be absolutely sure that your own hands are free from violence and hatred, lest she weigh her scales for you as well! The symbol for Maat is the pure white feather.

The binding itself is a very simple matter. A poppet can be sewn to represent the malicious person. Fill it with earth (grave dirt if you can find it), bating, rosemary, sage, a piece of smokey quartz and a piece of amethyst. Also enclose a piece of the person's fingernails, a lock of hair, or another personal item. Their handwriting can be enclosed if you have nothing else. Photos can also be rolled and placed within the doll. If your intention at any time during the ritual is to harm that person, remember that you will only bring harm upon yourself — so be very, very careful.

If you cannot do the ritual right away, store the doll (with the head still open) in a white cloth. During the ritual you will sew up the head while connecting the psychic link. Then you will proceed to sew the arms and legs of the doll together. You will finish by wrapping the doll mummy-fashion with a black ribbon. Bury the doll when you have completed the ritual.

A person can also be bound using mental capabilities. Laurie Cabot says that whenever she sees a terrorist or murderer on the television, she binds him by placing a mental white "X" over the face. I envision them wrapped in mummy fashion in white gauze.

Turning Back vs. Binding

This subject treads, in many minds, that fine line again of ethics. Before you make the decision on whether or not you wish to employ this method, you should consider that your aura naturally "turns back" a great deal of negativity and unbalance as long as you are healthy in body and mind.

To turn back negativity is to become a mirror, where the energy that is sent to you bounces back to the initiator, leaving you unaffected. There are those that feel you are acting as personal judge and jury when you do this. Others think that because you have not actively generated the negative energy, you are not responsible for it — you are only reflecting something meant to harm you.

A great deal of protection magick employs "sending back" negative energy. Talismans, protective jewelry, strengthening one's shield — all are methods of sending energy back from whence it came. There is an old Pennsylvania Dutch custom wherein if you have been the recipient of negative magick, you should take off your shirt and pinch it between the door and the lock, thereby squeezing out the ill will and sending it back.

Placing a sample of a person's handwriting and capping it tightly in an old Bell jar is a way to stop malicious gossip. When the danger is over, unscrew the cap and burn the handwriting. Mirrors can also be used to turn back negative energy. However, if you employ such a method, never turn the mirror on yourself during the ritual and do not allow anyone to look into the mirror at any time. Trust me on this one!

Summary

This chapter carried a great deal of information and is the foundation of practical magick. You can influence almost any part of your reality with candles, colors and sympathetic magickal functions. The information given can be used every day to obtain your desires and protect you.

Practical magick is a means of bringing mundane matters into form — money, better employment, success, love and health. There are no exotic or expensive items used; all equipment can be found on hand. We've also touched lightly on ethics and ethical behavior in the use of magick. Remember to do all magickal endeavors with grace, love and faith.

You have now completed the next step in your Craft training by learning the fundamentals in performing magick. I suggest you practice the building blocks presented in this chapter before moving on. Once you have had some experience casting spells, you will be better able to continue your education in the Craft.

Suggested Reading List

Raymond Buckland, *Practical Candleburning Rituals.* Llewellyn Publications.

Raymond Buckland, *Practical Color Magick.* Llewellyn Publications.

Gerina Dunwich, *The Magick of Candle Burning.* Citadel Press.

R. G. Torrens, *The Golden Dawn: The Inner Teachings.* Samuel Weiser, Inc.

Gems, Herbs and Healing

Living Magick

Unlike candles or manufactured tools, gems and herbs are animate — meaning they carry life properties of their own, regardless of human interaction. Before a Witch can properly use these natural instruments, he or she must understand the act of showing honor and respect to these life forms and link with their natural intelligence.

It is my firm belief that all Witches, somewhere within their study, should examine Native American religions and the practice of Shamanism. These individuals mastered the art of communication with the earth and all her inhabitants, much as our own ancestors of the Old Religion did. Shamanistic principles have a great deal of information that is important to the New Generation of Witches.

In their book *American Indian Ceremonies,* Medicine Hawk and Grey Cat tell us that:

> *Each individual is literally a cousin, a brother, a sister of everything . . . In everything is some spirit stuff which is the true existence of the cosmos: The same spirit stuff is within each individual human.*

The Native American believes that all parts of the Universe are sacred. To use the benefits of the Universe, one must become part of it to understand it. This should be true for the Witch, as well.

The gifts of the Medicine Wheel can be intermingled with the properties of the modern Witch and his or her Craft with fluidity. However, one must study both in their separate forms to practice them in harmony.

Thanking the spirits of animate objects is both important and appropriate. A simple blessing will suffice, or you may wish to do something more elaborate, like leaving a gift behind at a favorite tree or rock. This is called a "give-away" and is most appropriate when dealing with humans, natural spirits and power animals.

When I was a child I heard a theory on boulders as they relate to the Universe. All rocks are living, the theory said, but their movement is so slow that it is not detectable to the human eye. Since most people are of the "show me" variety, the rocks have kept their secrets well hidden through eons of time. Not long after I heard this story, I saw something similar on one of the Star Trek adventures.

I thought this was clever and tricky, but forgot the story until years later, when I began to work with gems and stones. It hit me then that there was truth in such an absurd and unusual theory.

The Properties of Rocks

Gems and stones carry the living force, or energy, just as you do. For centuries, various religions have integrated the use of them into their practices. Many Jews believed that the amethyst brought forth visions and revelations. Often, gems and stones would be placed on tools of war for protection — such as a shield, breastplate, or arm band.

In Native American practices, gems and stones were collected and utilized for their healing, protective and scrying properties. Gem power was, and still is, an actual belief and not a legend or story to them. Gems and stones were also revered for their spiritual properties and considered as aids in personal enhancement and growth.

Also, you will hear stones and rocks called precious and semiprecious. Precious stones are simply those that are hard to get, such as rubies, diamonds, emeralds and sapphires. All other stones and gems are considered semiprecious. For example, if the world's supply of quartz crystals suddenly dried up or simply became difficult to obtain, clear quartz would be considered a precious stone. Already I am sure that you have seen the prices jacked up for quartz crystals simply because they are "in demand," but there is not a shortage of them.

Gem Energy

The energy force of gems and stones can be absorbed into the human body. They can be used in an overt magickal act (such as a spell or hands-on healing), and in non-active situations (such as enhancing your own spiritual qualities and power through jewelry, or by taking a ride in your pocket). They can also assist in meditation.

Since we absorb the energy of gems and stones, an overload can occur. If you begin to feel uncomfortable with any gem or stone, cease use and experimentation for the moment. Later, you can run a test to determine if it was the gem/stone or some other factor. Several "try-outs" should be run during different moon phases, not only when difficulties arise, but for general reference as well.

There are some families of gems/stones that you may never be compatible with. For instance, green malachite and I do not get along. How can I tell? Physical symptoms can manifest, such as headaches, an upset stomach, disorientation, or a light-headed sensation. You may not feel quite "in touch" with the world at large. A general air of imbalance is another warning sign, as well as irritability.

Although gems and stones have overall properties and meanings amassed through the years, each person interacts differently with them due to individual spiritual and physical chemistry. For instance, a snowflake obsidian may protect my purse, but it might not protect yours. You will find special stones that are just for you. River beds and streams are wonderful places to find these stones. You don't have to know the properties or the name; they should be considered special gifts from the Universe, and their use will be made plain to you.

Color should also be taken into consideration when using gems and stones. Remember the color chart in the last chapter? When experimenting with stones, remember to check that chart. Often a particular meaning or usage escapes us, but if we stick with the color chart, we can find what we are looking for. For instance, we may forget what rhodocrosite is for, but we know that it is pink. The color pink is for loving, healing, and soft emotions. Therefore, we know this stone has something to do with these principles, though we just can't pinpoint all the details immediately.

Using Gems and Stones

All gems and stones should be cleansed, consecrated and empowered. You can let them soak in a glass of spring water, or hold them in a stream or under a running faucet. Moonlight and sunlight are also excellent cleansers.

Wear gems and stones as close to the body as possible. Place in a pocket, purse, or wallet. Pouches can be fashioned from leather or silk. They can be sewn in the hems of skirts or pants. Garters of gems can be created, as well as belts and headbands.

Use masking tape to secure them under desks and chairs in a workplace, office, home or dashboard and seat of a vehicle. You can place them behind pictures, doors, under the carpet or in the corner of a room — just about anywhere you feel you need to use the energy of the stone.

Always remember that the size of the stone is not important. You don't need a fifty-pound piece of rose quartz to bring a maximum amount of loving feelings into your life. A small piece, no bigger than the end of your little finger, will do the trick nicely.

Gems can be placed on magickal tools, as well, with glue or wire. Some beautiful pieces can be made, such as goblets, Tarot boxes, wands, baskets, and herb containers.

·☽ ☾·

The best way to begin using stones and gems is to sit in a quiet place and hold them one at a time in your left hand. Let the energy of the stone move in your palm. Imagine that it is a delicate being you don't want to squash.

Be aware of what you are feeling. If nothing seems to be coming through, don't get frustrated. Instead, open your third eye chakra center and look at the stone from that angle. Continue to experiment with your right hand. Write your sensations in your workbook. Switch to your left hand. Are the sensations different, and if so, how? When you have finished with each stone, re-read the interpretation of that stone.

Aventurine (Color: green, blue, or red): Appears tightly packed with metallic speckles. It is sometimes called Indian jade. A nice good-luck gift with the distinction of adding that extra favor or push in a winning direction.

Agates (Color: varied): There are several types of agates. **Banded:** Relieves stress/emotional pain. **Dendritic:** Milky-white with blue/black spots; protection in travel. **Indian:** Eye formation in center of stone. Used for bodily protection or survival. **Moss:** Milky with moss inside. Also tree agates and fern agates. These are healers, stimulating wound closure. Acts as a cleanser, stimulator and strengthener. Its liquid appearance and smooth surface are great soothers for children's minor "accidents." **Plume agate:** Milky with fiery red grasses inside. Good for visualization practice and reaching desired goals. Agates in general combined with other stones and gems make for excellent magickal results. They act much like the binding runes as they provide an active link for the harmonious blending of several properties.

Amber (Color: yellow or orange): Fossilized resin of extinct organic matter. This is an all-purpose gem. It is an excellent protector of children and a spell strengthener, and can stimulate the flow of money toward you. A High Priestess of a coven may wear amber as well as jet beads to signify her position. Amber is said to be one of the most magickally used stones by the Witches of the Old Religion.

Amethyst (Color: transparent crystalline purple): Used to transform negativity and strengthen the third eye vision or your intuitive sense. Put it under your pillow or on the headboard of a bed for one who suffers nightmares or disturbing dreams. Always have a nice piece in the room where you entertain outsiders, such as friends or clients (and especially family!). This gem is good for headaches and preventing overindulgence in alcohol.

Bloodstone (Color: very dark green with red or orange spots or bands): The bloodstone is really a jasper, but because of its unique properties I have listed it separately. It is also called a heliotrope. Keep this in mind when stone shopping since different dealers and stores use a variety of names. The bloodstone is an aid in removing both mental and physical blocks. It has been used for centuries in healing of both internal and external difficulties. If you embark upon the healing of another person, keep a bloodstone in your pocket to protect yourself, as well. It is also carried to avoid wounds, bring money, increase production, protect pregnant women, and provide "cloaking" when you do not want to be seen. In our home, the child that sees another hurt runs to tell me to "get the bloodstone!" These stones are nice give-aways as well. It is said that when their energy is used up, the red spots turn to white. The stone should then be returned to the elements from whence it came.

Carnelian (Color: translucent red or orange): This is a very special agate. It is the success stimulator for career minded individuals. A powerful action stone — things move very fast with this one. If you think you will be entering an arena where your thoughts will be "scanned" by another person and you do not desire this, carry the carnelian!

Fluorite (Color: variegated translucent blue, purple, pink or blue-green): Fluorite is seen as interlocking cubes or gives the appearance of two pyramids fused together. This is a relatively "new stone." Fluorite is great for use during meditation to contact your higher self and can assist in tuning you in to the Akashic records, enabling you to answer some of those haunting past-life questions. At first you may experience mere flashes, but they often contain all the answers necessary to formulate a complete scenario. Others use it to strengthen analytical and intellectual abilities.

Geodes: Stone balls with crystal, amethyst or topaz centers. Others are a collection of mineral deposits that dazzle the eye when the stone is sliced. These are often called "thunder eggs." They stimulate dance and the free spirit. In magick, a geode can be used to concentrate power prior to its release.

Jaspers (Color: varied): Hard, opaque stone. They are known as the "rain gatherers." Jaspers strengthen your energy flow and relieve stress. **Red:** Night protection, defensive magick and the return of negative energy. **Green:** Healing. **Brown:** Grounding and stability.

Malachite (Color: blue or green with variegated bands): This stone has a truly unique ability — it breaks into two pieces to warn you of imminent danger. Also believed to greatly enhance vision questing.

Moonstone (Color: pink, white, blue or green): All hues are soft. This is one of my favorite stones. It promotes love, compassion and sympathy both in yourself and others. Also the gem of second sight, it enhances psychic powers and should be kept with divinatory tools. If you have over-extended yourself with dream work and need a pleasant night's rest, place the moonstone under your pillow. The moonstone can also assist in unblocking emotions between two lovers, helping them to communicate in an atmosphere of unconditional love. Some of my most exciting and successful experiments have been with the moonstone.

Obsidian (Color: black): A type of volcanic glass. Pebbles are called "Apache tears" of which I have heard several ideas on the legend, including their formation by either Mother or Apache sisters when brave warriors died in battle. As their tears hit the earth, they turned to black transparent stone. The obsidian is basically a stone of protection, although mirrors of obsidian have been used for scrying purposes. Snowflake obsidian is my absolute favorite. If I put it with my money I never run completely dry. If you feel too many people are taking advantage of you, carry a piece of this gem with you to screen out this pushy energy.

Rhodochrosite (Color: variegated pink and white): The "energizer" of the stone family. If you are feeling a little tired but you have got to finish that project, let this stone help you out.

Rose quartz (Color: pink): This is a quartz crystal with a soft, rosy hue. Another excellent give-away stone as it always encourages peaceful and loving feelings. It promotes beauty, love of self and of others. Set a piece in your home or office environment. When your children are having an argument or an especially bad day, have them sit quietly and hold the stone. Soon there are smiles all around! This stone is also excellent for a friend or family member who is experiencing profound grief over the loss of a loved one.

Smokey quartz (Color: translucent grey/black): This stone is clear quartz that looks like it has been infused with a heavy dose of soot. It is another energy generator and a protective stone. My husband has a lovely faceted piece set in a silver star. He hangs it on the rearview mirror of his truck not only to protect it from vandalism, but also to keep it in running order. I borrowed the stone for my car when I took a load of Girl Scouts on a long trip because nobody in my house thought my car would make it. We had no problems, but my husband's truck broke down while I was gone!

Sodalite (Color: deep blue with strands of white): Often confused with lapis lazuli. An excellent stress reducer, this stone enables you to go through the day without being affected by minor upheavals or emotional turmoil. It is also a good meditative stone, especially when teaching adults.

Sunstone (Color: tangerine): Native to Oregon. This stone looks like a slice of orange, and even feels like one! The first time I held a piece, I instinctively put it up to my nose, expecting a citrus scent. This is an energizer and a cellular healing stone. It is often associated with the Sun and the element of Fire, and used in cancer recovery.

Tiger eye (Color: honey-brown with banded tints): This is a stone of luck and fortune, but is also known for its truth-discerning capabilities. It is a stone of honesty. Anyone attempting to lie to you while you are carrying this stone better be careful, as his cloak will be removed. Often others will blurt the truth or you will find out in the same day that you have been deceived. Veils are lifted with this stone. It also assists in accurate judgement calls. **Falcon's eye** is a danish blue in color. It is not as outgoing as the brown version but it is very effective in situations you believe have zoomed way off their mark. It will draw you to a more sure-footed path and back in control.

Turquoise (Color: baby blue): Looks like baby blue bubble gum. A highly absorbent stone, it drains of color if in contact with your flesh over a period where you are in a highly stressed mode. Turquoise is the "speaking stone." It enhances verbal communication and allows thoughts to flow in perfect sentences. If you are nervous about giving a speech or presentation, wear turquoise around the throat. Turquoise is considered to enhance love, heath and happiness, as well as functioning as a protector of the spirit. Perhaps we should urge both the Senate and the House to re-do their chambers entirely in turquoise and tiger eye!

This list of gems and stones is by no means complete. They represent those stones I have personally worked and experimented with. None of the stones should be ingested; they should be carried or worn when personal contact is required.

The best way to familiarize yourself with gems and stones is to work with them yourself. Don't forget to record your experiences with various stones in your notebook. Try mixing the stones together to see how their energies work together and balance one another.

Crystals

I use crystals often in my magickal workings, which is why I have left them for last. When you pick up a crystal imagine that you are plugging it into your energy system, much like plugging a television into an electrical socket.

Crystals have a variety of uses. They can enhance psychic powers, aid in vision questing and be worn as protective shields. They are used for prophecy, energizing, and thought storage retrieval. They are excellent projectors, and many a magickal wand has been capped with them.

Crystals are unique because they can be "programmed" by yourself. This is done by holding the crystal to your third eye and focusing on a specific thought form, such as protection.

A crystal's power is enhanced by direct moonlight, which performs a cleansing function, as well. Rituals are conducted at the Full Moon with crystals at each Watchtower or on the altar. Often a Tarologist will carry crystals with their cards to act as protectors and enhancers. Bracelets of leather and crystal can be worn on either wrist to enhance your projection capabilities. Draw the wrists together and let the crystals touch as you project your thoughts or energy. Crystals are often used in dreaming by placing one under the pillow and programming it for a specific function before you fall asleep. In healing, crystals can be placed around the body in various patterns to bring the bodily systems into balance. Used with gems and stones, crystals can direct their energies to specific chakra points when placed on the body to clear blockages. Crystals on a headband can assist in the projection of your thoughts to another person, or enable you to vision quest with more clarity.

Crystal usage is almost unending. They are great all-purpose pieces and wonderful give-aways. If you lose a crystal, don't fret. Perhaps it is only taking a vacation to cleanse itself, and will return. Or it may be gone forever, its work with you completed.

Take good care of all your gems, stones and crystals. Many are subject to chipping or cracking. Store them in separate pouches. If you are into sewing, you can design a pouch of your own to hold several stones in pockets. I have seen some beautiful circular draw bags with pie-slice pockets.

Keep a record of successful uses of your stones and gems. This will assist you in the future in your magickal workings and counseling of family and friends.

Plants and Herbs

I like to believe that faeries are really the spirits (or collective unconscious) of plants that mimic human form when the desire moves them to do so. All plants and herbs, like gems and stones, have a life force of their own. Although you can purchase plants and herbs through many shops and mail-order houses, I prefer to harvest my own. Most of the plants and herbs listed in this chapter are those I am most familiar with because I harvest them myself, and they grow in the climate where I live. I suggest that after you read this chapter, you become familiar with those plants that are native to your area, and learn to work with them first.

Magickal Uses of Herbs

Amaranth (cockscomb): repair a broken heart
Apples: healing and love
Basil: love, wealth and protection
Bay: wisdom, protection, psychic powers
Birch: cleansing
Carnation: protection and healing
Catnip: cat magick
Cedar: purification and healing
Cinnamon: spirituality and healing, cleansing
Clove: money and protection, cleansing
Clover: money, love and luck
Cornflower: psychism
Garlic: protection and healing
Ginger: money, success and power
Holly: dream magick and balance
Iris: wisdom
Ivy: protection and healing
Lilac: protection, beauty and love
Marigold: dreams, business or legal affairs
Marjoram: protection, love and healing
Mint: money, luck and travel
Mistletoe: protection, fertility, healing and psychism
Orris root: divination
Rose: love, psychic power and divination
Rosemary: love, power, healing, sleep
Sage: protection and wisdom
Thyme: healing and psychic powers
Willow: love and divination

Medicinal Uses of Herbs

Anise: tea form — treatment for colic; sedative

Basil: tea form — colds, flu, cramps, bladder

Bay: do not take internally — use as poultice on chest for bronchitis and chest colds

Black pepper: take at first sign of any disease

Bonset: tea form — laxative and fever

Caraway: mild stimulant for digestion

Cayenne: fast recovery, stops internal and external bleeding, said to prevent heart attacks and also helps with depression and headaches

Cinnamon: ground or taken with milk — good balance after a heavy meal or dessert; also used for diarrhea, dysentery or general indigestion

Cloves: chew for toothache, also good for nausea or vomiting.

Fennel: tea form — to expel mucus

Fenugreek: tea form — also to expel mucus with bad cases of bronchitis

Garlic: high and low blood pressure; removing parasites and infections

Ginger: tea form — for cramps and nausea; externally for stiffness; add in cooking to detoxify meat, especially chicken

Rosemary: tea form — for treating headaches or body aches

Thyme: tea form — to rid of intestinal worms; can also be used as a mouthwash

Tumeric: added to warm milk — regulates menstrual cycle

Harvesting Plants and Herbs

Part of the magick in plants and herbs is the ability to harvest them. Visiting a sun-dappled forest or wading through a field is an exciting and peaceful way to commune with the Goddess. The supplies you will need for gathering, drying and storing herbs are simple and can be obtained with very little expense.

In the spring, when the last of the snow begins to melt from the ground and frost is a companion no more, I bring out my "gathering basket." This particular basket was a Yule gift, made of intertwined branches as thick as your thumb. On the outside rim I tie thirteen bows with brightly colored ribbons, each about four to five inches in length. The ribbon color is your preference, but I usually use the colors of Earth Mother — green, pink, lilac, white — the hues of the flowers and greenery of spring. I place the basket on the family altar and perform a "Gathering Ritual" which includes a cleansing and consecration of the basket and my bolline. I prefer to do this ritual on the New Moon, as it signifies the beginning of an enterprise.

I also check my herb supply. This is a collection of bottles and jars that are relatively the same size. During the winter they are arranged alphabetically; come spring, I arrange them by harvest date. On each bottle or jar is a label with the name of the herb, if it is poisonous, and the date it was harvested. Below this I have briefly indicated its uses. All bottles and jars are cleansed and consecrated before use. If I feel I need more bottles, I prepare them to be included in the Gathering Ritual as well.

Over the winter months, I have sewn several pouches and open pillows for this year's crop. I check this supply to see if I need to do any last-minute stitching. Invariably, I add a few for good measure. This is also the time I begin to gather supplies for my indoor herb garden. I purchase seeds, trays and potting soil. At their correct planting time, I do a Planting Ritual.

Throughout the spring and summer as the herbs come into their harvest time, I take the basket outside on sunny mornings (after the dew is gone) and gather what I need. I never gather an over-abundance, especially with the plants that I know will prosper until the first frost. I want their full potency for winter stock. If the plant is one that has a short growing season, I watch it carefully until I know that its time is soon coming to a close. Then I gather a major crop of those. Of course, the climate you live in has a great deal to do with harvest times and availability of certain species of plants. Since my life is dictated by the central Eastern climate, so is my gathering time.

To harvest a plant, I first take hold of it gently and mentally express my love and gratitude for its beauty and use. Then I explain why I am cutting the plant. At this time, some Witches draw a clockwise circle on the ground in front of the plant, others draw a clockwise circle around the plant. This is to protect its energy as you are cutting it. Use the bolline to take what you need. When cutting plants like roses, lilacs, etc., you should have some knowledge (as we spoke of before when dealing with trees) of proper pruning. Again, I suggest the purchase of a book on where and when the safest cuts can be made, or visit your local library or greenhouse for this information.

If the harvest is a small one, you can dry the herbs on a paper towel in an airy place where they will not be disturbed. Drying time varies with each plant. If you have gathered a rather large amount, bind them with twine and hang them to dry where the air will circulate around them.

When they are completely dry, bring out your mortar and pestle and crush the plants. I do not make them into a powder at this time; I like to leave this for the actual magickal application of the plant.

When the new plants are dried and crushed, I empty out last year's stock and replace it with the new plants. I also put the new harvest date on the label. Last year's harvest, along with the plants that have not been included in this year's storing process, are scattered outside.

On the eve of the harvest, I take some tobacco or fertilizer and sprinkle it around the plant in respect for the spirit housed there. If I am out gathering away from home, I take the gift with me and give thanks right after the cutting.

When you first begin to work with herbs and plants you can use them in small pillows, medicine bags, mixed with incense or in potpourri. Always keep track of your measurements so that you can repeat the mix when you like.

Empowering Plants

Herbs and plants should be charged before use. In this way you mix your energy with that of the plant to bring forth a desired response. During this process you must tell the herb or plant exactly what its use will be. This is important — this is the combined focus of yourself and the spirit of the plant.

Philters are mixtures of herbs and oils that are not ingested or brewed. They can be placed near doors or windows. Tape a vial to the table you use for divination. Cooking herbs can be magickally empowered, as well.

Garlic is a very healthy plant. It assists in preventing cold symptoms. Empower it, and it will have twice its strength. Teas can also be empowered. Those for restful sleep, such as camomile, can be charged for pleasant dreams.

To fully educate yourself on herbs and plants, search the library. Holistic health magazines and books are excellent forms of reference. I have also listed some books in the suggested reading list at the end of this chapter.

Healing

By now, you can see that each skill area has its own level of expertise. Some things will come very easily to you, others will not, and you will have to work hard to improve your performance. It is possible for you to spend months, even years, perfecting one particular skill, leaving other interests totally dormant. Your learning and expertise will move in cycles. This month you may be interested in gems, run several experiments, and have a great number of successes to make you confident to move into another area. Maybe you will come back to the gems a few months from now, a year from now, or maybe even longer than that. It is said we all travel around the Medicine Wheel, sometimes learning, sometimes teaching, other times lying dormant for introspection.

When individuals become familiar with your "Witchy" side, they may ask you to assist them. Perhaps they have trouble sleeping, can't get rid of a headache, are having trouble with an errant son or daughter, etc. There is nothing wrong with helping these people as long as you keep some important principles in mind.

First, you are operating under the definition of grey magick (simply for lack of a better term). This is doing a service or using your skills for another person, at their request. Always remember to ask the person's permission to perform any magick or use your skills for them. There are times when they will ask for help outright and you won't have to do this, but more often than not, people find it difficult to ask you for help because they don't really want to admit that you may be able to do something about it.

What I usually say is,"I would like to help you, but I need your permission first." Then I explain exactly what I think will help them, such as an empowered gem, a binding rune, a bag of herbs, etc.

For instance, a acquaintance of mine was having troubles with her mother, who had abandoned her when she was small, and returned to ask the girl if she could represent her as the Mother of the Bride at the girl's wedding. The young woman was horrified because naturally she wanted the woman who had raised her to fill that place by her side. She was terrified of the scene that would ensue when she told her birth mother that she did not want her to represent herself in that manner at the wedding. I offered the girl a piece of empowered rose quartz and told her to keep it with her whenever she was near the birth mother, even if she was only having a phone conversation with her.

Now, before I continue this story, I'd like to interject that I personally did not work any magick for the young woman. I gave her a tool and told her what to do with it. Magick has the best chance of success where the strongest emotion lies.

All differences were absolved and the wedding was a huge success; however, there was one problem. The birth mother was struck by a medical difficulty and had to enter the hospital for a short time right over the week of the wedding. The young lady was worried that perhaps, in some way, the rose quartz or what I had told her was at the bottom of the medical problem. I assured her that rose quartz loving feelings of compromise would never strike anyone ill. As she walked away, though, I wondered how deep-seated her emotions may have been at the time of the crisis.

Work magick that encourages the other person's participation, if at all possible: the act of carrying a gem, the use of positive affirmations, etc. If you give a gift for healing purposes, either mental or physical, be sure to tell that person exactly what it is for and how they should use it. You must be specific on every point they may question you on. This helps them participate in an educated manner in their own healing process.

Above all, however, you should closely scrutinize their mental health when sharing your knowledge. This is something I did not do then, but do now. Take the time to study them closely while they are speaking to you. You may be hearing one thing, but they may feel in an entirely different manner. I did not take into consideration this young woman's strong feelings on the subject of being abandoned, simply because I had never experienced it myself. When things are closer to home you think along those lines; when they are far from your life pattern, you must be more observant.

Never tell anyone that you can definitely "fix" a problem. Instead, explain that you may be able to help. You are not perfect, and because of numerous variables you may encounter a failure. If you have insisted you could solve the problem, and fail, you not only lose face for yourself, but for your religion as well. There are times when you will definitely fail because the person you are assisting doesn't really want help. They want attention and being healed will cause a lack of attention directed toward themselves.

Never set yourself up as a replacement for proper medical care. Always suggest that they see a physician, or politely ask if they have consulted one. Never tell them to stop taking a prescribed medication. Instead, if it is obvious that the medication is incorrect or even if there is some doubt in a recommended surgery, encourage them to seek a second opinion. The idea is not to get them to fear medical technology but to use it to the fullest.

Remember that most difficulties, especially sicknesses, begin in the mind of the individual. The word "dis-ease" is a perfect example of this. When a person comes to me with an illness or problem, we always talk about it in depth, including any psychological angles that have developed either prior to or at the onset of the sickness. Many medical problems are brought on by stress of one type or another. Remove the stress, and you have a good chance of removing the medical problem. Many times stress has blocked a chakra center in the body and once this block is removed, the illness will pass.

Your healing should always work in conjunction with that of a medical professional, if one has been sought. Never talk down the doctor because if you chip at his reputation or decision, you are also chipping at the patient's judgment in choosing that physician or practice.

Do not be offended if individuals seek you out when they are only in trouble or sick, and don't bother with you any other time. These are the proverbial fair-weather friends; it is inclement circumstances that bring them to your doorstep. An important lesson to learn is that you do not own people, nor is it your job to control their thinking processes. If they come to you, be thankful that you have been given the opportunity to assist them.

People pass in and out of our lives like the ebb and flow of the tides. They cannot make things stand still, although they may try. Learn to change with the times and the emotions of others. Honor these tides of life instead of seeking to harness them.

Most of your magickal endeavors for other people will come in the form of healing, protection and love. There will be times, but less frequently, when you will help them in their personal prosperity. Why less? Because most people do not like to admit that they have money problems.

Never forget that there are times when you will not need magick at all. Instead, you should become a good listener. Witches should be the best listeners ever produced by the Universe. From listening to things both deafening and those unheard, you will learn. People will think you are the greatest person in the world if you simply learn to keep your mouth shut and your ears open. They will walk away from you thinking you are a very special person indeed!

Don't overlook mundane help, either. A gift of food, clothing or money can be helpful, too. These are just as magickal in nature as casting a spell or performing a ritual.

Healing Yourself

Of course you should take preventative measures with your health; keep yourself fit, eat right, don't go out in the rain without your overshoes, etc. But we do get sick, and when we do, our self-confidence goes right down the tubes while our fever rises. I personally think that healing oneself of sickness is the hardest of all the skills to master. But it can be done!

I tried many methods of self-healing when I had a medical problem — and failed miserably with every one — until I came up with the vacuum concept that was mentioned earlier in this book in the chapter on meditation. I stumbled across the floating globe concept by accident when reading an article somewhere. I thought, however, that the technique did not make sense because the referenced globe did not seem to be disposed of properly; it still left negative energy hanging around "out there." So, I came up with the vacuum concept with the subsequent lowering into the ground.

The next time I had a medical problem, I used this technique and it worked! My sniffles were gone in a matter of minutes. I tried it again when I strained my hand (a writer with a strained hand cannot exist happily!), and within fifteen minutes, the symptoms were gone.

If you are extremely ill — with the flu, for example — keep up the process and continue to take any prescribed medication. You will heal faster.

Learn to understand your body signals. You know what it feels like when a headache is "just starting" or you feel the "flu coming on." Immediately use the vacuum meditation, even if you have to go to the rest room at work to do it.

If you have a particular herbal mixture that helps to heal specific ailments that you have now and then, use them as soon as possible. I used to have terrible bouts with bronchitis and pneumonia. My father, who is really into herbs, gave me the following recipe:

> 1 oz. tomato juice
> ⅛ tsp of cayenne pepper
> ¼ tsp of black pepper

Mix together, and take this for three days each morning and drink the remainder of the tomato juice in the one-serving container.

I can honestly tell you that I have not had a serious cold or infection since I have taken this remedy when I had a respiratory infection, and I have shared it with numerous people who indicate the same. But I have to remember to take it! It is great not to have to take those cold medicines that leave you groggy or nervous. However, as with all home remedies, consult a physician first since there is no guarantee they will work for you.

The Power Pouch

The Power pouch is much like the Shaman's Medicine bag. The pouch should be hand sewn from leather or soft cloth. The color depends on the nature and purpose of the bag. The bag itself can contain anything — herbs, gems, crystals, feathers, pieces of inscribed paper, etc. Each item should be empowered before it is put into the bag, and then the entire bag should be empowered through ritual if possible. The bag can be a one-time affair or something to be used often. They can be as ornate in design as you please, or plain.

The Medicine Shield

Although the Medicine shield is most often attributed to the Native Americans, Witches can use them, too. The act of making a shield is just as important as using the finished product.

Shields are made to eliminate the destructive influences in your life and turn away evil and difficulty. A shield is basically the culmination of a protective act of purpose. They are made for victory, courage, protection, psychism, growth and healing. The shield eventually takes on its own identity; some are male, female, or balanced between the two. It acts as a mirror between yourself and the world around you, both physical and in other dimensions.

The shield does not have to look like the ones in the old cowboy and Indian movies. It can take any magickal shape, although circular ones are the most common today. It can also be made out of anything, including paper. They have two parts: the under-shield with special protective or magickal significance, and the outer covering. They, too, can be as elaborate or plain as you desire. Shields must be awakened or empowered. This should be done in a special ritual composed by yourself.

Healing Another

The laying on of hands procedure is an acceptable one in many religious structures. The trick is to keep yourself from getting sick!

There are definite guidelines for healing other people. They have to want to get better, they must believe in themselves, and they must believe in you. They should also have some type of belief in what holds the world together, something that makes it possible for them to get well, such as God, the Goddess, the Universe, The All, Skyfather . . . something.

An outline for diagnosis and treatment follows. Be sure that before attempting any healing for a physical or mental ailment that you perform the first two steps.

1. Have the patient draw on a piece of paper exactly where they are having a difficulty on their body.

2. Ask the following questions:

    Have you seen a physician?

    If so, what was the diagnosis?

    Have you had a second opinion?

    Are you taking any drugs or medication?

    Do you drink or smoke?

    Do you have a chronic condition?

    What is the history of your family disorders?

    Are you pregnant?

    What are your sleep patterns?

    Are you under a lot of stress?

3. Do a physical examination.

4. Explain the healing process to the individual.

5. Cast the magick circle.

6. Invoke the Goddess.

7. Perform the healing process.

8. Thank the deities you have called.

9. Close the circle.

The Laying On of Hands

Have the patient sit or lie comfortably. Cast a magick circle in the manner that you think will be desirable to the patient. For example, if they are jumpy, do it in your mind; if they like the mystery, cast a full circle complete with incense and water, etc. Open your chakra centers and begin to build your power through chanting, singing, or simply thinking quietly. Everyone has their own style.

Step 1: Lay your hands on the patient and check their chakra centers. Determine what is blocked or too open. If there is a disease, you will remove it with your left hand, and shoot it out your right hand at the vacuum globe.

Step 2: Take your hands off the patient and shake off any excess negative energy. Step back if it is necessary for you to get out of any residue.

Step 3: Put your right hand on the affected area and raise your own power from your center, out through your hand, and into the person. Watch as this power works entirely through the person's body. As you do this, imagine the Golden Light of the God and Goddess surging down from the heavens and instilling the person with energy. When you are finished, turn off the globe and ground yourself. Shake out any excess energy and put your hands under cold running water.

The second step of this process is the most important. If you don't do this, you will likely become ill yourself. I cannot begin to count the times I was successful in healing my children, only to find myself ill the next day. I could not fathom what I was doing wrong; those guys on television just laid their hands on people, and in ten seconds, "Praise the Whatever!" (Hey, these are the things solitaries run into!) I knew the television stuff was just crap, but come on, faith healing does exist, the least they could do is fake it properly!

I finally figured out that I was drawing the negativity into myself and not disposing of it properly. When I got that perfected, I stopped getting sick.

Absent Healing

This procedure is used when you cannot, for some reason, be with the person who is ill. Many methods can be employed. Candle magick, poppets, the Tarot and runes are just a few suggestions. You can also visit the person in their dreams and do the vacuum meditation in the astral. Again, you should have the person's permission before using any of these magickal practices. Keep an accurate record of the healings you perform so that you can duplicate them as the need arises.

Summary

This chapter has covered many vital magickal applications. You will find gems and herbs extremely useful in many situations. Combine them with sympathetic magick and holiday rituals. The possibilities for their use are almost limitless. Herbs and gems are considered practical magick — that which comes from the Earth Mother. It is the use of the elements of the Universe. Use it wisely.

Suggested Reading List

Dr. John R. Christopher, *School of Natural Healing*. Christopher Publications.

Scott Cunningham, *The Complete Book of Incense, Oils and Brews*. Llewellyn Publications.

Scott Cunningham, *Encyclopedia of Crystal, Gem and Metal Magick*. Llewellyn Publications.

Scott Cunningham, *Magickal Herbalism*. Llewellyn Publications.

Scott Cunningham, *The Magic in Food: Legends, Lore & Spellwork*. Llewellyn Publications.

John Lust, *The Herb Book*. Bantam Books.

Medicine Hawk and Grey Cat, *American Indian Ceremonies*. Inner Light Publications.

Dorothee L. Mella, *Stone Power*. Warner Books.

Wally and Jenny Richardson, *Spiritual Value of Gem Stones*. DeVores & Company.

Michael G. Smith, *Crystal Power*. Llewellyn Publications.

Michael Tierra, C.A., N.D., *The Way of Herbs*. Pocket Books.

Section Four

Challenging Shadows

Telepathy, Psychometry and Mind Power

Not Just for Psychics!

How many times have you gazed at another person, desperately wishing that you could read the thoughts bouncing to and fro behind that passive face? How many times have you sat quietly alone, wondering if another person was thinking of you?

"Tuning" into people's thoughts is not as difficult as everyone has led you to believe! The main requirements for this feat are patience and perseverance — that's all. You don't have to have suffered a severe blow to the head, been struck by lightening, or been a victim of an extra-terrestrial spaceship ride. Telepathy is not just for psychics; don't let them kid you.

First, you already know that thoughts are energy vibrations. You also know that they are detectable through scientific experimentation and equipment. Therefore, there is no sound reason for you to hold a mental block on your capabilities as either a sender or receiver of thoughts. You can be just as calibrated as any scientific tool; you only have to practice!

"Telepathy" is the process of tuning into the thoughts and emotions of another individual. The telepathic process can be broken into assimilation of data, both physical and mental. To enhance your abilities, you should become aware of any situation or process that can aid you in understanding the human individual.

Why? Because being of a telepathic nature is not just hearing what the other person is thinking, like dialing up a radio show or switching channels on the television. Nor is it simply experiencing pictures that prance before your inner eye. It is the ability to gain a total composite of the thoughts and feelings of another person by using whatever tools are available to you, such as your physical senses. Truthfully, it is a rare individual indeed who can actually "hear" with an inner ear exactly what another person is thinking in the verbal language that you normally use for communication purposes.

Most often you will pick up the vibrational patterns of that person, such as general mood, emotional changes, and health. Being telepathic is to be sensitive to these energy vibrations and their fluctuations, whether they are emitted by people, plants, animals or astral entities. It is also the art of attuning to the physical actions of others.

Body Language and Telepathy

The discovery in the sixties and seventies that non-verbal communication can provide a reliable assessment of human thought patterns led to countless books and discussions on the subject. It was the "in" thing, and it was "hot." Because of the time period in which these studies were conducted and implemented (flower power, peace demonstrations, and psychedelic advertising), the topic of body language was generally considered a fad that finally wore itself out as cocktail conversation or a method of priming a victim for a one night sexual encounter. With the progress of time it was promptly dropped from popular notice, along the the path of "What's your sign?"

You may not know it, but your subconscious has been studying the art of interpreting body language ever since you were born into this lifetime. Our subconscious already monitors the physical gestures of other humans and feeds them into our unconscious assessment process. Often, our conscious mind is so busy evaluating what a person is saying, along with obvious facial expressions, that we tend to ignore what our own subconscious is trying to tell us. Sometimes we may have sensed a feeling of unease when the conscious data was in direct conflict with the information simultaneously supplied by the unconscious.

Understanding and learning to evaluate body language is valuable to the Witch, as we are often placed in counseling situations. It is also the first step in sensitizing ourselves to the telepathic information readily available to us.

Reading Facial Expressions

Expressions of anger, astonishment and happiness are the most obvious indicators of a person's internal thought processes. However, they are not entirely reliable. Remember, theatrical mimicking of appropriate expressions is used more than even we ourselves would care to admit.

For example, your best friend has confided to you a deep secret and you have given your word that you will not repeat it. Several days later, you are approached by a mutual acquaintance who questions you closely about your best friend. You honor your vow by feigning a variety of emotions, using contrived facial expressions to make your answers appear believable. I'm not suggesting that you have lied about the subject, but merely danced around with words to protect someone you care about. Therefore, facial expressions, although the most obvious body language, are not necessarily reliable.

Look more at skin and eye coloration change. The draining or heightening of color in the face or neck can indicate emotions or thought patterns. Eyes are definitely windows to the proverbial soul. Almost all eye colors change tint when the body is undergoing strong emotions, whether they be anger, sympathy, grief — even when a person is lying! You must be very observant to catch these coloration changes, and they most often happen with severe emotions. These changes are more noticable in individuals with lighter-colored eyes than in those with darker hues. However, I have watched distinct color changes in brown-eyed people undergoing great emotional stress.

For example, very blue eyes may pale during certain emotional circumstances, or they may get extremely vibrant or turn more to a green color. Brown eyes can pale in color, become extremely dark (almost black), or turn tawny gold or hazel.

Eye direction can be another indicator. When people lie, they tend to look in the same direction each time they prevaricate, but it is not the same for every person. Some may look to the left, some to the right, and some straight ahead. People also look in specific directions when formulating concrete physical recall, and a different direction for abstract recall, so don't jump quickly to conclusions on the veracity of their statements on this point alone.

Granted, none of the above does much good if you are dealing with a stranger. (Except for one case, which I'll get to in a minute.) Eye color and directional gazes can be studied over a period of time. Your first exercise will be to view five people for three weeks, watching facial expressions, eye color and direction during different situations.

There is one particular eye characterization that is difficult to explain, but seems to remain the same in individuals who are either mentally unbalanced or of a criminal nature. I first noticed the phenomenon with someone I knew very well. The eye appears to have an unusually thick dark ring around the iris, while the inner portion of the iris is much lighter in color. The eyes are usually held unnaturally open, hence the term wide-eyed. But it is not just things you can see physically; there is a cold, unhealthy feeling that seeps over you when you look straight into their eyes.

The next time I noticed this odd characteristic was at a grocery store. There was a young man standing outside, and I passed close enough to get a good look at his face. I turned to my husband and said, "That guy has crazy eyes. I'm telling you, he's bad business."

My husband didn't say too much and we drove on. That night as we were watching the late news on television, guess who had just been caught for robbing a different store? You got it. The man I had seen that very day!

Since then I have watched several documentaries on criminals just to examine their facial expressions and eye coloration. Many of those interviewed did have "crazy-eye." Although I've seen this trait more in men, on occasion I have met women who carry this same "look."

Body Positions and Gestures

Body positions and hand gestures are definitely a more reliable indicator of what a person is thinking and feeling, even strangers. Personal movements are excellent barometers for checking or enhancing your own mental presentation of yourself.

For example, a client comes to you for a Tarot reading. If this is his first time, he may seat himself across from you, fold his arms over his chest, cross his legs and position his body away from you, towards the nearest exit. You, in turn, cross your ankles.

Both you and the client are taking defensive positions against each other. His signal by not only "locking up" his body but leaning toward the door, indicates he is not going to be initially receptive to what you have to say. Your crossed ankle response is a subconscious indicator that you sense his unease. Men also show their openness of mind by unbuttoning their suit coats, sweater, or vest. If the top layer of clothing (such as a suit coat) remains buttoned in a comfortably heated environment, you have a slight problem on your hands.

Let's get back to the client. Realizing that he is on the defensive, you should unlock your ankles and lean slightly forward while he is speaking, but not so far as to invade his personal space. Ask him leading questions and give him plenty of time to elaborate. To show that you are interested in what he is saying, assume the "thinker" position, placing your fingers near your temple or under your chin.

My husband muses (not always happily) that people tell me just about everything. Believe me, I don't know their deepest, darkest secrets, but simply listening to what they are saying and asking leading questions often opens various flood-gates of information. Learning to keep your mouth shut often pays off. Anyone, whether they be on the job, at a party, or interested in your magickal work, will walk away from you thinking you are the next best thing to sliced bread if you learn to zip your lip.

A female client may show her defensiveness by crossing her arms across her chest, or showing an obvious unwillingness to put her purse down out of sight. If she clutches it close to her chest or fiddles with it on her lap, you are in for a tough read. If either sex keeps their hands predominately in their pockets, whether it be pants, skirt, sweater, blazer, suit coat, or regular coat (baring it is not 50 degrees below zero in the room) they are holding many secrets.

By now, the client should be using their hands in symphony with their words. As you do a reading, watch their reactions carefully. If they lean their elbows on the table and cup their hands in front of their mouth, they may be hiding something from you. If a person plays with their glasses by cleaning them, taking them off and rubbing the bridge of their nose, etc., they may be vying for time before they answer a direct question.

A pen in the mouth is another indication that they are not ready to speak. If the client is playing repeatedly with an ear or touching your arm while you are speaking, they may wish to interrupt you. Feet on the table or steepling fingers is a sign that the individual feels totally in control of the situation, and may be playing you for all the situation is worth.

Likewise, if the feet are propped up on a desk or chair, they may feel they are totally at ease, yet controlling in a non-threatening manner. Adjusting clothing and rapid eye blinking is a sign of definite nervousness and possibly a pack of lies.

Hand rubbing is a gesture of expectancy, while wringing or tightly clenched hands indicate nervousness or a total blocking of what you are saying to them. If these things begin to happen, take a moment and regroup your own thoughts. Where is the conversation heading?

Hands that drift are another sign of discomfort. Know any key or change in the pocket jinglers? I wouldn't be surprised if they were preoccupied with the dollar.

Other significant gestures are how a person may walk or stand. Poor posture indicates low self-esteem or that something unfortunate has happened to that person, especially if the eyes are down and unfocused. Feet apart in the standing position shows self-confidence and strength — the ability to hold their ground.

Of course, all these gestures may have unrelated causes. For instance, if a person has poor dental work or warts on their hands, they may try to cover what they are sure will be a distraction to you or an embarrassment to them. Feet could be propped up because they are prone to swelling of the ankles, or the woman may be clutching her purse because she has just made a fantastic business deal and is carrying a $50,000 check!

How can you tell the difference? Well, sometimes you just can't, but a good indication is the repetition of gestures in a given time period.

As an example, remember our client? By now you have placed him totally at ease. His suit coat is open, both feet are planted firmly on the floor and he is leaning toward you. His pupils are dilated, indicating a sense of intense interest (providing you are seated in an adequately lighted room). His arms are open; one on the table, one resting lightly in his lap.

Suddenly, he rubs his eye! Now what can that mean? You know you haven't said anything unusual in the conversation; in fact, you have been listening and his thoughts are clear and focused. The modulation in his voice has not changed. Therefore, the hand to eye movement is not significant, unless it is repeated and accompanied by further gestures.

Some gestures will be apparent to you immediately; others you may have to practice to notice. As with all skills, the one of observation must be practiced. It is also lots of fun to monitor your own gestures as well. You will soon become a cultured communicator!

Linking Telepathic Skills and Body Language

Guess you have been wondering what all this stuff about body language has to do with telepathy or even magick, huh? First, you are starting to program your mind to accept new data in an unusual way. You are also teaching yourself to be more physically observant of people and things around you.

Becoming skilled at monitoring body language links subconscious messages to conscious ones, removing that block that "crosses" your mental signals. You will know when you have mastered it because as you look into another person's eyes, you have the odd feeling of being able to see right through them and deep into their spirit. This is an astounding experience, and even though they may not consciously signal that you have made contact, their subconscious will register the knowledge.

Understanding body language also gives you more confidence when you attempt to use your telepathic abilities. One of our greatest difficulties in using mind-reading skills is our own self-doubt and fear that we will interpret something totally incorrectly, making a major blunder. Often the insights on an individual's behavior are almost astounding, but when they verbally deny what you are saying, doubt enters your mind and you lose confidence in your own capabilities. They smoke screen you so well that you don't even realize your first assumptions were correct.

Don't be worried about sensing "chronic" problems that are not verbally verified. I can think of several cases where for weeks I would receive the exact same impressions when talking to a person. I may feel that they are very tired, and tell them so. They may say, "You said that the last time we spoke!" trying to give you the impression that you are wrong and you have not thought carefully about what you are saying to them. I usually say, "The feeling persists, and I bet you have not been sleeping well!" They may not answer, but their body language will tell you if you are correct or not.

In another case, for months whenever I met a certain person I would instinctively ask, "What's wrong?" This person got very irritated with me and asked me to stop making this remark every time we met. Much later I found out that she was an alcoholic and not in the mood to talk about such a subject with an acquaintance — who could blame her?

Belief in your skills is vitally necessary for them to grow stronger and more precise as you continue to use them. Granted, you will not always be correct, but you will be closer to the truth more often than not.

Empathy

Empathetic sensations are extremely common among those people practicing various forms of higher consciousness. Empathy is telepathy in a less refined form. To be an empath is to experience the same emotions as the person who is near you or speaking to you. This does not come from the full assessment of body language and facial expressions. You are not exactly aware of what a person is thinking, but you are very much aware of what they are feeling. Practice raising your own energy and meditation techniques to open the channels for empathetic exchange.

Empathetic feelings and sensations are sneaky. Have you ever stood beside a total stranger and experienced a wave of despondency when you are aware that everything in your life is perking along just fine? Often, these feelings stealthily integrate themselves into your own mental communication system so silently that you may mentally or physically react as if they are your own!

"Shields up!" should be your first response in such a situation. Assessing the body language of those around you is the second step. Empathy is a wonderful experience and a good indicator of what another person is feeling. However, empathetic experiences should be controlled to protect your own mental health.

For example, if you were sick with the flu and your friend Suzanne has just experienced a devastating crisis in her marriage, it isn't going to do you any good to let her feelings wash over your mental message system. Remember, you don't have to be standing beside your friend to experience her pain. She could be in Vermont or Japan, frantically telling you all the gory details via the phone. The distance will not lessen the empathetic process.

An emergency can be devastating for both the empath and the victim if the empath does not learn to block out the feelings of fear and helplessness. Often victim and empath will feed off each other in a crisis situation if the empath has not immediately shielded him or herself.

The first type of mental communication you experience will most likely be that of empathy — simply because feelings vibrate at a faster and stronger rate than thought-words. Also, we do not always formulate our thoughts into words. We often think in pictures, feelings and sometimes, words.

Emotions set off physical reactions and chemistry changes in our bodies. Sometimes these indicators are subconscious, whereas a sentence such as, "Are you going to eat toast for breakfast this morning?" would not cause the same type of energy fluctuation within or without the body.

Voice and Tone Inflection

Although it seems obvious, voice tone and inflection are important when assessing communication with others. Often we are so busy contemplating what we want to say next that we fail to hear the tonal quality of others. You don't need a musician's ear to detect emotional cadences or voice patterns. You do need to quiet your own inner discourse to hear properly.

Individuals who work a great deal on the telephone develop an "ear" for emotion through voice quickly because they deal with numerous "unseen" individuals and therefore become acute in picking up slight inflections and tonal quality. To enhance your own abilities, trying turning off the picture of your television set and listening to the sound of the actresses and actors. Done over a period of a few weeks at fifteen minutes at a time, you will be surprised what you will learn to pick up.

Accents can assist you in determining an individual's place of origin or where they have spent a great deal of time. Although this is considered an obvious trait, we tend to disregard it. But by listening closely, you can get a general idea of a person's education, family background, financial stability and the society they are most comfortable operating in. Although not entirely accurate, it may answer questions when you observe unusual behavior. You should also try mimicking various accents as individuals will feel more comfortable if your inflection matches theirs.

Thought Transference

Telepathy is normally considered thought transference. By now, you know that this is not entirely true. Thought transference happens all the time; you just are now aware of it. It is never a coincidence. The more receptive you become to your environment and human nature in general, the more proof you will have of your own telepathic abilities.

There are two general types of transference; sending and receiving. Some of us seem to be naturally better at one or the other. Your own abilities will increase as you practice both aspects of sending and receiving data and emotions. Do not give up if one comes more easily to you than the other.

The basic rule in thought transference is not to concentrate — meaning do not strain to achieve your goal. Instead, calm yourself, open your chakra centers and imagine you have plugged into the switchboard of the collective unconscious. Focus an image, emotion, or message for sending purposes. To receive, make note of the first thing that comes into your mind, not the logical process that occurs after the thought.

A Witch's first impression of an individual is usually accurate. Why? Because we allow ourselves to open and be washed by the essence of the individual we are meeting. We are "scan lining" them, so to speak. What ever we pick up first is 85% accurate, give or take previous neurological programming that may get in the way of our scanning faculties. Sometimes we say, "All Christians are the same," or, "I never met a Karen I liked," etc. These blockages and prejudices must be realized and passed over when scan lining.

·☽ ☾·

You should practice using all the information that has been given to you thus far. Keep accurate records in your notebook. When running experiments, remember that the human mind absorbs material and works at its peak in ten-minute bursts. We tend to peak in the first and last three minutes of each burst. This is one reason why a lengthy ritual can slice off a large portion of productive energy (referred to as the cone of power). Although good results can be obtained, optimum success most likely will not materialize with everyone in the group.

Working with a Partner

To be realistic, you can only do so much experimenting with telepathy on your own before you will need to select a partner to run such tests with. Experimentation with another person is basically a support mechanism to prove to yourself that you are capable of both sending and receiving thoughts and emotions.

Finding someone you can trust is vitally important. I have been in a situation where as much as I wanted to believe my partner was telling me the truth, I doubted it because their nature in other areas of their life was one of deceit. Even their body language screamed that there was a problem. Therefore, after several months of experimentation I took all the results I had tallied by that time and scrapped them. This was a devastating experience, but a lesson well-learned. Later I ran the experiments with a new partner and tallied many of the same results; however, I could not comfortably use any statistics from the first experiments to even match them against.

When you are working with another person in any magickal endeavor, remember that everyone's vibrational rate is different. For example, perhaps you and Harry have been working for months on sending numbers, patterns, or colors to one another and you have both tallied a high number of hits. This does not mean that you will be able to have equal success with Charlene. You will, however, begin to notice coincidences and energy transference with other people, including Charlene, that you did not recognize before.

Don't be discouraged if you think you are not getting through to someone. It is necessary to assess the physical signs both of yourself and the other person you are trying to contact. Perhaps they are not allowing their subconscious to send the appropriate signals to their conscious mind, or maybe they are well aware of the messages but literally fear saying anything because they think it is wrong, bad, or downright crazy!

Do not limit your telepathic abilities to humans. Plant and animal contact is enjoyable and enlightening. I suggest laying your hands on a plant while communing with its spirit, but I do not recommend the laying on of hands when working with animals. Animals tend to misunderstand your physical gestures due to either their training or their wildness.

Ethics and Mind Reading

Is the practice of telepathy ethical? Telepathy, in itself, is a natural occurrence. We send and receive messages all the time without our conscious mind being aware of it. The question of ethics should be considered only if you are using the skill to "push" an individual to do something that he or she would not normally think of doing, or if you are using the information you gather in a harmful or negative manner. Always keep in mind that you are fully responsible for your own actions and reactions. Because you are human, though, there are going to be times when you are simply going to say, "Cut and be damned." We will study such scenarios and what can happen later on in this book.

Is It Possible to Make Things Happen with Your Mind?

This is what magick is all about — making things happen with your mind. Telepathy and empathy are important skills in your Craft training. In the future you will need them.

Psychometry

The ability to pick up an object and receive emotional or visual perceptions of the owner of that object, or thought forms that have attached themselves to it, is called psychometry. It is a heightened state of telepathic receptivity that can provide concentrated information on a particular person, place, or thing, and any emotional attachment to that object. Psychometry comes in handy in LDR's, where the querent is not present.

Even if you do not sense the residual energy consciously on the objects you are holding, remember that you are receiving information subconsciously. Don't fret if you do not see pictures or a video tape in your mind about the person or event attached to that object, or feel emotions that are surely connected with it.

Remember, too, that you have spent a great deal of your life blocking out this information, so don't be surprised that your off/on switch is rusty or stuck for a bit. As with your other skills, practice brings you closer to perfection.

Considerations

The older an object, the more astral impressions or vibrations it may contain. Take a photograph as an example. If the picture was taken last week, you could possibly receive the following impressions:

> The factory where the film was made.
> The store where it was sold or developed.
> The person who took the picture.

The person who handled that photo last.

The individual in the picture.

And the list could go on.

By taking this example further, think about a picture that was taken 75 years ago. What type of list would you have then? Think about it.

More critical experiences involving objects may overshadow others. For example, perhaps the last owner of a crystal ball had a life-altering vision while meditating with it. Then you, and most others who touch it, would first glimpse that experience before any other mundane occurrences involving that crystal ball, such as the last time it was packed away.

Another impression that may surface first is one where the situations and events surrounding the object have been repetitive in nature. If every time a locket was passed from mother to daughter was on the day of her wedding, then the first impressions may be of sadness, fear, excitement, trepidation, etc. These types of objects are said to be "haunted" in nature because even the most non-sensitive persons could be thrown into a state of unhappiness or melancholy when touching the object.

Worse, if the case history of the object is known by the current owner (such as a supposed curse on the piece), then the owner may experience the same physical loss or situation because they expect it to happen! They subconsciously believe in the curse; therefore, they will it to happen.

Negative energy patterns can be cleansed from various pieces by using the techniques in our cleansing and consecration lesson, or by the power of the mind if those required items are not handy. In this case, you would will the energy to leave the object and sink to the ground where Earth Mother will neutralize it.

If you do a great deal of networking through the mails, try to ascertain the "mood" or any other information that may be contained in a letter before you open it.

You could also ask a friend to gather various objects from their family. These objects, including their history, should be familiar to your friend. Place the object in your left hand and try to pick up any information either about the object or about the owner. Say the first thing that comes into your head. Discuss the results with your friend. Try not looking at the objects at times when you hold them, and try holding them in different hands or placing them over your third eye. Which method gives you the best impression?

A third exercise is to ask a friend to give you photographs of people and places they know. Hold the photographs in your hand and try to determine where they were taken, how old they are and the emotions of the people at the time. Keep a record of your impressions and discuss them with your friend.

Psychometry is not just a receptive activity. You can charge an item with a specific memory or function, much like a talisman or charm. Auto-suggestions can be placed in an object's astral sphere by yourself to ensure implantation on another individual's mind.

For example, if you wish to give a friend power and energy, hold a crystal to your third eye and concentrate on that emotion. If you give a loved one a piece of jewelry, fill it with your unconditional love. To keep someone from touching a favorite possession of yours, place a mental "do not touch" sign on it, or imagine that it is too hot to touch.

Mind Power

In this chapter we have discussed using the conscious and unconscious mind in a variety of methods. But how powerful is it, really? Can it can create an entire illusion in which to live, or is the illusion the reality?

If you have faithfully studied all the chapters preceding this one, you are realizing that the world and its reality are no longer what they were when you began. The parameters are no longer solid; past limitations no longer apply. There are no speed zones, either, but there are a few bumps along the way!

You are different from most people. You understand that you are responsible for your own actions, and you can control your own life. Perhaps you are not happy with everything, but at least you understand that you are not drifting aimlessly in a sea of humanity. You know that if you are diligent your efforts will be rewarded.

Perhaps you sometimes hesitate to use your skills, wrapped up in personal arguments of ethics, or you may think that you would like to do something the hard way on purpose — without the use of magickal expertise. You may feel that you are cheating if you use magick, or are taking the easy way out. Psychic skills are an inherent part of our human nature. What is truly unnatural is to stifle them or to allow another to squash them for us. There is plenty for everyone in this Universe; you will not be taking from someone to achieve your goals.

The most dangerous of enemies to many magickal people then, from Druids to Witches to Ceremonial Magicians, are not people, but thought forms. In most cases, we have manufactured our own foes. Consider this small list as our worst, most deadly enemies:

Doubt

Low self-esteem

Inflated ego

Intolerance (not so much of other faiths, but those individuals who practice within our own ranks)

Procrastination

Greed

Jealousy

The list goes on, but you get the point. Our minds have the capability of digging us into a hole or putting us on top of the world. The choice is always ours.

We also wonder, why, if our "powers" are so great, we are not experiencing a better harvest in this life time. Or worse, we fear our own power by worrying that we have inadvertently caused harm to either ourselves or someone that we love by "wishing" and not considering the basis for our desires and the results that may occur.

There are many cautions when working with a magickal system, enough to deter even the most willing student at some point in their practice. This is a natural reaction; temper it with this thought: I believe that the Universe contains and is built on a Grand Plan, made up of more details and connections than we can possibly imagine. If you think you are out there sitting on a limb alone, you are not. The magickal problems you wrestle with have been put to the mat by many before you, from the priests/esses of Atlantis to the Druids, the Knights of Templar, The Order of the Red Garter, The Order of the Golden Dawn, Robert Cochran, The Frosts, and even, I am sure, Raymond Buckland. Some have tried and failed, others have succeeded and won.

I also believe that there are breakwaters provided for us by the Grand Plan, if we choose to heed them, and if we use them when needed. Magick can not be rushed, it should be savored. It should also be fun! If you become too serious, you are surely heading for disaster and will miss the knowledge of the lighter things of this incarnation.

Increasing your mental abilities can be done through education and practice — two rather dull words. Here are some fun things you can do to increase your mental powers.

Focus

Mind power works if you can focus properly. We've talked a great deal about pulling off this feat, but we've not really ripped it apart. Just exactly what is the best way to focus? Do you just stare at the person or object and hope you are getting it right?

No. To focus, imagine that there are two perfect circles of energy, one on each side of the object or person. Take your index fingers and hold them out so that they are pointing directly in front of you. In the air, take your right finger and draw a circle clockwise. At the same time, let your left index finger draw a counterclockwise circle. This is what you should imagine when you begin to focus — two circles moving in opposite directions.

Now, bring the circles together slowly, until one is on top of the other as you reach the middle of the object. Imagine you can hear the vibration of energy. When both circles come together, they will now move in unison in a clockwise direction over the object. It is now when you interject your thoughts to obtain what you desire.

Fixing Machinery without Your Hands

This is great practice and you don't have to be capable of taking the machine apart and putting it back together again. In fact, it is better if you don't know the details of how the machine is supposed to work — only that it works when you flip the button, turn the key, etc.

Let's say that the neighbor's car will not start. Stand or sit perfectly still. Close your eyes and imagine that all the parts of the engine that are supposed to work are in perfect condition. Put yourself in "tune" with the engine. Visualize it running and hear the sound that it will make (this is very important). Then, forget about it. The car will usually start — maybe not immediately, but you will have a high rate of success. This works with computers, printers, chain saws, lawn mowers, microwaves, etc. And yes, I have tried and succeeded with each of these. Practice this, and you will never have to sit in traffic behind a stalled vehicle, or in one!

Finding Your Personal Parking Space

Nobody likes to walk a mile from the parking lot to the store or mall. As you get into the car, envision where you wish to park. First row, second, etc. Visualize only the empty space. I usually choose a row and think of four or five spaces in that row. I very rarely don't get the space that I want.

Getting Money Fast

In their most recent book, *Spells and How They Work,* Janet and Stewart Fararr give us this little hint from a Romeny friend: say "Trinka-five" several times. Believe it or not, this works! I've tried it and my daughter has tried it. We both had plenty of money when we needed it.

Finding Lost Articles

Visualize the item that is lost. Surround it with golden light and attach a silver cord to it. Mentally draw the cord toward you until the object is in your hand. Forget about it. The object should show up in the next hour or so, but it could take much longer. Just forget about it. If it is supposed to come back to you, it will. If you feel you were not focusing properly, do it again at a later date.

One note here: gems and stones should never be considered lost. When you have outgrown them, they pass on to others who need them more. Never be unhappy over the loss of a crystal or other favorite gem. Know it has gone to where it is needed most.

Traffic Lights

No one likes to stop at traffic lights unless their child has unbuckled their seat belt or they desperately need to light a cigarette with a match. Here is a little rhyme to use before you get in the car or when you've just been stuck at the fifth red light and you have to be somewhere twenty lights away, ten minutes ago.

> *Count of one, this spell's begun*
> *Count of two, all traffic lights in tune*
> *Count of three, all lights stay green for me!*
> *One . . . two . . . three!*

Hit the steering wheel lightly three times with your open right hand and say:

> *So mote it be!*

Visualize green traffic lights all along your route, then drive and forget about it.

Getting Unstuck in the Snow or Mud

First, don't panic. Second, don't grind the engine. As you move from reverse to drive, gently rocking the car and easing on the gas pedal, imagine that four huge polar bears are tethered to the front of your car with a heavy silver cable for snow, or four mastodons for mud. See them pulling your vehicle to freedom.

You may heartily laugh at this one, but I have never gotten stuck in the snow when I was driving. I have also gone up steep highways in a Camaro, Aries, Hornet, and a clunky station wagon whose brand will remain nameless, in snow and ice while I merrily passed trucks, four-wheelers, tractor trailers and cars with chains!

Protecting Yourself at Blind Intersections

There are times when all of us hold our breath as we venture out of a blind intersection or while we are zipping down a highway that has crossroads without lights. When the intersection comes into view, imagine a force field wall that closes off all entrances and exits to the highway or road. As you pass through, keep the wall intact; when you have passed by, open the wall or visualize it away.

Using the Universal Telephone Line

Think of a person you wish to contact. You can imagine them picking up the phone to call you, or you can just say, "How are you doing? This is Sally. I haven't heard from you in a while and am wondering if you are okay."

Keep the message simple and think it over and over and over again. Make note of the time you made the contact and when that person actually does call or visit you. With enough practice, you will most likely hear from them within a 24-hour period.

Why 24 hours? First, you are not ordering them to call you. Rather it is a message of, "Hey, I am still on this plane. Give me a call." For instance, Sherry is my best friend. We have known each other for many years. We found a few years ago that we were so close, we could contact each other telepathically by accident, so we decided to try on purpose. Now we do it all the time.

Sometimes when I contact her, she doesn't call for a day or two, or sometimes three. Why is this? Did I fail? No. Sherry has two children, a home, a job and a husband, as well as various hobbies. Her thoughts are directed in many areas of her life and she may not always be receptive to my message, or she may be tired or involved in some project and not ready to call. In sending a telepathic message to Sherry I am not infringing on her free will, I am just letting her know I'm thinking of her.

Often she will call me and say, "Were your ears ringing yesterday?" or I will say, "It's about time you called me, I was just thinking about you!"

Getting People to Remember You

If you want a woman to remember you, focus directly at her and smile. Let your warmth of good intentions enter your mind. If you want a man to remember you, focus directly at him, but do not smile. Instead, tell him (in your mind of course) that you mean no harm, that you are not a threat; however, you do demand respect.

Remember that everyone has two personalities or more. Basically, the one you see and the one you don't. Individuals are multi-faceted, and you must keep that in mind especially when dealing with strangers.

When meeting a couple, concentrate on the member of your own sex first. Let him or her know that they have nothing to fear. If you are overly attentive to their partner, you are just asking for trouble.

Summary

From body language to mind power, you now have a whole new series of Craft tools to use to make your world a better and happier place. As with any other magickal endeavor, your ethical standards should always be observed. Snooping, eavesdropping, and gathering information for malicious purposes will only cause you harm in the end.

Mind power should be used by the Witch and never disregarded as too difficult to perform. We can make peace in our time possible, if we only apply our skills to their fullest potential. One person can make a difference; you just have to try.

Suggested Reading List

Melita Denning and Osborne Phillips, *The Development of Psychic Powers.*
    Llewellyn Publications.

Diane Mariechild, *Mother Wit.* The Crossing Press.

Michael Miller and Josephine Harper, *The Psychic Energy Workbook.* Aquarian
    Press.

Richard Bach, *Illusions.*

Mark Twain, "The Mysterious Stranger." (short story)

Astral Projection, Bi-location and Power Animals

This chapter is considered an intermediate one. It is assumed that you have already mastered creative visualization and practiced a satisfactory meditation process often.

·☾ ☽·

Astral projection has been scientifically categorized as an OBE (out of body experience). Astral projection is the practice of actually projecting your energy body away from your physical one. This "body of light" is connected to the physical body by a silver cord that does not detach until the death of the physical form.

An OBE most commonly occurs during the sleep cycle, but can happen during meditation. Daydreaming provides an additional vehicle for astral projection.

How Do You Know If You Have Experienced an OBE?

The following sensations can be credited to OBE's:

1. The sensation of floating above your body, seeing the actual physical form below you and either actually "seeing" or being aware of the silver cord. This usually occurs in that twilight time we associate between full wakefulness and the actual sleep cycle.

2. Experiencing a "whooshing" sensation as you awaken from sleep. Sights flash by swiftly as you resurface into the body.

3. The inability to move limbs — a type of temporary paralysis when you are barely awake. This passes quickly, but can produce a disconcerting type of inner hysteria if you are not expecting it.

4. An especially vivid dream where people, places and things appear larger than life or extremely colorful. Often you will be unfamiliar with both the places and the people involved.

OBE's are a natural but not always remembered occurrence. Everyone travels at some time in their life in the astral plane. However, people who ordinarily feel that they must be consciously in control of every aspect of their lives have difficulty going into an OBE state without the dream as a vehicle. This is not a terrible thing. It just means that they have to release their fears of not being in control.

Many psychiatrists and other therapeutic counselors now use the OBE in moving the individual toward total mental health. Those difficulties worked out in the OBE state tend to cut normal counseling time by months, sometimes even years. The counselor, by allowing the "higher self" of the individual to take over much of the process, is able to retain an uninvolved status, thereby becoming more effective in treating the client/patient.

Sleeping Like the Dead

Ever hear the expression "sleeping like the dead"? When one is in such a deep state that they can not be roused easily, or at all, they are most likely on an astral journey. Therefore, this statement is aptly used. The body is physically in the bed but the body of light, with the conscious mind contained in it, is on vacation. This is why it is so difficult to awaken an individual in this state. They are unconsciously quite comfortable with astral projection, and do not see the immediate need to return to consciousness just because you want them to.

Although I mentioned that this is not a lesson in theory, one should be introduced for your consideration. Those individuals that remain in a comatose state for any period of time may be purposefully there to work out specific Karmic structures in this physical lifetime. "Pulling the plug" then, would have even deeper impacts on the "puller" and the "pullee."

·☾ ☽·

There are three ways to approach astral projection and reap its benefits: the dream state, the meditation state, and bi-location (which includes the Watcher and body-double).

The Dream State

Before you go to sleep each night, program your mind by telling yourself that you will recall your astral travels. It may take two or three weeks before you are able to have very good recall, but don't rush it. The remembrances will come.

If it takes longer, try writing some affirmations each day to reinforce your night time message. Nightly meditation will also be of great assistance. Don't forget to keep that note pad and pen by the bed to record your travels.

The better your recall, the more control you will have over the experiences that occur in the dream state. Eventually, you can plan where you wish to go, what you wish to accomplish, and who you would like to meet.

The Meditation State

Experiencing astral projection in the state of meditation leaves you with more conscious control of the OBE. You can choose any body position you desire; however, more success may be achieved through the prone position (as this is what both your body and unconscious mind are used to when OBE's are accomplished in the dream state). However, if you feel you would be more comfortable sitting up, by all means, do it!

As mentioned earlier, you should have a good meditation system that you are familiar with. If you have difficulty with either the meditation or the ascent to astral travel, you may wish to purchase cassette tapes currently on the market that assist in this procedure, or are straight, soft music.

Everyone is capable of conscious astral travel, just as everyone is capable of performing magick. The only barrier erected is the individual's personal fear of the unknown and the false assumption that they will not be in control.

Procedures for Conscious Astral Travel

First, ensure that you will not be disturbed. This is a definite prerequisite for any type of magickal or astral activity. Take several deep breaths and relax your body. Open each of the seven chakra vortexes, then the vortexes in the hands and feet. Surround the body with the blue light of protection. Imagine a golden light pulsating within your body. This is your light body. Let it rise from your physical body, retaining your physical structure. (Later, you will learn to shape this light body at will.) Move your consciousness into the light body and imagine that your physical body is safe and will remain that way, fully functioning, until your return. Since you think it — it is so.

At this point, you may proceed in one of two ways. You can travel around the room and become comfortable with being in the astral, or you can go directly into either the astral or physical plane.

Some individuals prefer not to look at their physical bodies because they fear that the body has ceased to function, which is not the case — but the sight can immediately pull you right back into that body in the bat of the physical eyelash, with your heart beating like crazy.

This brings up a very important point. Individuals with heart trouble should not consciously attempt an OBE as it alters respiration and heartbeat. If you are terrorized by the thought of astral projection, do not force yourself to practice it. Perhaps your fear will lessen at a later date and you will be more comfortable with the skill. If you have a history of heart trouble or respiratory disease, I do not suggest consciously attempting an OBE.

I mentioned earlier that you can travel in two dimensions, the earth one and the astral (there are others, but let's stick to these two for now). You may be comfortable working more in the one than the other. Working in the astral is called vision questing and is the route that many shamans follow.

What Purpose Can Astral Travel Serve?

Like any skill, it will provide what you allow it to provide. Some seek only a vacation experience; to visit places where the body can not either afford or physically go. Others seek knowledge that cannot be found elsewhere. There are people who arrange meetings in the astral or on the physical plane while in the OBE state. Later, they compare notes. Some individuals merely use it for experimental purposes.

When you return from your excursions in the astral, you may wish to hover first around your body, or join it immediately. If the physical body is disturbed during an OBE you will return to the body with that "whoosh" sensation. Sometimes the environment will speed past you in a blur. Don't worry about it, it is a fantastic experience.

I would also like to mention that you have what is called an "ocular voice" when in the astral. It is a strong, piercing vibration that you can use to protect yourself if you feel threatened. On this plane it comes out like a silly croak, but on the astral it can cut an unwanted entity to pieces.

Practice Makes Perfect

Once you have learned the skill of conscious astral projection, choose some places in the physical plane that you can visit that are easily accessible to you in the waking state. Make it a public place, unless you have arranged with a friend to visit them. Time your astral travels so that you can visit the site in the next 24 hours. Keep a record of your astral visit. Write down the things you remember, such as the varieties of plants in the flower bed, broken pavements or window panes. Perhaps you have noticed a traffic light that was out of order, an unusual billboard, a new store, etc.

The following day, visit the site and check off all the things on your list. Don't have heart failure if something is incorrect. Traffic lights can be fixed, flower beds replanted, side walks repaired and billboards changed. Practice until you are confident enough to try the next exercise.

·☾ ☽·

This exercise requires a trusted friend. Set a pre-arranged time where you will be going into an OBE situation. During this time, they should be monitoring what they are doing and their surroundings, and monitoring whether or not they are aware of your presence. Later, meet and compare notes. Keep practicing until you are both proficient. Keep accurate records of your experiments.

Bi-location

If you are having trouble obtaining a decent OBE through either the dream state or meditation state, you should try bi-location. Also, what if you desperately need to know something, but can't lie prone in your office or dining room to enter the astral? The answer then, would be bi-location.

Bi-location is basically the same procedure as that used in the meditation state, save for one basic twist — you are more "in control." A sitting position is best for this procedure.

During bi-location you are vaguely aware of what is happening around your physical body. You never entirely lose control (conscious recognition) of the television behind your closed door, the sound of the dishwasher out in the kitchen, or the furnace kicking on in the basement.

Go into your normal meditation structure. This time, however, form in your mind a body that much resembles yourself — not a light body, but a ghostly one. Think of him or her as a type of drone where all things experienced by the entity are fed directly to you — much like a computer link-up. Guide him/her out of the door, out of the house and into the world. When you have finished, bring the entity back and have its body melt into yours. This "being" can also function as the Watcher.

The Watcher

The Watcher is a replica, just as in the process of bi-location. In this instance, it is not necessary to travel with the Watcher. If you wish, you can instruct it as it stands before you. Tell it what specific information you desire and what time to come back. Now, go about your normal business.

At the specified time, take your seat again and greet the Watcher. Ask it to impart all the information it has gathered. If you cannot understand the information, don't worry. Let it merge with yourself, knowing that all the knowledge you seek will be imparted to you in a manner which you can understand subconsciously. Later, the knowledge may surface as a memory or your subconscious may sort things out faster and you will find that you are suddenly aware of the answers to your questions now that all the data has been assimilated.

The practice of the Watcher is not a new one. People involved with the occult have been using this technique for a long time.

Remember that the Watcher is part of you, not a discarnate entity. If you wish to call such an entity, that is another ball-game entirely. So, if you are squeamish about ghosties and things that mysteriously go bumpity-bump, you are not dealing with that kind of manifestation in the Watcher. You are only working with yourself.

Extended Bi-location

A body form to guide is not always needed in bi-location. Recently I read someone use the term "over-looking," which is exactly what you can do. Your mind can over-look an event or place. It is possible for you to sit in your chair, go into meditation, and go directly where you wish (sort of looking over someone's shoulder) and not experience any "going to" or "coming back" processes as you do in standard astral projection techniques. One second you are here, the next you are there, with no travel time involved. One can also merge with another human being — thought I don't really recommend this for a variety of reasons, including ethics.

If you should fall asleep during conscious astral travel, don't worry about it. Your mind is familiar with astral travel in the dream cycle and will bring you back safely, as it has always done before.

Body-double

The ability to make the astral body appear to others as a solid, physical object is called body-double. This is an advanced technique, one that takes a great deal of skill and concentration; though the less you consciously try, the better you will get at it.

The trick is to learn to mentally solidify and make apparent the alternate form. Occasionally, your use of bi-location and the Watcher will automatically become body-double if you have practiced either technique a great deal. In attempting the body-double technique, you will have to work with a trusted partner who can monitor your success.

Power Animals

Power animals are and are not a part of the Wiccan or Witchcraft Traditions. They are used by Native Americans, shamans, and other tribal organizations and traditions. Covens usually have a totem animal that is only known to those within the group.

Why are we discussing totem animals in a lesson on astral projection? Because in the astral, you can merge with your totem and become the animal with your own intelligence intact. This is called shapeshifting.

·☾ ☽·

Witches are said to have "familiars," animals who live with them and assist them in their magickal endeavors. Cats are high on the list, but dogs, snakes, ferrets, and other small animals have been known to serve that function in physical form. Familiars are not just any animal. They are a special psychic derivative of a particular species of animal who compliments your spiritual self.

Just because a person has a cat that lives with them does not indicate that that person is involved with the Craft. Not all Witches work with physical familiars due to space limitations, rental rules, family allergies and schedules. A familiar actually represents all the good qualities of that species. It provides the Witch with a link to the power of the animal kingdom — the essence of that power. Hence, the term "power animal."

Power animals do not have to be physically domesticated and living in our homes to assist us. They function quite well in the astral; in fact, perhaps even better, as we can not keep a wolf or a panther in our apartment on the seventeenth floor, or in a home that also houses many young children.

Not all small animals normally kept as pets carry the essence we may need. If panther medicine is needed, a rabbit is not going to do any damn good.

Many Witches choose one power animal that closely represents to them their function in this life time, or provides the medicine (energy) that they must be equipped with to practice a particular type of magick. There are Witches who work with a variety of animals but keep one or two, even three in particular esteem.

Your main power animals come to you either by an affinity for the animal itself, or through astral travel and meditation. There are cards on the market today that can assist you in choosing your animals as well as providing a divination tool. These are called Medicine cards. If you feel the selection is too limited, you should use other methods in conjunction with the cards when studying each animal's medicine.

Each animal has a particular function or essence that is attributed to it. There are books that can tell you what the Native Americans felt about each animal and its power, but you should not rely on these interpretations alone, either. I suggest that you study the different animals first-hand, read about them, how they function in the wild, how they relate to humans, and finally, what their magickal attributes are.

Meeting Your Power Animal in the Astral

There are two ways you can meet your power animal in the astral plane and discover which animal medicine is right for you. First, you could write and perform your own ritual to call the essence of the animal that would suit you best and assist you in your present magickal workings. If you are not comfortable with the ritual format you can go into the familiar meditative state, walk through the astral forest and meet the animal.

When the first technique is used, that of the ritual, you will most likely see a picture of the animal in an unlikely place, or even see the animal in its natural form. There may be a synchronistic conversation where the topic is of the animal, or you find a book about the animal, etc. When you catch that first glimpse of that particular medicine, you will know it in your heart.

If you meet the animal in the meditation, converse with it. Anything is possible in the astral, right? So, ask questions and get to know your new partner.

If you have seen the animal after a ritual, plan some time to go into the meditative state to cement your relationship and get to know the animal and the essence it represents.

What Do You Do with a Power Animal?

Now that you've got the animal, what do you do with it? Power animals are great advice givers, often representing our higher selves that we haven't been paying attention to lately. In a meditative state you can ask for their assistance on problems that have been nagging at you. At times, two power animals can work in conjunction with each other, as long as they want to. I have had some truly interesting and fruitful conversations with mine.

Power animals can assist you in the waking state as well. Perhaps you are trying to teach someone a particular theme and they are having difficulty understanding it. Ask wolf for assistance; she is the great teacher.

Remember the old adages: clever as a fox, strong as an ox, etc? Perhaps you need camouflage — then ask Brother Fox for assistance. If you seek wisdom, ask the Eagle. The Lynx knows the art of keeping secrets, and the Swan guides one into dreamtime. The Panther is a good protective animal, though she does have a sarcastic, laid-back nature.

Power animals are not limited to mammals. The reptilian and insect kingdoms can be just as helpful. Children can also be taught to work with animals and have a great deal of success with them. My youngest daughter can still relate her experience with Sister Dragonfly! It was the biggest one I have ever seen. Dragonfly tells us how to break through illusion and how to gain power through our dreams and goals. She teaches higher aspiration.

Honoring the Power Animal

The act of honoring an animal is not an act of worship, but is the acknowledgement of their power and their being as brothers and sisters of the entire Universe. The energy of the animals, birds, and other creatures that assist us should be honored. For too long we have subjugated these creatures who are our equals in the system of the Universe. The Native Americans leave tobacco as a gift, scattered on the ground. You could also burn incense in honor of the animal. When I do a full ritual, I always remember my power animal and honor it with a gift of some sort. A crystal or gem on your altar is also a lovely gift.

Shapeshifting

There are two types of shapeshifting: changing your light body in the astral to a power animal, and changing your physical form on the earth plane into an animal. Perhaps this is where the lycanthropy legend actually began. Very adept shamans are said to be able to change their physical human forms into that of animals.

There is also a middle ground we should not miss. During certain ritual dances, humans can be possessed by the animal spirit. Although they outwardly do not become the animal, their bodies may contort or move in the fashion that the animal is most comfortable. Vocalizations are also heard, such as the cry of the Eagle, scream of the Falcon, etc. These power dances are not harmful, as long as they are done within some type of magick circle. Inwardly, the individual melds with the animal. The human's sense of smell or sight may be heightened, there could be increased dexterity in the limbs, or a feeling of savage power that the animal may represent. It is exhilarating and enlightening.

In the astral, taking on the shape of the animal is not particularly dangerous. I had only one glitch, and that was in the form of a panther, where I had to learn to control the beast and not let it run away with my (or its) strength.

In order to keep accurate track of your astral studies, you should use your notebook. Be sure to write the date, time, moon phase, weather conditions, and your own health at the time of the travel. Also indicate the reason for the exercise.

Physical Familiars

If it is possible for you to have a physical familiar, by all means, do so. Just make your choice very carefully. Sometimes though, they choose you.

We had a very interesting experience when choosing our family familiar. My husband is allergic to cats; therefore, my favorite choice was out. I performed a ritual for the familiar that was suitable to our family. In my mind I had a German shepherd, because I felt it would be best with the children. For two weeks, I worked on a visualization of seeing us with the dog working well both in mundane and magickal matters, and it had to be a male. Female dogs and I have a history of not hitting it off.

One afternoon I stopped in at the newspaper where I work to submit a story. They also run an advertisement sheet for yard sales and other things. Somehow the conversation turned to the fact that I was looking for a nice animal for our family. They told me a gentleman was advertising to sell a sheltie.

My question was, "So what's a sheltie?" I didn't want a small excitable dog, nor did a want a monster, either. "It's sort of like a collie," they said, "except a bit smaller."

I took the number and called him later that day. I told him I had several children and was looking for a good companion for them.

"Well, I've been getting $200 a piece for these pups," he said. My heart sunk. I hadn't seen the ad and knew I could not pay that much money for a dog, even the one of my dreams.

"This is our last one," he continued. "My wife says he's got to go. It's just a pup, about four months old. He's trained and just been to the vet's."

I apologized for bothering him and told him I hoped he found a buyer soon.

"You mean you're not interested?"

"It's not that," I explained, "it's just that $200 is a little out of my price range, not that the dog is not worth that kind of money."

There was a pause on the line, and then he said, "Be at my house at 4:30 this afternoon." He gave me the directions. I was totally confused; I had just told the man I couldn't afford the dog.

I started repeating myself, and he said, "You got four kids, right?"

"Well, yes."

"And you need a dog, right?"

"Yes."

"Well then, come get him. He's yours . . . for nothing!"

Needless to say, the spirit of our dog chose us. It was later I realized that he matched many of the country-type pictures I have around the house. In fact, I didn't notice it — someone else pointed it out. Even though shelties are small, this one is about the size of a collie. Beats me, folks!

Summary

The skills in this chapter will give you a great deal of mobility, both in the physical and non-physical planes. They take practice and focus to achieve. Use the skills with a strong ethical conscience. Snooping in other peoples' business is not the Witches' style.

If you plan to work with another individual, be sure they will be aware of your visits. If they are properly protected, they can give you a terrible headache if you have not warned them you are coming. It is not that they will strike out to purposefully harm you, but they may have protective magick that will turn you away quite neatly.

Never be afraid of the astral, but never assume that all things in the astral are only of a positive design. Remember that you have no barriers in that plane, and that your personal magick will respond faster than in the physical plane. Happy trails!

Suggested Reading List

Lynn V. Andrews, *Jaguar Woman*. Harper & Row.

Melita Denning and Osborne Phillips, *The Llewellyn Practical Guide to Astral Projection*. Llewellyn Publications.

Enid Hoffman, *Develop Your Psychic Skills*. Whitford Press.

The Medicine Cards and Text. Bear & Company.

The Summerland: Death and Reincarnation

A Place to Go

All religious systems have a place where the soul ascends (or descends) when the physical body can no longer function. In Craft belief, we call this place the Summerland. We have no Hell, or place of terror or damnation. However, that's where the agreement stops on the subject of the hereafter, save for the concept of reincarnation.

Birth and death, two ancient mysteries, have been the root of many a serious conversation and heated discussion. Where do we go when we die? When does the soul enter the body? Why am I even here, on this planet, in this time?

Each of us forms opinions and theories on these questions fairly early in life. Usually our considerations are based upon the teachings that have been imparted to us by our parents or the religious leaders of the time and our society. There comes a point, however, when each of us begins to question what we have been told about things that cannot be seen or proven by experimentation of our own design. This questioning process may start with something small and insignificant, and later blossom to more headier topics.

For instance, one day you may realize that Uncle Harry, who your mother has always idolized, is truly a rat, let alone a downright jerk. From that day on, you begin to look around at other people (no longer seeing them as towering elders to be respected) and see them as human beings with insecurities, lack of control, and a limited amount of wisdom. At some point we finally begin to usurp the myths and pre-packaged explanations of the adult world (that really isn't so very grown-up, after all).

Few world religions do not believe in reincarnation — the logical process of living, dying, and living again on the earth plane. Some religions also believe in transmigration, where an individual's soul may enter not only the body of a human, but the body of a plant or animal.

Most people, however, believe in something after physical death, but the "what" is still up for discussion. In most Witchcraft Traditions, reincarnation is the accepted theology for dealing with the subject of death and rebirth. We move with the seasons, the cycle of the Wheel, the turn of birth, death, and rebirth. That part of it usually isn't questioned because it is logical.

What is questioned is the space between the living experiences, the number of lifetimes, and the reasoning for going through each one. Also intriguing is "who we were," with whom, and when.

The basic premise of reincarnation is that you choose each particular incarnation to work on different aspects of your development. Most often we are not here for one purpose alone, but several. Thus, we can accept with relative ease the situations that revolve around us and those individuals we encounter along the way. As Richard Bach once said, "If you are still living, you're not done." In his book *Illusions,* he writes:

> *The bond that links your true family is not one of blood, but of respect and joy in each other's life. Rarely do members of one family grow up under the same roof.*

This theory could explain the enormous amount of attraction we may have for one particular individual who may, at this point in time, be a perfect stranger to us.

Many Witches believe that groups of souls become incarnate at the same time in different areas of the world to work together toward a common goal. Hence, you may hear yourself called "my brother" or "my sister" even though there is no blood relation and you may never have even met each other face to face.

Witches are not the only individuals who hold this collective reincarnation theory. Many people involved in the New Age movement believe this also.

What happens between incarnations is a puzzle to many. Do we float around as ghosts? Do we fill the position as "Guardian" of a loved one or a stranger? Do we become Angels? And what are Angels, anyway? Are they beings like us, or very unlike us? Do we go to another planet, or perhaps to another dimension with living, breathing people who are more evolved than ourselves? Or do we go to a place to rest and relax, shoot the shit with those we missed in the last incarnation, and prepare a complete documentary of what we have learned and what we didn't?

Well, I believe that we could do any of those things; that we have a definite choice in the matter, unless we have been particularly rotten, and that there is some type of "holding pen" for truly perverted people (I hope). Though I don't believe in the typical Hell, I certainly hope there is something like it for people like Hitler and a few other bad eggs I can think of. Witches, of course, don't believe in Hell. But I do believe that we can create our own right here on this plane, both for ourselves and for others.

It is logical to assume that most people go to the Summerland. This is the resting place — the way station, if you will — for souls to recover, and to disseminate and categorize information and lessons we have learned. It is also a place where they can plan what they are going to do next, either by haunting the local graveyard to prove to us earthlings that there is life after death, or to go back and assist and fix the things that need it, or to go further on.

This is where the statement, "There are no victims, only volunteers," comes into play. I believe that you can choose your parents, the society in which to return, the type of career you will have, who you must help or what you must do (that feeling of you've got a purpose, but you don't know what and time is running out) and I believe you choose your own time and method of death. You also choose your physical condition, your body chemistry and your DNA structure — which is why some of us have the capability to be rocket scientists and others fill the roll of artist or writer. This does not mean that everything is set in stone when you get back here, but that you have laid out an itinerary and whether or not you choose to follow it once you get here is totally up to you.

Reincarnation then, is logical. It slights no one. All men and women are "created" equal, you get to decide what human attributes and detriments you wish to work with.

I recently read a statement noting that there are more people alive today than if you added all the people up since time began. Does this throw a kink in the reincarnation theory? If all those people are alive today, they they can't all have been reincarnated from an earth life. This is true. However, I believe that there are many souls here at this time who have not been earthlings before. Society today plays hard with the idea of other inhabited planets and dimensions. Just about everyone these days has seen at least one UFO. Could it not be, then, that many souls here now are from various planets, perhaps sent here to protect Earth Mother, or bring some type of religious or scientific awakening?

I also believe that there is a core group of "Old Souls" — those that have lived several lifetimes, perhaps enough not to come back, but they choose to do so anyway in order to perpetuate a thought or deed that will assist humankind in its collective destiny.

A great deal of Craft ceremonies revolve around life, birth, death, and rebirth. This is shown in our major holidays, each attributed to a particular cycle of growth. The major theme is not that they happen only once, but are repeated as the human cycle of life, growth, and death are experienced a multitude of times — both mentally and physically.

When you come right down to it, most of us do not fear death; what petrifies us is how it is experienced. No one wants to know pain, and each of us holds both a fantasy of exactly under what circumstances we would like to go, and under what conditions we would never want to go. For each person, this best/worst scenario is different, and that is what makes it so odd. I may have a great fear of being eaten by a lion (though I live in the heart of Texas) and you may be deathly afraid of an element, such as fire or water.

We can peg three theories on this subject. Perhaps something happened in our childhood that so influenced us that we hold that fear close to our hearts. Or, we could have died that way in another incarnation (I can still vividly remember the day my youngest son, at age three, described to me how he had died in a plane crash that went into the big water — "No one came to get me out . . ." His description was really creepy.) Or we may be slated to die that way in this incarnation, and therefore stay as far away as possible from what we most fear.

These emotional feelings are very real and affect us in many ways. There are people who won't set foot near a large body of water, or refuse to get in any type of boat at all. There are those that dislike high places, those that are afraid to fly, afraid of closed spaces, groups of people, chronic or terminal illness, etc. They carry this fear to what modern science describes as a "phobia," where all rational thought stops, and raw fear completely rules the waking mind.

Some phobias can be worked through with the use of hypnotism, past life regression, and/or meditation techniques; others require the assistance of a trained professional. In fact, working through present life difficulties is how our modern masters of the mind stumbled onto past life regression therapy in the first place.

Remembering Past Lives

Why bother to remember who we were if we came here for a purpose we already know about? And if we are truly capable of living many lives, why can't we remember more than bits and pieces, if at all?

It has been said that perhaps we cannot remember any past lives because, as a result of a safety mechanism, we are ensured that feelings of guilt, sadness, and remorse do not affect us on a conscious level while performing the tasks in this incarnation.

Did you ever notice that there are things that you just cannot abide? Like people making fun of another's physical deformity, or anything bad happening to a child? You can't even watch a movie about things like that. Perhaps you are experiencing old guilt feelings, where you by accident or design did something that you now abhor.

Even before I knew that it was possible to live again, I hated being a child. I despised it. Often I would sit in our backyard and ponder this intense dislike of being a child "again." It was not that I had a bad childhood; quite the opposite. My parents weren't rich, but they weren't destitute, either. They didn't drown themselves in booze or drugs. They didn't beat on each other, or me. And what arguments they did have, I never heard.

But in my heart, I knew that things were not as I was being taught, and the frustration I experienced was great indeed. I knew what I learned in Sunday school was wrong . . . that I was being taught an incorrect theology; but I didn't know how to word it, and certainly couldn't, at that age, discuss it with my parents. It is one thing to be frustrated over known variables, it is another to be clawing at the heavily shrouded truths that lurk among us.

A child is not in control of their destiny. They are stuck in the web of parental, educational, and social training. This is why it is important for the adult to never forget the time they spent in childhood, especially when they become parents themselves. It is necessary in some situations to "think like a child" in order to benefit fully from what is happening. It is also important to emphasize what a child may be feeling that you are responsible for. Was it really so long ago that you faced the same trials and tribulations as the little one that stands before you?

Past lives can be recalled through past life regression lead by another person, or they can be taped through meditation. There are various tapes on the bookstore shelves today designed to take you down through the cycle of remembering to obtain this information.

Basically on these tapes, one enters the meditation state and counts backwards in time. Random snatches may come to you, but if you do not have a definite need driving you to discover a particular incarnation, you may not be entirely successful. Usually you remember the most important events of the incarnation; the rest is fuzzy. Your mind sorts out what is most needed and discards the remainder.

In fact, it wasn't until my mother died that I began to search for the meaning of life and death and the possibilities of reincarnation. Usually, a person has some type of catalyst or event in their lives that sets them on the search for answers to life after death and possible life again.

There are various techniques for remembering past lives, including special decks of cards to assist you in opening the blocks. But before you run out and purchase such a tool, try your own meditation technique with a few different twists.

After you have opened your chakra centers and protected yourself in the usual way, design in your mind a very special place; a temple known only to you. It could be accessed through going into a large tree and descending stairs to an underground chamber, or walking to the sea to find a golden door that allows you to access another world — the world of past life knowledge. Once there, you may meet a being who will give you the information you seek, or perhaps you will come upon an old book wherein you will read the knowledge you require.

Another technique is to hold a piece of fluorite, open the chakra centers, protect yourself and let your higher self take the lead. After you have settled into your normal meditation routine, ask your higher self a question like "What past life occurrence has brought me this difficulty?" Often if we know the reason why something is happening, we can solve the problem or deal logically with the situation.

Sometimes past life experiences literally flash before us, and in a matter of seconds we know all the information that we need. All the pieces will fall neatly into place in an instant.

Remember that you do not need to know the whole saga of a single lifetime, just the area that directly affects the current situation. Although it would be nice to remember some of the mundane things (dates, places, times, names, etc.), it really isn't necessary to deal with all that information just to answer a simple question.

I need a specific event or series of circumstances to recall a past life. For example, if I am having a terrible problem with a particular individual who is close to me (whether I like them or not), I will use regressive meditation. My most successful recalls have been those in which I went into a meditative state and held a piece of fluorite. Fluorite is a new gem compared to crystal or rose quartz. Those in the New Age and occult fields are just now discovering its uses. The information I have received has been incredible.

In these examples, you are a bystander who only brings back information by watching what has occurred to solve a dilemma. It is also possible for you to bring back or reawaken a particular skill.

Discovering the hidden meanings of our problems is not the only avenue for the use of past life regressions. If we are lacking a particular skill in this life cycle, we can use regression to awaken talents that have been dormant until the present. Perhaps you have a mental block when writing, adding numbers, or gardening is involved. Perhaps your work appears less than adequate or is unsatisfactory to yourself. By asking your higher self during the meditation state to awaken gifts that you already hold, you can bring those talents to the conscious mind. This works well both in mundane and magickal matters. Perhaps you adore divination, but have not been able to progress further than a particular stage. By opening the valve of the subconscious you can draw from the well of knowledge, both within yourself and from the collective unconscious.

Drawing Your Own Conclusions

You must form your own theology on the cycles of life, death and what lies beyond. No one can tell you, "This is right, and that is wrong." When you are considering theories, don't forget the one on genetic memory which is responsible for many of our fight-flight instincts and who knows what else, including possible lineage from either apes or star people or both!

Theories on how it all works are as numerous as people both living and dead. Your best guide is to keep an open mind . . . and keep searching for the answers.

Death

In the Tarot deck, the Death card usually stands for great change and not physical death. We see it as the Dark Angel with sooty shrouds and ragged wings. We watch horror films involving death and destruction in hopes that we do not experience what we are seeing — that the visions are much like the Sacrificial King in function alone, allowing us to act out fantasy death to make it less real.

Although most people do not think about real death in general and steer away from it as much as possible, it continues to hold an alluring mystery for us. This point was brought home to me when I attended a party several years ago and watched a woman literally throw herself at a mortician.

For the life of me, I could not figure out why she was so entranced with a person who handled dead people for a living. To me, that was really gross stuff. But to her, it was exciting. Her conversation flipped constantly between how much she adored the man to exactly what his work entailed.

This individual was overwhelmed with the allure of death and those that handled it. It was a mystery, and perhaps she felt that by touching one who dealt with it every day she could keep the Angel of Death at bay. Personally, I was glad when the topic of conversation zipped to more amusing subjects.

Azrael is the proper name of the Angel of Death. His status in the "other worlds" is the same as that of the other Angels you hear of so often: Michael, Raphael, Ariel, and Gabriel. It is Azrael's task not to kill people (as we often think), but to take them when it is their time to their appointed place. He is, perhaps, the loneliest Angel of the lot. If you wish to learn more about Azrael and his world, check the suggested reading list at the end of this chapter.

One of the easiest ways to come in tune with Death is to visit several graveyards — some spooky and some not. This helps us to lessen the grip of fear when the subject reaches out to us. A walk on a summer day in a beautiful landscaped graveyard speaks to the soul in peace and tranquility. To wander among an older graveyard under a Full Moon in the autumn makes the blood rush with excitement.

One of the most exciting and touching adventures I have ever shared with another human was when my father and I went to some old graveyards in Massachusetts. We brought rice paper and special crayons designed for gravestone rubbing and brought back many beautiful pieces, two of which still hang in my dining room. People often think they are odd when they enter the home, but they are a part of our cycle and a project we shared together.

Death and Witchcraft

There are two of our holidays that specifically deal with death: Samhain — which is basically the final harvest and the time where the veil between the worlds is thin enough for even non-sensitive individuals to experience an alternate dimension — and Winter Solstice. This holiday is the divine struggle between the Holly King (who perishes) and the Oak King (who is reborn).

Work with dead souls is not usually done by the initiate; it is reserved for the second and usually third degree Witch. One must let go of a great deal of personal fears to set about conversing with the dead, as well as hold enough magickal wisdom and talent to control things if they get out of hand. Not all dead spirits (or living ones, if you prefer) are nice or even semi-intelligent.

However, there is no reason why you cannot honor your ancestors, even if you don't choose to work with them. During the Samhain celebration, one can set out the Feast for the Dead — an entire meal left on the table for those that have passed. The traditional cakes and ale may be taken outside after the ritual for the same purpose.

Our family leaves the jack-o-lanterns burning all evening in the front window, with the lights in the main room out. Beside the pumpkins, we burn black candles. We do not extinguish them, but let them burn for the duration of the night.

Divination is also performed on Samhain. It is suggested that two people work the Ouija board, if you choose to use that particular vehicle; but any divination tool you may have used as a solitary is acceptable.

Winter Solstice does not wholly concentrate on death, but on the cycle of sacrificial death and its subsequent rebirth. Mistletoe is gathered on this day as it is said to have the power over life and death through its magick.

Notice that Witches concentrate more on the cycle of life in their celebrations throughout the year rather than that of death, which is viewed as a temporary condition. Therefore, only a small part of the actual turn of the wheel is devoted entirely to the thought of death — that of the celebration of Samhain.

It is interesting to note that although Witches are quite comfortable with the color black for fashion dressing, one will see them wearing white at a funeral of any beloved person. As death indicates rebirth into a purer form or light form, white is used to reflect that thought. It is a Witch's way of honoring the dead.

There is a cycle of grief when the death of a loved one touches your life. Witches are extremely sensitive to friends who have experienced this grief process. As a solitary, your first act of aiding another may be due to a death. Even as a solitary, I performed four funerals in one year. My funerals are different from ones you may normally experience. The grieving person and I spent time together, honoring in ritual the person who passed away. As priestess, I then opened the gates to the Land of Death and call on the Goddess to carry messages from the living to the dead (for goodness sake, don't forget to gate!).

Another custom is to light a candle on the anniversary of a loved one's death in honor of the gifts they gave to us while on earth.

The Responsibilities of Death and Birth

If you plan to be a leader of an organization of Wiccans or Witches, or choose to be a High Priest or Priestess of a coven, you would be expected to be able to perform a handfasting ceremony (marriage), a christening (for the birth of new babes) and funeral rites.

However, these functions are not solely related to a group of Witches. As a solitary, you will have family and friends that will ask you to "bestow that extra blessing," so be prepared for it. At these times you are viewed much like the Fairy Godmother in the tales of old. There is something exciting and special about your presence, as you really may be able to bestow something magickal to the occasion. Those that honestly believe in your capabilities truly wish the function to be performed and those that don't are not comfortable with the thought of pissing you off (even though you probably wouldn't be angry in the least).

The only occasion in which you must worry about legalities is the handfasting ceremony. Each state carries different laws on the subject of performing a marriage, so you will have to do some research on the legal implications. It is my belief that handfastings are far more sacred marriages than those conventionally performed by any state or standard religion. In this ceremony, you are creating a bind that will exist after this incarnation is over. Since this is such a solemn occasion (as well as joyful), Witches can first be handfasted for one full year on a trial basis. At the end of the year, if both partners are in agreement, the ceremony will then be held beyond the bounds of time.

In welcoming a new baby, it is your function to give them a magickal name, if you have been called upon as a representative of their faith. Before choosing the name you should carefully consider the child's heritage and perform a specific meditation with that child as your focus. When it is your turn to bestow the name, a gift should be included that the child may keep as a talisman, such a piece of jewelry. As a solitary, your gift should not be a "baby thing," as the parents will get lots of those. Yours should be both elegant and full of power.

Why discuss handfastings and christenings in a chapter on death and reincarnation? A marriage denotes the partial (note I say partial) death of self and the incarnation of a new life form — the union. A christening of a child denotes a celebration of their rebirth to this earth plane, where death has gone before. As an adult, it is your duty to protect them until they can assume this function for themselves. Any child who has a God-Father and a Goddess-Mother (gee, I wonder where they originally got the idea?) is certainly a lucky child indeed!

Time and Perception

Up to this point we have discussed time as linear, where one event follows another. The human sees time, and in fact invented it, in order to give life a logical sequence for completing specified tasks as one grows to perform them.

A skilled Witch is capable of moving forward and backward in time, and is also capable of making time slow down or speed up. Why? Because time, as we have been led to understand it outside the world of Witchcraft, does not exist.

Time is not a linear function — past, present, and future are all one and the same. We have already discussed the technique for going backward in time to bring into the present either knowledge or skills to enhance our purpose. We also can go forward in time to future incarnations to fulfill the same purpose.

Did you ever consider that perhaps the legend of Atlantis did not occur in the past, but may be a place in the future? Hence, the legend lives, but nothing physical remains because it really hasn't been built yet. I am not saying this theory is correct, yet it gives you something to think about.

If not Atlantis, perhaps another place. Did you ever notice that the ideas of science fiction writers forty or fifty years ago are now a reality, and that we move ever closer to the "Federation of Planets"?

Could their muse have been tapping into the future? We all know that Leonardo da Vinci was a man before his time who is credited as a fantastic artist. However, he really considered himself an inventor by trade and he drew glorious plans for both air and water ships, the forerunners of devices that we use today. Perhaps his muse whispered these things in his ear as he painted the Mona Lisa to support his growling stomach. Indeed, she is probably smiling at the folly of the human who sticks to linear time, while her enigmatic smile has lived through life times — of which she is well aware. Or perhaps Leonardo himself brought his ingenious inventions back from the future.

To go forward in time, you can use the same meditation techniques as before, except this time, talk to one of your future incarnations. Be active instead of passive. Take a walk through the woods with them, or meet them in an unusual dwelling.

Cauldron gazing is good for seeing the succession of past and future lives, as well. Finally, if you are in need of advice, why not contact yourself in the future, asking for wisdom to solve a difficult problem?

Bending Time

You can bend time to your will. Let's say you are late for a meeting, and you have seventeen minutes left to make a twenty minute drive. What do you do? (Besides putting your foot to the accelerator and forgetting that the brake exists). First, calm yourself. A dead Witch from a traffic accident won't do anyone any good. Second, know that you will arrive on time. Don't get into logical arguments about it, just believe that you will get there when you need to. Don't let that fear crawl up your spine as you are driving. Listen to music; think about other things. Don't check the time on your dashboard, and don't drive like a maniac.

When you get to your destination, now you can check the time. If you have made it, you just bent time. If you didn't, try again until you succeed. Once you have achieved the goal, try shaving off the minutes, thirty seconds at a time.

Summary

The cycle of life and death is both uplifting and devastating. We must learn to endure and rejoice in both if we are to succeed in this life time. We must also satisfy our desire for knowledge of what happens to us after we cross from this world to the next. We may never have all the answers, but we can at least discover enough to continue along our path with relative ease.

Each individual requires different assurances and different answers. One single answer will not satisfy us all.

Time, and your perception of it, is all within the human mind. Humanity created time in order to live a more organized life, to be able to root ourselves in our own individual cycles. Time has no boundaries, save for those you put on it. You are really listening to the tick-tock of a non-existent clock.

You are capable of bending and shaping time, of travelling in and through it — around and beyond it. You can go backwards and forwards. All it takes is a little practice.

Suggested Reading List

Ken Carey, *The Starseed Transmissions.* The Talman Company.

Barbara Hand Clow, *Eye of the Centaur.* Bear & Company.

Chris Griscom, *Time is an Illusion.* Simon & Schuster Inc.

Jane Roberts, *The Education of Oversoul #7.* Pocket Books.

Dick Sutphen, *Earthly Purpose.* Pocket Books.

Leilah Wendell, *The Book of Azrael.* Westgate Press.

Leilah Wendell, *The Necromantic Ritual Book.* Westgate Press.

Your Future Lives. (Anthology) Whitford Press.

There's No Such Thing as a White Witch

When I had been studying the Craft for about two years, my husband said to me, "You know, there really is no such thing as a White Witch. The concept is a dream of perfection."

He is right. First, let me explain that the terms "Black" or "White" Witch have no racial connotations whatsoever. Someone, somewhere felt it necessary to draw the line between negative magick and positive magick in a way that the general population would understand. Hence, black was used for negative magick in the idea that no light is emitted from it, and white for positive magick with the meaning of pure light.

Depending upon where you live has a great deal to do with whether you term your practices as white/black or positive/negative. Where I live, in the belly of Pow-Wow country, people will readily understand white magick as being a good thing simply because for over one hundred years Pow-Wow's have been telling them that what they practice is "white" magick. Since people go to Pow-Wow's for healing and it works, they think that white magick must be all good, and since everything has an opposite — including the scale of hues — the opposite is black. Incidentally, Pow-Wow's are directly responsible for telling the general population in our area that Witches have always been bad and practice black magick. To a Pow-Wow, the Witch is the enemy! This is not an easy myth to destroy.

Just about every magickal text in print devotes at least one page, maybe even two, to a short discussion on magickal ethics. They give you the Rule of Three, and basically tell you that negative magick is a no-no, end of lecture. Is it really that cut and dried?

Nope. For the record, the Rule of Three is as follows:

Ever mind the Rule of Three
Three times what thou givest returns to thee.
This lesson well, thou must learn,
Thee only gets what thou dost earn!

On the surface, it seems like a relatively simple concept to grasp, doesn't it? Do something good for another person and it comes back to you three-fold. Do a nasty, and you get zapped worse that the effect of what you originally did. This doesn't necessarily mean that three bad things will happen to you. Just one very bad thing could happen instead, in the magnitude of a three-time zap. So what's so hard about that?

When one first begins working in magick, things fall under the exceptionally neat headings of Right and Wrong, simply because your magickal capabilities, knowledge, and expertise are limited to the basic fundamentals.

However, as your skills progress the line between right and wrong has a tenancy to blur; unless, of course, you are a Saint (which to be honest with you, is less than likely).

Determining boundaries becomes progressively more difficult as your capabilities strengthen. You may make mistakes — some very big ones — and things may get complicated until you work them out.

I believe one of the biggest problems Witches face today is the influx of Christianity and its "turn the other cheek" melodrama. More and more individuals are leaving the Christian Kingdom in favor of ours, but they bring with them brains that have been hammered for years with another philosophy.

The world is not run by the meek, and the meek aren't going to inherit it. The difficulty is not so much the doctrine itself, but those that carry it with them into various Craft organizations. If we laid down and put our paws up in the air tomorrow, our children would not be better for it.

Things You Should Consider in a Conflict

All things are drawn to you (or you are drawn to them) for a specific purpose. If you find yourself in a really tough spot, try to logically determine, as best you can, why this is happening to you. Here is where your skills are needed. By using divination, astral projection, protection magick, etc., you may at least be able to make a dent in the situation and stall for time until you come to a satisfying solution.

Common sense and wisdom should never play second fiddle to your magickal powers. A workable way to tackle a question is to sit down with a blank piece of paper in a quiet room, by a stream, or under a tree; any place where you know you will be undisturbed. On one side of the paper write the word

"Pro," and on the other side write "Con." This type of decision-making process can be used in a yes/no situation, or when you have to make a choice between two things. List all the reasons you should go ahead with your plan under the pro column, and all the reasons you shouldn't under the con column.

The trick here is to be totally honest in your assessment of the situation. Now, mentally review your paper. If the solution doesn't pop out at you, don't worry. Hold the paper in your left hand and go into your basic meditation procedure. Contact your higher self or the Universe and ask that you be provided with the best possible solution to the problem. If the answer does not blossom before you, tuck the paper in your pocket and go about your day in the usual manner. In the evening, put the paper under your pillow and instruct your dream self to assist you in finding a solution. When the solution does come to you and you are satisfied that you will take the best possible action under the circumstances, thank the Universe, and scatter the paper to the winds.

What is happening to you may not be the result of a past life boo-boo. One question I hear often when divining for magickal people is, "Is this difficulty a direct result of something I have done in a past life?" Too many people are willing to accept a bad situation by interpreting it as a punishment because of foul deeds done in another life time. For some strange reason, it makes the difficulty easier to rationalize and handle.

This gives us fine justification for rolling over and saying, "Gee, kick me again!" in a volatile situation, turning everything over to an Almighty Purveyor of Justice to squash their hopes and dreams without so much as a cry of indignation. "I must have deserved it" is not always a correct response.

Karma does not exist to be used as the easiest road in times of crisis. It exists to bring things into balance, yes, but the Universe does not revolve around this doctrine as the one and only rule. There are others. Cause and effect are important, but not everything.

You are here to learn many lessons, but you are also around to assist others in accomplishing their goals and lessons, as well. Not every situation you encounter is a result of the law of Karma. Not every difficulty you are involved in is a result of Karmic backlash. Likewise, not every person you meet is really someone you have known well or dealt with before.

If you are having difficulties with a specific person, stop and consider all the angles before getting angry. You must be an optimist in all situations; through this you can usually find a solution. When dealing with other people, don't believe everything you hear or have read. Gossip is a nasty bitch.

Think about how many arguments are started in one single day on the premise of misinformation. Not everything said or printed in black and white is true, and don't forget that truths differ among people. When you are in doubt about specific information, go to the source. Don't even bother with the tributaries.

If you find yourself in a verbal confrontation with another person, mentally step back from the heat of the moment to determine what is making you angry. Be honest with yourself; rationalization can get you into trouble. Remember that it is not your job to control the other person. It is your function to control yourself.

Check out the body language while you put your shields up. Once you determine why you are upset, you can attempt to figure out why the other person is having verbal heart failure. Maybe they are making you feel threatened or hurt. Bring your own emotions under control.

In a logical assessment, consider what is making the other individual angry. Is it misinformation? Has someone else hurt them (lover, boyfriend, parent, boss, etc.) and they are lashing out at you? Did you make yourself a prime target? Are they rationalizing, or did you really do something to piss them off? Are they on a guilt trip? Are you?

If you cannot resolve the situation and it is totally out of hand, calmly indicate that perhaps you should take up this discussion at a later date; but for goodness sake, don't haul tail and run unless, of course, you are being physically attacked and fight or flight becomes a necessary choice.

Hold your ground and stay calm in verbal confrontations. Do not take a defensive posture; take an offensive one. Speak in a clear, low voice. If the person screams even louder, speak lower and lower. Keep lowering your voice until it is barely a whisper. This works, and eventually the steam will go out of their locomotive mouth because they have to concentrate on hearing you and not on their anger. They will be left standing in a defensive position feeling totally foolish and looking equally stupid.

Consider that, at times, the best defense is no defense at all. There are situations where we can dig ourselves deeper by citing numerous counterpoints to an argument. Is this necessary? Is the accusation worth your time and effort? Or is your opponent really after the destruction of something that is not under fire? Perhaps you will be so busy dousing the flames you will lose something far more important. Do not hesitate to use strategy. For example:

Retreat is noble when continuance with the battle or the issue at hand would result in further losses or total annihilation of your resources. In order to return on another day, you must salvage all the warriors and materials possible.
—Leadership Secrets of Attila The Hun

Before opening your mouth in any confrontation, ask yourself this question: "Is it worth it?" Craft thought on casting spells for others, telepathic pushing, and power draining varies proportionately throughout the different Traditions and organizations. For example, there are those Witches who cast love spells on a specific person and think there is absolutely nothing wrong with this. And, of course, there are those that will tell you to bring love to yourself instead, without targeting a particular individual. In the end, the choice is yours — and so are the consequences. This is magick used in an overt manner, indicating that the consideration for the spell has been planned and strategy has been used. Whether it is right or not is not up for discussion at that point. But what do you do about an emotional thought form such as anger, jealousy or vengeance?

We all have these emotions. We would not be human if we did not. It is wise to remember that the subtle side of anger can be just as detrimental as casting a negative spell. In fact, it can be even more dangerous because of the amount of raw emotion involved. We know that no single individual is the epitome of good. Even the most calm and loving individual gets angry sometimes! Getting angry every once in a while is healthy. We must be able to vent our anger and frustration in order to stay psychologically sound.

What I have just described, then, is the perfect Catch-22 — and I daresay Yossarian would be proud at the analogy! But, that doesn't solve our dilemma, does it?

To run an experiment on action and reaction, go to a quiet lake, pond, or a smooth area in a stream. Take a small pebble in your hand and envision that you are the stone. When you throw it into the water, think "This is the action." Watch as the stone hits the surface and understand that the initial rise of water is the main consequence of the action.

Then watch as concentric circles flow from the point of impact. These circles represent the fall-out of your action, the stone hitting the water. Some of the circles are very definite in nature, others are almost indistinguishable in design. Carry this thought further and consider the impact of a good deed: the environment and all that is in it vibrates around the deed, and changes occur that are positive in nature.

Now imagine the impact as a negative deed, and ponder on the domino effect because of that action on the environment and those people that are contained in it. This example is a very good tool for teaching children as well as adults when they do not seem to be grasping the theology of action vs. reaction, and the fact that they are indeed responsible for their own actions.

As a magickal person, you carry the heavy burden that your knowledge imparts. Magick is not a sometime thing, but it should also not be considered a panacea, either. Common sense, wisdom, and strong values should already be an integral part of the Witch's life. Along with the multitude of good things magick can bring you comes the realization that you, and only you, are responsible for what you do, how you act, and the final shaping of your own destiny.

Where Is the Craft Heading?

Here is my theory, take it for what it is — someone's philosophy. It is my belief that first the male/female aspects of the Craft will become more balanced. As each woman yearns for the perfect male, and each male in turn searches for the perfect woman, then too the God and Goddess yearn for each other — the Ying and the Yang — the All . . . the One. Yet this whole will never again lose itself in either representation of one sex or the other. They will, finally, be together; equal.

At the same time, the breakdown of the patriarchal religions will be complete. If you have been watching your current events, you will have noticed that some of the big boys have begun to drop, one by one. The Savior of the Christians will finally have his bride — but it won't be the Church, as they would like you to believe. It will be the Goddess, in whatever form she sees fit to take. The Almighty Jealous Father syndrome will bite the dust.

An acquaintance of mine once remarked on how much knowledge of the New Age he has learned by tuning to one of the popular television church shows. It is one of those biggies that runs forever, with documentaries, game show techniques for the guilty to give money, and a talk-show atmosphere all rolled into one. He said, "You know, I learned so much because of the way they presented the New Age as evil, yet nothing I saw was particularly bad, and the point that they were trying to make was how much the New Age had infiltrated Christian doctrine. They were right about one thing," he added, "the fact that they showed me thirty minutes of New Age material certainly proved that they were assisting in the infiltration!" This individual was also astounded at the sophisticated marketing techniques used to keep the show in money.

I personally believe that women followers of the Christian doctrine are major catalysts of New Age phenomena. For too long the churches have accepted their money, their time, and their support without giving much in return. With the career woman now out and about, farming her kids to the closest day-care center (whether she likes it or not), dealing with both home and job, the church gave her nothing to lean on. No deity to relate to.

And unfortunately, in many cases, severe condemnation because she has to work to survive instead of caring for her little ones and being a good wife. Her husband is absolved from his affairs and she is to be supportive, no matter how many times she runs her fingers over the notches in the marital bedpost.

With a religion like that, who has to worry about some mythical place called Hell? She's already got a shitload of it. Definitely time to look for a new religious structure where women are not only supported, but accepted as equals. Enter the New Age, and the New Generation of Witches.

The men, too, are totally frustrated. His wife or girl friend has become a warrior right in his own bed. She competes with him on the job, nags him to share the work at home and take half the responsibility for the child, to boot.

He is supposed to be sensitive, but not weak. And he may no longer treat her in the centuries old "good-old-boy" fashion. If he pipes up and tells his wife that he wears the proverbial pants in the house, he has another thing coming. Not only from her, but from her friends, her mother, her sisters, and from women he didn't even know existed.

It used to be you could have a nice wife and a nice mistress and never the two should meet. Furthermore, neither wife or mistress were permitted to switch roles; it would have been un-Christian and certainly un-American.

Now these roles are no longer separated and he'd better be happy with what he has chosen, or his days are surely numbered!

I also believe that men, too, are not finding the support they need within the major religious structure. And since it is a patriarchal structure at this time, they can choose whether to go with the flow of equality, or hang on for dear life to the last vestiges of power in the struggle between the roles of men and women. Their religion is not telling them how to cope with a woman who is the mother of their children in the morning while putting them on the school bus, and Shaharazar after the lights go out. Their religion only tells them to stop it.

This is a mistake. It is not just the Christian doctrine that is fighting to survive without change; the Moslems are clawing to remain intact, as well as other equally unbalanced systems across the world.

Those that survive will be those that change. Those that change will move toward each other, in common equality. Those that do not change will die. I don't believe I will see it in my life time, but my children may actually experience the moment when all religions suddenly realize that they are heading in the same direction (which they are). And, one day, they will be One.

Coming Out of the Closet

To Tell or Not to Tell . . . That Is the Question

Once you have become comfotable with your beliefs in Witchcraft, you should sit back and consider how strong your personal convictions are. Do you think they could stand the onslaught of the general public? What will you lose if you begin discussing the Craft with family members, coworkers, local government, church groups and friends? What will you gain?

When I first began writing this book I was a closeted Witch. No one, save my husband, knew my personal beliefs. As the book took shape, so did my life in the Craft. I began teaching my children, my friends, and now those that have come to my door for assistance.

It has been a slow process, this removal of myself from the dark secrecy of my faith. I do not live in a large city, therefore the minds of the many are not open to change or easily re-educated. It has not been easy. I lost my job and found deceit, and I lost a few vapid, selfish friends — but I found a wonderful complement of brothers and sisters. I am now an individual that belongs to no one, but shares with many.

I began by telling my father, then my children and my two best friends; I went on to others that had known me for several years, and progressed to those who did not know me well at all. I told my new employer before I even accepted the job. But through it all I was as careful as I could be under the circumstances. I felt it was important for people to know me, then know what I am. I also felt it was important that my children not be targeted unnecessarily. Why should they suffer for my faith, when in the future they may choose something entirely different?

Last month I was told by a new friend, "Gee, you're so normal!" And that's just the point. If you are working as a solitary practitioner, there will come a time when the Craft becomes so much a part of your life that you will no longer worry about "what everyone else thinks."

Magick is for everyone; the Craft is for the few strong souls who can stick with it, live it, and share it with others until it is fully accepted by society. Then our time of waiting will be over, and the New Generation of Witches will succeed in matters beyond our dreams.

As someone who works with magick, sooner or later you're going to be found out, anyway. Let's face it. You will probably carry yourself differently (confidence does that to a person). You may become articulate, more sensitive, more ethical; happier, richer, healthier. You will succeed in your dreams where others spend their lives wishing instead. Eventually, people will wonder what you are doing right!

People may also fear you. Not because you have threatened them, but because you obviously are not enjoying the same tragedies they are. They will really become suspicious of you if you don't tell them what you are in to. Also, Witches are truth bringers and sayers; many people do not live by the truth and won't particularly care that you do. You are now a wolf, not a sheep.

Questions

Answering questions about your beliefs may be difficult at first. You want to tell the truth, but you know that you may not be completely understood. Common questions from people that do know you are "How do you know you are a Witch?" and "What do Witches do, exactly?"

The first question is rather a stupid one, but it can tie your tongue nevertheless. They are asking you this question because they do not associate Witches with religion; they are associating you with history and a power source (usually not a good one). Your best response is to ask them what religion they practice and how they know they are of that religion. If they don't follow any particular religion, ask them instead how a Christian knows they are a Christian, or how a Moslem know they are a Moslem.

In response to "What do Witches do?" or "Tell me all about Witches," be very careful if you are not familiar with the questioner. Instead, get them to talk about themselves by using the conversation techniques you have learned. They may never get an answer to their question on the first meeting, but they will walk away thinking you are a great person anyway because you listened to them.

How do you steer them away from the topic of Witchcraft if you find yourself in a time or place that is not suitable for such a discussion? This is an easy one; just ask them exactly what they wish to know. Most often their questions are vague and you can give them an equally vague answer and ask them something about themselves. Since it is human nature for people to love to talk about themselves, you will have them chattering away in no time.

If you feel they deserve a good answer, ask them to phone you later or arrange for a specific meeting, instead of whispering in the middle of your child's piano recital or in the dugout of your Sunday softball game.

Disagreements

Conversations don't always go like movie dialogue, where you can understand everything that is being said and there appears to be some type of logical thread to the train of thought. Real people do not talk that way. They talk too fast, skip sentences, and get angry before the breath is out of the kind syllable that preceded it. If you are not carefully monitoring the situation, you can look like a total fool.

For example, at a writers' meeting last year a conversation got out of hand when one of the members (who I did not know well) picked up the star pendant (it was not a pentacle, just a star; but it was charged) on my chest and proceeded in quick bursts of rapid dialogue to tell me I was wearing a Satanic symbol.

I wasn't ready for this, though I should have been. "It is not!" I snapped. "Yes it is!" he shouted. And we went back and forth like children until I was able to interject a few more words than "No," and he backed off. The rest of the group was staring at us like we had just stepped from the twilight zone. As I sit here now, I can not believe how stupidly I reacted. I had sprung to the defense of my beliefs and blown my cover forever.

In the long run, it worked out well. Most of the people in the group now know I am either a Witch or a person interested in the occult. Some give me wide berth; most don't. And that particular individual no longer attends our meetings. Lesson learned. If you are going to wear magickal jewelry in public, be prepared at any time to explain it, or any other unusual thing you do or say.

Some New Generation Witches do not move beyond the "flash" of the Craft. These are the people who waltz about town, invariably dressed in black, with tons of magickal jewelry dripping from just about every protruding part of their body. We all go through this stage, but we all don't get stuck there. If your dress and mannerisms are constantly screaming "look at me — oogie boogie!" you are begging for trouble.

Indeed, writing this book was another step out of the closet both for myself and my family. Although many people knew I was writing a book, they weren't interested and I kept conversation low-key on the subject, but when Llewellyn accepted the manuscript, things changed drastically. When hit with, "What is your book about?" I invariably drew a blank.

At first, I said, "About how to make your life better and be happy," but that sounded rather lame, even though it was true enough. The summer before the manuscript was accepted I tried my best to integrate myself in my own community so they would know I wasn't a beast. With hesitation, I began answering, "It's on the occult, and how to make life work for you in a positive vein." That sounded sort of snotty, though, so finally, I began to break down and say flat out, "It's about Witchcraft," and let the chips fall where they may.

I Need Help

Try never to turn anyone away who needs help, unless you are so over-taxed you feel you will not be able to assist them. Help can be given in magickal and mundane matters, from good advice to a spell or ritual. Likewise, never offer help if you are not capable of assisting. It isn't fair either to them or to yourself.

Explaining

One way to educate those close to you is to give them Marion Weinstein's book, *Positive Magick,* or Scott Cunningham's book *The Truth About Witchcraft Today.* I recommend Marion's book for individuals that are not comfortable with the "W" word; this one is best for them. Both books are marvelous for anyone else. Be prepared to answer their questions as they read. Try not to get on the defensive if you can help it.

The way you live will also be a testament to your beliefs. By serving others, you will indeed serve yourself.

Living in the Closet

Some Witches prefer never to come out of the closet. They see the Craft as a totally religious belief and don't feel the need to share it with the world in general. There is nothing wrong with this as long as you are completely comfortable with it.

I have a friend who feels this way about the practice of the Craft. Although he frequently mixes with magickal people, discussions on the Craft with normal people are usually off-limits. You may feel this way, too. He does recommend that when you are ready to tell your family or close friends to have your dissertation prepared, and to center yourself before the discussion begins.

Witchcraft is going to go where you — a member of the New Generation of Witches — want to take it. It is your time now.

Your Own Circle

There comes a time on your solitary path that you may feel you need the company of living and breathing magickal friends on a regular basis. When I finished the first draft of this book, I didn't have a circle. The next summer, my next door neighbor and I got to talking and decided that we would like to work together. One day she asked if another friend of hers could join us. No problem; Jean and her friend had been close for years. A safe contact. A few weeks later one of my students joined the group. And it grew, and grew, and grew!

Now we call ourselves the Witches of the Round Table (WORT) and we meet once a week to chat, work, and enjoy each other's company. Our extended group numbers over twenty. Are we all Witches? No. Has the group grown into a "group mind"? Yes.

In the beginning I decided that due to our small town environment and the fact that there were few degreed Witches within driving distance, I would have an open circle. This means that anyone of any positive faith could participate. After all, we were and are all geared to a more spiritual life, and we all wanted to help other people with our work.

Interestingly enough, we all consider ourselves equal. The Witches aren't better than the Catholics; the OTO ladies aren't a cut above the Witches. We have a good group that works hard to bring about positive change for everybody.

Therefore if you in East Podunk, don't assume you are all alone just because of your environment. My friend Lord Ariel Morgan of South Carolina says, "Honey, this is not the Bible Belt anymore! I got news for them; this is the Girdle of the Goddess!" We, the New Generation of Witches, are everywhere!

·☾ ☽·

This book represents one phase of your training in the art and science of Witchcraft. It is hoped that you will continue your studies. Details of subjects such as working with the dead, sex magick, weather magick and the art of hexing have not been discussed in detail. Each of these areas requires wisdom and expertise beyond what has been offered here. Neither did we discuss women's mysteries and their applications, which would fill an entire text on its own.

If you have completed all the exercises and experiments presented herein, there is no reason on this planet why you cannot call yourself a Natural Witch; a real member of The Craft.

> *Thou art now a Natural Witch . . .*
> *Neither bound by Tradition nor Degree, but by thy*
> *own principles and deeds. May you continue to*
> *walk wisely on the Path of Enlightenment.*

Silver RavenWolf
aka Jenine E. Trayer

Suggested Reading List

Janice Broch and Veronica MacLer, *Seasonal Dance*. Samuel Weiser, Inc.

Marian Green, *A Witch Alone*. Aquarian Press.

Janina Renee, *Playful Magic*. Llewellyn Publications.

Just for Families

Ashleen O'Gaea, *The Family Wicca Book*. Llewellyn Publications.

Margie McArthur, *WiccaCraft for Families*. Phoenix Publications.

Ceisiwr Serith, *The Pagan Family*. Llewellyn Publications.

Appendix 1

A Smattering of History

Those of you who have worked through the completion of this book are the New Generation of Witches. Some of you will go on to join small covens, others will join one of the Wiccan churches that are springing up across the nation. There are those who will continue to practice the Craft alone; and of course, there will be a few individuals who will migrate to other magickal religions.

For the New Generation of Witches, a foundation has been laid by those who have dedicated their lives to the Craft and the people it serves. Who are these movers and shakers of the New Age of the Craft?

The list that follows encompasses many of the individuals who have given more than 100% of themselves to the betterment of their religion. They may not agree with each other on every issue, but each has made a definite contribution. If you hear these names, prick up your ears and listen. If you get a chance to meet any of these people, remember that they have worked long and hard for some of the freedoms you are enjoying today.

Margot Adler
Raymond Buckland
Z. Budapest
Laurie Cabot
Deidre and Andrus Corbin
Scott Cunningham
Janet and Stewart Farrar
The Frosts
Selena Fox
Donald Michael Kraig
Dr. Leo Martello
Rosegate Coven

Pete Pathfinder
Lord Serphant of Serphant Stone
Starhawk
Diane Stein
Doreen Valiente
Marion Weinstein
Otter and Morning Glory Zell

On May 22, 1988, the Church of All Worlds sponsored a Resolution at the Ancient Ways gathering in Northern California. Although this document caused much political upheaval among the Pagan community, its final, much re-written version was accepted by most of the larger organizations and covens in the Craft environment. The Earth Religion Anti-Abuse Resolution 1 reads as follows:

> *We, the undersigned, as adherents of Pagan and Neo-Pagan Earth Religions, including Wicca, or Neo-Pagan Witchcraft, practice a variety of positive, life-affirming faiths that are dedicated to healing, both of ourselves and of the Earth. As such, we do not advocate or condone any acts that victimize others, including those proscribed by law. As one of our most widely-accepted precepts is the Wiccan Rede's injunction to "harm none," we absolutely condemn the practices of child abuse, sexual abuse, and any other form of abuse that does harm to the bodies, minds or spirits of individuals. We offer prayers, therapy and support for the healing of the victims of such abuses. We recognize and revere the divinity of Nature in our Mother the Earth, and we conduct our rites of worship in a manner that is ethical, compassionate and constitutionally protected. We neither acknowledge nor worship the Christian devil, "satan," who is not in our Pagan pantheons. We will not tolerate slander or libel against our churches, clergy or congregations, and we are prepared to defend our civil rights with such legal action as we deem necessary and appropriate.*

What is important here is not who signed and who didn't. This statement went far beyond human egoism by showing the entire Pagan community that there are enough active Witches and Pagans who are willing to work together to assist their community — and that we are our own worst enemies.

Why should such a negative statement be a benefit? Because to conquer your enemy, you have to know that it exists. For many years we have concentrated on defending our religion against the opinions of outsiders. It is high time we understand that strife among our own causes the most difficulties in our religion. Persecution by others now falls neatly into the number two slot of our political worries, only occasionally sliding up to number one.

Why am I telling you there is strife in our community in a text such as this? To keep you from falling into the same rose-colored trap that I did. I was running a bi-annual newsletter when the Resolution was proposed. I thought it was great; all these people getting together to further a positive impression of the Craft by written documentation. Not that it hadn't been done before, but the public does not swallow the truth as easily as it lives for lies. Therefore, any type of proclamation was better than none.

To my absolute amazement (and many others, as well) I discovered that everyone did not feel the same way I did (pretty egotistical on my part, wasn't it?). Strife was afoot in the Pagan community; could you beat that?

I realized that our religious community is like any other — we are made up of human beings, and we carry different opinions. But what about all that stuff we are supposed to live by? You know, perfect love and perfect trust . . . we tell everybody we are the Wise bunch. What gives?

Every person's truth is different. I have watched prominent Craft members being trashed by not so prominent ones, which in turn makes everybody prominent. Ahem.

I have seen covens and newsletters deteriorate beyond repair due to jealousy, selfishness and greed. There are Witch Wars of power. Who gets to be top gun or kiss-my-feet priestess? Maybe one group is getting too big, they make too much money or they are liked by too many people. If they can't be squashed in the conventional way, subversive moves are used.

I have even witnessed mail-writing campaigns in which the initiators hoped they could completely destroy a particular individual or group — and more than once, in which the attackers didn't have the guts to sign their names, Craft or otherwise.

If you think this is all tripe, your are correct. But it happens.

A Witch War usually begins without wisdom and with lack of forethought. Like most conflicts, they are senseless, bloody in the aesthetic sense, and the antagonists leave the rest of the community to pick up the pieces. Wars often take place in more densely populated areas of our community, where three or more groups are practicing the Craft; however, if pure power is the object, it could span the entire country if the participants put their minds to it. Such a waste of time and energy!

This is what the movers and shakers of your community are spending their time on right now. Yes, they still work to protect the religion from the rampages of the general public, but many of them are concerned with the unity of our religion without stepping on everyone's Truth. Not an easy task, is it?

On the heels of the Resolution, the Church of All Worlds published *Witchcraft, Satanism and Ritual Crime: Who's Who and What's What*. Released around the Summer Solstice in 1989, this one booklet has been instrumental in the positive positioning of many Witches and Pagans across the United States and overseas. The text had been prepared to combat negative propaganda against our community. The first printing ranged around 1000 copies. Demand was so high that in November 1989, 2000 more copies went to press.

This publication has been placed in police stations, libraries, newspaper offices, schools, social service agencies and churches. It has been favorably reviewed and recommended by leading police journals and orders have come from as far away as the former Yugoslavia and New Guinea. Funds generated by this project have gone, for example, to help pay for therapy for victims of ritual abuse. At the writing of this book, CAW plans to print 2000 additional copies, due to recent Hollywood pictures that have been perceived to trash our religion.

Pete Pathfinder of the Aquarian Tabernacle Church should also be included in this short history lesson. With much hard work and perseverance, he gained three seats for Wiccans in 1990 on the Oregon InterFaith Council, where many of the major religions have had seats for quite some time.

The Rosegate Coven out of Rhode Island made a giant leap for Witches when they gained the first non-profit status for a Wiccan organization. Now they are springing up all over the country.

Several Wiccan organizations, including Church of All Worlds and Circle Sanctuary, were instrumental in running a huge Pagan politicking campaign against ABC Television. We fought as a single community, and now they at least know we are here, and that we are not about to let the world roll right over us anymore.

Laurie Cabot began the Witches League of Public Awareness, an instrumental organization in our community designed to protect all Witches from discrimination. Dr. Leo Martello formed the Witches' Anti-Discrimination Lobby for much the same purpose. Both organizations have been highly successful.

Z. Budapest, Starhawk, Doreen Valiente, the Farrars and Marion Weinstein have written best-selling books and have travelled all over the country dispelling the myths that surround us. They have helped thousands of people with their positive thoughts, words, and deeds.

Not to mention Margot Adler, who cracked the frozen lock on our history and shared it with great care and expertise, or Raymond Buckland and Scott Cunningham who stepped forward and showed the magickal community that one does not have to follow a rigid set of rules in order to delight in the practice of the Craft.

Still another is Donald Michael Kraig, author and former editor of *Fate* magazine, who when Witches were being trashed in Florida, wrote an excellent piece in his editorial that reached the huge readership of *Fate* magazine.

If you plan to be a leader in our community, then you had better be prepared for the bad as well as the good. You must be calm, not jump to conclusions, not listen to gossip and above all, learn to be fair! There are lots of kids and grown-ups in the sand box, and I assure you there are enough pails for everybody! We are responsible for our own actions.

Each day our history is written. Not every Witch assists in a big way to write it, but each one of us should remember to keep our heads when reading it. Since we all see things differently, we must be sure to weigh both sides of any given argument before adding our own truths to the bubbling cauldron.

Appendix 2

Guide to Pagan Newsletters and Services

In this section are listed groups, journals, newsletters, and services. As with all things that change, I cannot guarantee that you will be able to contact all those listed here; addresses may change or groups disintegrate over time. However, if you do experience a problem in contacting one of them, you can always write to the WPPA and ask for further assistance.

Alternate Perceptions
Eagle Wing Books, Inc.
P.O. Box 9972
Memphis, TN 38190

Azrael Project Newsletter, The
(Gothic, Macabre)
5219 Magazine St.
New Orleans, LA 70115

Bats 'n Bellfire
P.O. Box 20368
Las Vegas, NV 89112–2368

Calendar of Events for DC, MD & VA
Vision Weavers
P.O. Box 3653
Farfax, VA 22038–0653

Calendar of Events (National)
890 Alhambra Rd.
Cleveland, OH 44110–3179

Celtic Connection
P.O. Box 177
Curtain, OR 97428

Church of Iron Oak/Voice of Anvil
(ATC affiliated)
P.O. Box 060672
Palm Bay, FL 32906

Council of the Magickal Arts
P.O. Box 6756
Abilene, TX 79608–6756

Connections
1705–14th St., #181
Boulder, CO 80302

Craft/Crafts
P.O. Box 441
Ponderay, ID 83852

Crow's Cause
P.O. Box 8281
Roseville, MI 48066

Dear Brutus Press
Apartado 36 Coban,
Alta Verapaz, Guatemala

Divine Circle of the Sacred Grove
(Druid, Wiccan)
16845 N. 29th Ave., #1346
Phoenix, AZ 85023

Goddess Journal
450 Hibbs Ave.
Glenolden, PA 19036

Green Man, The (Men)
P.O. Box 641
Point Arena, CA 95468

Hawthorne Spinner, The
P.O. Box 706
Monticello, NY 12701

Hermit's Lantern, The
9724–132nd Ave. NE
Kirkland, WA 98033

Hole in the Stone Journal
3595 W. Union Ave.
Englewood, CO 80110–5215

How About Magick (HAM)
(For children)
P.O. Box 624
Lakewood, OH 44107

International Red Garters
c/o N.W.C. (British traditional)
P.O. Box 162046
Sacramento, CA 95816

Keltria (Druid)
630 N. Sepulveda Blvd., Suite 909
El Segundo, CA 55433

Leaves (Celtic)
Temple of Danaan
P.O. Box 765
Hanover, IN 47243

Magick Words
3936 S. Semoran Blvd., Suite 433
Orlando, Fl 32822

Moonbeams Journal
P.O. Box 6921
Colombia, MO 65205–6921

Moonlight & Memories
4 Spring Lane
Framingham, MA 01701

New Dawn Publishing Co.
608 Huntington St.
Watertown, NY 13601

New Moon Rising
P.O. Box 1731
Medford, OR 97501–0135

Notes From Taychopera
P.O. Box 8212
Madison, WI 53708

Oak Leaf
P.O. Box 1137
Bryn Mawr, PA 19010

Of a Like Mind (Womyn centered)
P.O. Box 6530
Madison, WI 53716

Our Pagan Times
P.O. Box 1471
Madison Square Station
New York, NY 10159–1449

OWW—Of Writers and Witches
c/o WPPA
P.O. Box 1392
Mechanicsburg, PA 17065–1392

Pagan Dawn
BM 7097
London, England WC1 N3XX
United Kingdom

Pagan Educational Network
P.O. Box 1364
Bloomington, IN 47402–1364

PagaNet News
P.O. Box 61054
Virginia Beach, VA 23466–1054

Pagans For Peace
P.O. Box 2205
Clearbrook, BC V2T 3X8
Canada

Panegyria
(Aquarian Tabernacle Church)
P.O. Box 57
Index, WA 98256–0409

Phases—Temple of
the Triple Goddess
7625 N. 19th Ave., #121
Phoenix, AZ 85021

Phoenix Publishing
David Brown, Publicist
P.O. Box 10
Custer, WA 98240

Sacred Earth Journal
193 Sugarwood Rd.
Plainfield, VT 05667

SageWoman (Womyn centered)
P.O. Box 641
Point Arena, CA 95468

Seeker, The
P.O. Box 3326
Ann Arbor, MI 48106

Silver Chalice
P.O. Box 196
Thorofare, NJ 08086

Silver Pentagram, The
P.O. Box 9776
Pittsburgh, PA 15229

Terminal Journal
60 E. Chestnut St., #236
Chicago, IL 60611–2012

Thoughts
3 The Pines, 100 Bain Ave.
Riverdale, Toronto, Ontario M4K 1E8
Canada

Unicorn, The
9724 132nd Ave. NE
Kirkland, WA 98033

Upper Group
RR2, Box 2574A
Harrison, ME 04040–9455

Wanderer's Network, The
P.O. Box 1583
Clovis, NM 88102

Occult Supplies

The Sacred Grove Apothecary
1605 N. 7th Ave.
Phoenix, AZ 85007
(Enclose $5.00 for catalog—great medicinal and magickal selection—DSG is a member of the Black Forest Family)

Crossroads Metaphysical Bookstore & Coffee House
224 Howard Ave.
Houma, LA 70363
Ray Malbrough, Llewellyn author, is co-owner. Ray is a member of the Black Forest Family. Ray specially blends several magickal oils, candles and incenses adding incredible punch to his stock. Crossroads serves Wiccan and Santerian customers. Herbs, powders, oils, candles—the staff will burn candles for you or prepare a special candle tailored to your personal needs. Catalog available for $5.00.

Morganna's Chamber
242 W. 10th St.
New York, NY 10014
Morganna has unique and unusual stock. Be sure to visit her when you tour the Big Apple! Morganna is a member of the Black Forest Family.

Magus Books
1316 SE 4th St.
Minneapolis, MN 55414
1-800-99MAGUS
They can find any unusual book you are looking for. Also, Magus Books will help you put up your web page and can host your web page. They are fantastic in helping you get your own domain name and can answer any of your technical questions.

Strange Brew
2826 Elmwood Ave.
Kenmore, NY 14217
(716) 871-0282
Great herbal selection! The owner makes her own oils and they are wonderful.

Mansions of the Moon
1215 S. Main
Old Forge, PA
(717) 457-STAR
Don't miss out on this great store. Vinnie has both Wiccan and Santerian products. He will also burn candles for you or prepare special candles for your personal needs. Vinnie has an event-oriented store with authors visiting regularly.

Appendix 3

The Wiccan/Pagan Press Alliance

The Wiccan/Pagan Press Alliance began in the brilliant mind of John Kurluk of Baltimore, Maryland. In September of 1989, Silver RavenWolf took over the project, which at that time had a total of thirteen members.

The WPPA is non-denominational. We represent all positive religions. For example, we currently have members who are of the following beliefs: Wiccan, Native American, Shamanism, Nordic, Celtic, Egyptian, Thelemites, Magicians, Classical, New Age, Spiritualists, Metaphysical and Womens'/Mens' spirituality. We have Christians, Astrologers, Psychics and Druids. The WPPA does not belong to any church, as it is an entity in its own right. It does, however, belong to the WARD (Witched against Religious Discrimination) for Pennsylvania.

The WPPA is designed as a networking system for editors, authors, writers, artists, illustrators, goods and services people, and the Pagan community at large. We offer such services as Editors' Search wherein these individuals can publish information on what they need in submissions for their presses.

We have a Writers'/Artists' bank where individuals can advertise their expertise to editors who are looking for something in particular, be it Celtic knot designs or dissertations on sex magick.

The WPPA assists new editors and writers in the fields of Pagan publishing and writing. We often act as a funnel for the community in general, whether they are looking for help to work out a personal or occupational problem, or just need to get in contact with a particular magickal faction.

We started the first syndicated article system for magickal people in the

United States, wherein Pagan newsletters can share articles that they feel will be of interest to the entire community. We created the first magickal press cards for our editors, the first editor lending library, and the first major awards for small magickal presses.

The WPPA publishes one newsletter: *The Midnight Drive,* which is a monthly publication on what is happening in the community and the Pagan publishing environment.

We fully support any magickal writer and do our best to promote their work, whatever the form.

We are a husband and wife team: MindWalker and Silver RavenWolf. MindWalker handles the advertising and production, and Silver gets all the other fun editorial and directorate duties. Our extended staff is Breid Foxsong, Senior Archivist, a publisher out of Kenmore, New York. She is a great assistance to the WPPA and just about the closest magickal friend we've got.

One does not have to be an editorial member of the WPPA to take advantage of its services. We do our share of Pagan politicking for the community.

We are here to assist any individual, provided the request is reasonable. We do ask that a legal-sized self-addressed stamped envelope (SASE) accompany all correspondence. If the SASE does not appear with your letter, you may not hear from us.

If you wish to receive a sample copy of *The Midnight Drive,* please send $4 for postage and handling. A subscription to *The Midnight Drive* is $18 per year (subject to change with the economy). If you are an editor of a press, please indicate such when contacting us.

WPPA
P.O. Box 1392
Mechanicsburg, PA 17055

Index

ORDER LLEWELLYN BOOKS TODAY!

Llewellyn publishes hundreds of books on your favorite subjects! To get these exciting books, including the ones on the following pages, check your local bookstore or order them directly from Llewellyn.

Order Online:
Visit our website at www.llewellyn.com, select your books, and order them on our secure server.

Order by Phone:
- Call toll-free within the U.S. at 1-877-NEW-WRLD (1-877-639-9753). Call toll-free within Canada at 1-866-NEW-WRLD (1-866-639-9753)
- We accept VISA, MasterCard, and American Express

Order by Mail:
Send the full price of your order (MN residents add 7% sales tax) in U.S. funds, plus postage & handling to:

Llewellyn Worldwide
P.O. Box 64383, Dept. 0-87542-791-x
St. Paul, MN 55164-0383, U.S.A.

Postage & Handling:
Standard (U.S., Mexico, & Canada). If your order is:
Up to $25.00, add $3.50
$25.01 - $48.99, add $4.00
$49.00 and over, FREE STANDARD SHIPPING
(Continental U.S. orders ship UPS. AK, HI, PR, & P.O. Boxes ship USPS 1st class. Mex. & Can. ship PMB.)

International Orders:
Surface Mail: For orders of $20.00 or less, add $5 plus $1 per item ordered. For orders of $20.01 and over, add $6 plus $1 per item ordered.

Air Mail:
Books: Postage & Handling is equal to the total retail price of all books in the order.
Non-book items: Add $5 for each item.

Orders are processed within 2 business days. Please allow for normal shipping time.
Postage and handling rates subject to change.

To Stir a Magick Cauldron
A Witch's Guide to Casting and Conjuring
Silver RavenWolf

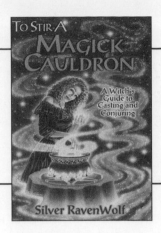

The sequel to the enormously popular *To Ride a Silver Broomstick: New Generation Witchcraft*. This upbeat and down-to-earth guide to intermediate-level witchery was written for all Witches—solitaries, eclectics, and traditionalists. In her warm, straight-from-the-hip, eminently knowledgeable manner, Silver provides explanations, techniques, exercises, anecdotes, and guidance on traditional and modern aspects of the Craft, both as a science and as a religion.

Find out why you should practice daily devotions and how to create a sacred space. Learn six ways to cast a magick circle. Explore the complete art of spell-casting. Examine the hows and whys of Craft laws, oaths, degrees, lineage, traditions, and more. Explore the ten paths of power, and harness this wisdom for your own spell-craft. This book offers you dozens of techniques—some never before published—to help you uncover the benefits of natural magick and ritual and make them work for you—without spending a dime!

Silver is a "working Witch" who has successfully used each and every technique and spell in this book. By the time you have done the exercises in each chapter, you will be well-trained in the first level of initiate studies. Test your knowledge with the Wicca 101 test provided at the back of the book and become a certified Witch! Learn to live life to its fullest through this positive spiritual path.

1-56718-424-3
288 pp., 7 x 10, illus., softcover   **$14.95**

To order, call 1-877-NEW WRLD
All prices subject to change without notice

To Light a Sacred Flame
Practical WitchCraft for the Millennium
Silver RavenWolf

Silver RavenWolf continues to unveil the mysteries of the Craft with *To Light a Sacred Flame*, which follows her best-selling *To Ride a Silver Broomstick* and *To Stir a Magick Cauldron* as the third in the "New Generation Witch-Craft" series, guides to magickal practices based on the personal experiences and successes of a third-degree working Witch.

Written for today's seeker, this book contains techniques that unite divinity with magick, knowledge, and humor. Not structured for any particular tradition, the lessons present unique and insightful material for the solitary as well as the group. Explore the fascinating realms of your inner power, sacred shrines, magickal formularies, spiritual housecleaning, and the intricacies of ritual. This book reveals new information that includes a complete discussion on the laws of the Craft, glamouries, and shamanic Craft rituals, including a handfasting and wiccaning (saining).

1-56718-721-8 $14.95
7 x 10, 320 pp.

Beneath a Mountain Moon
A Novel of Suspense & Witchcraft

Silver RavenWolf

Welcome to Whiskey Springs, Pennsylvania, birthplace of magick, mayhem, and murder! The generations-old battle between two powerful occult families rages anew when young Elizabeyta Belladonna journeys from Oklahoma to the small town of Whiskey Springs—a place her family had left years before to escape the predatory Blackthorn family—to solve the mystery of her grandmother's death.

Endowed with her own magickal heritage of Scotch-Irish Witchcraft, Elizabeyta stands alone against the dark powers and twisted desires of Jason Blackthorn and his gang of Dark Men. But Elizabeyta isn't the only one pursued by unseen forces and the fallout from a past life. As Blackthorn manipulates the town's inhabitants through occult means, a great battle for mastery ensues between the forces of darkness and light—a battle that involves a crackpot preacher, a blue ghost, the town gossip, and an old country healer—and the local funeral parlor begins to overflow with victims. Is there anyone who can end the Blackthorns' reign of terror and right the cosmic balance?

1-56718-722-6
360 pp., 6 x 9
$14.95